The Short Oxford History of Europe

The Nineteenth Century

The Short Oxford History of Europe

General Editor T. C. W. Blanning

NOW AVAILABLE

The Eighteenth Century
edited by T. C. W. Blanning

The Nineteenth Century
edited by T. C. W. Blanning

IN PREPARATION, VOLUMES COVERING

Classical Greece
The Romans
The Early Middle Ages
The High Middle Ages
The Late Middle Ages
The Sixteenth Century
The Seventeenth Century
The Early Twentieth Century
The Later Twentieth Century

The Short Oxford History of Europe

General Editor T. C. W. Blanning

The Nineteenth Century

Europe 1789–1914

Edited by T. C. W. Blanning

OXFORD
UNIVERSITY PRESS

Great Clarendon Street, Oxford OX2 6DP

Oxford University Press is a department of the University of Oxford.
It furthers the University's objective of excellence in research, scholarship,
and education by publishing worldwide in

Oxford New York

Auckland Cape Town Dar es Salaam Hong Kong Karachi
Kuala Lumpur Madrid Melbourne Mexico City Nairobi
New Delhi Shanghai Taipei Toronto

With offices in

Argentina Austria Brazil Chile Czech Republic France Greece
Guatemala Hungary Italy Japan South Korea Poland Portugal
Singapore Switzerland Thailand Turkey Ukraine Vietnam

Published in the United States
by Oxford University Press Inc., New York

© Oxford University Press 2000

British Library Cataloguing in Publication Data

Data available

Library of Congress Cataloging in Publication Data

Data available

ISBN 978–0–19–873135–1 (Pbk)

13

Typeset in Minion
by RefineCatch Limited, Bungay, Suffolk
Printed in Great Britain
on acid-free paper by the
MPG Books Group, Bodmin and King's Lynn

General Editor's Preface

The problems of writing a satisfactory general history of Europe are many, but the most intractable is clearly the reconciliation of depth with breadth. The historian who can write with equal authority about every part of the continent in all its various aspects has not yet been born. Two main solutions have been tried in the past: either a single scholar has attempted to go it alone, presenting an unashamedly personal view of a period, or teams of specialists have been enlisted to write what are in effect anthologies. The first offers a coherent perspective but unequal coverage, the second sacrifices unity for the sake of expertise. This new series is underpinned by the belief that it is this second way that has the fewest disadvantages and that even those can be diminished if not neutralized by close co-operation between the individual contributors under the directing supervision of the volume editor. All the contributors to every volume in this series have read each other's chapters, have met to discuss problems of overlap and omission, and have then redrafted as part of a truly collective exercise. To strengthen coherence further, the editor has written an introduction and conclusion, weaving the separate strands together to form a single cord. In this exercise, the brevity promised by the adjective 'short' in the series' title has been an asset. The need to be concise has concentrated everyone's minds on what really mattered in the period. No attempt has been made to cover every angle of every topic in every country. What this volume does provide is a short but sharp and deep entry into the history of Europe in the period in all its most important aspects.

Sidney Sussex College   T. C. W. Blanning
Cambridge

Contents

Conclusion: into the twentieth century

T. C. W. Blanning

List of contributors

T. C. W. BLANNING is Professor of Modern European History at the University of Cambridge and a Fellow of Sidney Sussex College. He is also a Fellow of the British Academy. His recent works include *Joseph II* (1994), *The French Revolutionary Wars 1787–1802* (1996), and *The French Revolution: Class War or Culture Clash?* (1997). He has also edited *The Oxford Illustrated History of Modern Europe* (1996) and *The Rise and Fall of the French Revolution* (1996); as well as (with David Cannadine) *History and Biography: Essays in Honour of Derek Beales* (1996) and (with Peter Wende) *Reform in Great Britain and Germany 1750–1850* (1999).

NIALL FERGUSON is Fellow and Tutor in Modern History at Jesus College, Oxford. His books include *Paper and Iron: Hamburg Business and German Politics in the Era of Inflation 1897–1927* (1995), *The Pity of War* (1998), and *The World's Banker: The History of the House of Rothschild* (1998). He has also edited the best-selling collection of essays *Virtual History: Alternatives and Counterfactuals* (1997).

COLIN HEYWOOD is Senior Lecturer in Economic and Social History at the University of Nottingham. His publications include *Childhood in Nineteenth-Century France* (1988) and *The Development of the French Economy* (1995). He is currently working on a history of childhood, and a study of the town of Troyes in the nineteenth century.

A. G. HOPKINS is Smuts Professor of Commonwealth History at the University of Cambridge and a Fellow of Pembroke College. He is also a Fellow of the British Academy. His publications include *An Economic History of West Africa* (1973) and (with P. J. Cain) *British Imperialism: Innovation and Expansion 1688–1914* and *British Imperialism: Crisis and Deconstruction 1914–1990* (1993).

PAUL W. SCHROEDER is Professor Emeritus of History and Political Science at the University of Illinois. He is the author of several books and many articles on the history and theory of European and world international politics. His most recent work is *The Transformation of European Politics 1763–1848* (1994), a volume in the Oxford History of Modern Europe series.

JAMES J. SHEEHAN is Dickason Professor in the Humanities at Stanford University. Among his numerous publications on German history are *German Liberalism in the Nineteenth Century* (1978) and the classic *German History 1770–1866* (1990). His history of German art museums is forthcoming.

ROBERT TOMBS is Reader in French History at Cambridge and a Fellow of St John's College, Cambridge. His books include *France 1814–1914* (1996) and *The Paris Commune 1871* (1999).

Introduction: the end of the old regime

T. C. W. Blanning

Europe changed more rapidly and more radically during the nineteenth century than during any prior period. Perhaps most fundamentally, its population more than doubled, from 205 million in 1800 to 414 million in 1900, not counting the 38 million who emigrated to other parts of the world in the course of the century. The economy grew even faster, as the per capita Gross National Product (GNP—i.e. the total economic output for every European) increased by 120 per cent between 1830 and 1913. More visible to contemporaries than the apparently modest rates of annual growth that underlay this secular figure was the communications revolution. In 1800 the wealthy travelled by horse-drawn carriage and the poor walked; in 1900 the wealthy travelled first class on the railway or were driven in their own automobiles, while the poor travelled third class on the railway and by omnibus, tram, or underground railway. The first Paris Metro line opened in 1900, carrying 15 million passengers in its first year of operations (a figure that had increased twentyfold by 1909). On 17 December 1903 the first flight by a powered aircraft pointed the way to an even more revolutionary acceleration in the pace of travel. Messages had long been travelling above ground, thanks to the invention of the telegraph in the 1830s and the telephone in the 1870s. The more earth-bound written word was also spread further and faster than ever before, as the mechanized printing presses and paper-making machines brought the unit cost of newspapers within reach of working-class pockets. This was accompanied and encouraged by the virtual disappearance of illiteracy from western, northern, and central Europe. Nor was this transformation confined to the European continent. The imperial powers, led by Britain, subjugated huge tracts of the world, to the extent that—as Tony Hopkins tells us in Chapter 6—even the penguins of the Antarctic had to acknowledge their sway. No wonder that the French poet Charles Péguy could write in 1914 that the world had changed more since he started going to school in the 1880s than during the two previous millennia.

All these changes, and many more besides, are described and analysed in the chapters that follow. And so are the forces that made for less eye-catching but equally significant stability. Indeed, a good case could be made for electing to live in the nineteenth century in preference to any other epoch, if only because it was relatively so peaceful. Wedged between two world-historical struggles for French and German hegemony respectively, the only major wars during the ninety-nine years between Waterloo and Sarajevo were the short, sharp conflicts leading to Italian and German unification. In proportion to the population, *seven times* fewer men died in battle than during the previous century. That is why Paul Schroeder announces provocatively at the beginning of Chapter 5 that he will concentrate on explaining peace. Nineteenth-century Europeans proved to be the beneficiaries of an intense learning process imposed on the great powers by Napoleon after 1805. So rapacious and brutal was the treatment he meted out to the powers he vanquished that even the dimmest of them had to recognize that a new basis for international relations had to be found. Essentially, the international politics of the eighteenth century, based on the competition and conflict engendered by an obsession with the balance of power, were replaced by a system based on concert and political equilibrium.

Less fortunate were the non-Europeans, for whom this more civilized code of conduct did not apply. Indeed, it is arguable that the resources and energy the Europeans saved by peace at home were diverted to expansion overseas. Old colonial powers such as Britain, Russia, Portugal, Spain, The Netherlands, and France were joined by newcomers such as Belgium and Germany in the conquest of the world. As Hopkins shows us, by the end of the century exploration had been succeeded by partition, and partition by occupation. It may be doubted whether the Christianity that the Europeans also brought was deemed adequate compensation by the native populations on the receiving end. Nor was this expansion confined to territorial acquisition: the European powers used their muscle to turn nominally independent states into semi-colonies by imposing one-sided trade treaties. The 'invisible empires' established in the Middle East, China, and South America could be just as exploitative as the more formal versions. Only the United States of America and Japan showed they had learned from the European example, the first by creating a domestic empire at the expense of the Spanish and its own aboriginal population and then adding an overseas empire in the Pacific and Caribbean, the second by colonizing Korea and parts of China. The crushing defeat inflicted on the Russians by the Japanese in the war of 1904–5 showed that the balance of power between Europe and the rest of the world was changing.

Significantly, it was defeat in that war that helped to ignite the first great crisis of the Tsarist regime, in the shape of the revolution of 1905. Arguably the Russo-Japanese war also represented the first clatter of pebbles heralding the landslide of 1914. Since it was also defeat in war at the hands of the Prussians and their German allies that put an end to Napoleon III's empire in 1870, the importance of international peace in maintaining domestic stability is easy to appreciate. It also helped to preserve the prestige attached to land and the power enjoyed by its owners. If Blake's 'dark satanic mills' seem a more appropriate image for nineteenth-century society than Constable's *Haywain*, it should be remembered that most Europeans continued to earn their living from agriculture throughout the century. In 1900 that applied to between a quarter and a third of Dutch, Belgians, and Swiss, between a third and a half of Germans, French, Irish, and Scandinavians, and between a half and two-thirds of Italians, Spaniards, and Austro-Hungarians. The figure for the largest country— Russia—was 80 per cent. Moreover, political arrangements took a long time to catch up with economics, as landowners continued to wield influence out of all proportion to their economic contribution. Even in Britain, 'the workshop of the world', the deference paid to landowners ensured that as late as the 1880s there were still 170 MPs who were the sons of peers or baronets. Landowners had helped themselves by founding political parties and pressure groups to protect and promote their interests, proving just as adept as their commercial or industrial rivals in exploiting the opportunities presented by the development of new media.

Paradoxically, the tenacious power of land was also demonstrated by its disruptive potential. Although contemporaries were especially fearful of the cities and their 'dangerous classes', it was in the countryside that most violence erupted. The urban poor were assimilated relatively quickly by social and cultural institutions, but the peasants proved much more difficult to control. For example, although it was events in Paris, Vienna, Milan, or Berlin that caught the eye in 1848, the revolutions of that year were also rural, and it was in the countryside that their fate was decided. Wherever political and social violence remained endemic—in Ireland, Spain, southern Italy, Hungary, and Russia—it was in large measure because 'the land question' could not be resolved. It was in Russia that the solution was most difficult to find and it was in Russia that the consequences of that failure were to be the most explosive and far-reaching. 'Peace and land' was to be the slogan of 1917: hence Richard Pipes's sage verdict that the Russian Revolution was first and foremost 'a mutiny of peasant soldiers'.

If the 'long nineteenth century' ended in the conflagration of the First World War and the Russian Revolution, for most of its course it had been marked by international peace and the continued dominance of the landed interest. The cultural equivalent of this consistency was the vitality of religion and the churches. In his chapter on 'religion and culture' in the volume on the eighteenth century in this series, Derek Beales ended with the sentence: 'The nineteenth century, in the Catholic as well as the Protestant lands of Europe, would be an "Age of Religious Revival".' It is a theme taken up repeatedly in this volume too. The churches that emerged from the searing experience inflicted by the French Revolution and Napoleon were leaner, fitter, more missionary, less aristocratic in their social composition, more populist, and—in the case of the Catholic Church—more ultramontane. They were correspondingly better equipped to deal with a polarized world in which both belief and unbelief were propagated with ever-increasing stridency. If the nineteenth century was the century of popular science, Darwin and Nietzsche's proclamation of the death of God, it was also the century of monastic revival, Victorian piety, St Bernadette of Lourdes, and the Vatican Council's proclamation of papal infallibility.

Peace, land, and faith were the rocks on which the old order stood, but there is no rock so hard that it cannot be eroded. As James Sheehan shows in Chapter 4, although religion was indeed central to the century's concerns, it was no longer an accepted fact of cultural life: it was now a problem. If the churches were less complacent and more assertive, so were those who rejected their authority altogether. Even—perhaps especially—countries previously associated with monolithic orthodoxy, such as Spain or Russia, experienced the rapid rise of militant anti-clericalism and casual indifference. Christians could live with the provocations of intellectual gadflies like Voltaire (indeed they needed each other), but the challenges posed by Comte, Marx, Darwin, Huxley, or Nietzsche were of a different order. As the great cities mushroomed, communications expanded, and opportunities for secular recreation proliferated, the churches could not run fast enough even to stay in the same place. Their impressive capacity for political organization and popular mobilization could not disguise their relative move towards the margins. In the last general election in Germany before 1914, the Catholic Centre Party performed creditably, winning ninety-one seats, but was overshadowed by the triumph of the Social Democrats, who won 112 seats and 35 per cent of the popular vote. Christians themselves were keenly aware that the ground was moving beneath their feet, a mood caught with special eloquence by Matthew Arnold in his melancholy poem 'Dover Beach', which Sheehan quotes in his chapter.

So, if it is possible, or even likely, that more people worshipped a Christian God with more understanding and intensity than ever before in Europe's history, the *perception* of contemporaries was that an age of faith was making way for the age of Mammon. The same shift in perspective underlay the emergence of the 'social question', which was to be just as fiercely debated. As Colin Heywood writes in Chapter 2, the nineteenth century was self-consciously an age of improvement but was no less haunted by the plight of the poor. The critiques of Proudhon, Marx, or Chernyshevksy, the novels of Dickens, Balzac, or Freytag, the poems of Hood, Hugo, or Heine, the paintings of Courbet, Millet, or Leibl, even Richard Wagner's monumental *The Ring of the Nibelung* (cited by Niall Ferguson in Chapter 3) all testify in their different ways to this concern. No matter that the prophets of social meltdown proved to be wrong (except in Russia), no matter that capitalism proved able to increase the incomes of all classes, it was the perception of growing poverty and growing inequality that fuelled the drive for radical social change. Propelled by public opinion, encouraged by labour organizations, and intimidated by social unrest, governments felt obliged to respond. Legislation to improve working conditions, to allow collective bargaining, to provide social insurance, to establish recreational facilities, and a host of other measures, led to a fundamental shift in social power that in most countries helped to head off a socialist Armageddon.

Similar pre-emptive hedging and trimming also transformed the shape of European politics. In the aftermath of the Napoleonic Wars, anything that appeared to be associated with the French Revolution was under a cloud. Especially after their conference at Carlsbad in 1819, continental decision-makers, led by the Austrian Chancellor Prince Metternich, firmly resisted attempts to spread political participation beyond the traditional élites. As Paul Schroeder argues in Chapter 5, a clear distinction must be drawn between the 'Vienna system', which succeeded in its objective of maintaining peace abroad, and the 'Metternich system', which failed in its objective of preserving the status quo at home. The seizure of independence by the Greeks in the 1820s and by the Belgians in 1830, together with the successful revolutions in France in 1830 and 1848, showed that the central political lesson of the French Revolution—that no regime could be deemed legitimate that did not incorporate popular participation—could not be unlearned. Nor did those insurrections that apparently ended in defeat, as in Italy and Germany in 1848, fail to make an impact, for they hoisted signs that statesmen such as Cavour and Bismarck eventually followed. Even such a successfully conservative polity as the United Kingdom felt obliged to make major changes in 1829–32 and at regular intervals thereafter. Only the Russian and Ottoman empires remained true to autocracy, with predictable consequences. As Robert Tombs observes in Chapter 1, although taking different routes and moving at different speeds, nineteenth-century Europeans appeared to be travelling towards the same destination: liberal constitutionalism.

Their progress was accelerated by the need to adapt to social and economic changes, especially demographic, urban, and industrial expansion. As Niall Ferguson states, the nineteenth century was 'a watershed in European economic history'. This was not a sudden revelation, indeed most of the technological innovations dated from the previous century and even in Britain progress was gradual and fitful enough to cast doubt on the very concept of an 'industrial revolution'. But the secular trend was clear and the cumulative change unmistakable; by 1900 even the most diehard booby squire could see that a massive shift had occurred in Europe's economic balance, however much he might deplore it. One statistic cited by Colin Heywood is particularly eloquent: of the 100 millionaires who died in Britain between 1900 and 1914, seventy-two had a business background. Together with the communications revolution mentioned earlier, the colossal increase in productivity led to a commensurate expansion of the state apparatus. Although for most of the century the most popular economic theories called for free trade abroad and *laissez-faire* at home, industrialization was accompanied by bureaucratization. Perhaps the most striking statistics to be found in this volume are those that tell us that during the last third of the century the number of civilian government personnel increased from 224,000 to 304,000 in France, from 99,000 to 395,000 in Britain, and from 204,000 to 405,000 in Germany.

That was not the only field in which Prussia, and the Germany it created, came out top. In their different ways, each of the six authors shows that the nineteenth century can be called 'the German century' on the continent of Europe, as it was the 'the British century' overseas. In 1800 German-speaking Europe, divided into the myriad states of the Holy Roman Empire, could certainly boast an extraordinarily rich culture, especially in music, literature, and philosophy, but in every other respect was eclipsed by its western neighbours. By 1900 it was also the most powerful state on the continent and was challenging Britain for economic leadership. Especially in the new high-tech industries such as chemicals, pharmaceuticals, optics, and electronics, the Germans were proving much more adept at exploiting scientific discoveries in the marketplace. Moreover, an increasing number of those discoveries stemmed from their own research laboratories, which provided the institutional underpinning to discover and sustain individual inventiveness. The benefits long outlived the regime: between 1900 and 1930 twenty-six German scientists won Nobel prizes, more than a quarter of the total awarded. Nor was their supremacy confined to 'hard science'. In the economically unproductive but not unimportant field of history it was the Germans with their new research seminars who led the way.

Powerful, prosperous, and cultured, the Germans of 1900 had every reason to feel pleased with themselves. In one important respect, however, they lacked self-esteem, for a combination of unfavourable geography and delayed nationhood proved to be an insuperable handicap for such a latecomer in the scramble for overseas colonies. In terms of both quality and width, German possessions ranked only with the empires of third-rate powers such as Portugal and Belgium. Not surprisingly, this discrepancy alarmed as much as it galled, especially those Germans influenced by Social Darwinist notions of the survival of the fittest. So there came an increasingly strident demand for 'a place in the sun', to use the memorable metaphor coined by the new Foreign Secretary, von Bülow, in his first speech to the Imperial Parliament in 1897. If that demand had been made in the middle of the century, it would not have mattered so much, as there was still plenty of the world to go round. Indeed, imperialism served as a safety valve for the European powers until the 1890s. But then, as Paul Schroeder argues, it proved to be dysfunctional: because the intensity of competition rose in inverse ratio to the territory remaining; because governments increasingly chose confrontation rather than power-sharing; because any kind of activity by another power in hitherto unclaimed territory was seen as a threat; and because the need to pursue world policy (*Weltpolitik*) came to dominate thinking about international politics.

Germany was bound to compete on the world stage—and it was equally bound to fail. That set the scene for the final erosion of the Vienna system and its later versions, which had served Europe so well for so long. As the great powers turned from seeking a balance in Europe to pursuing imperialist world politics, alliances hardened, compromises became more difficult, and minor incidents proved more dangerous. Although the Germans certainly contributed to this downward spiral, their counterproductive sabre-rattling, as in the First Moroccan Crisis of 1906 or the Second Moroccan Crisis (or 'Agadir Incident') of 1911, was only symptomatic of a general change in international conduct. True to his promise to concentrate on peace rather than war, Paul Schroeder demonstrates that the right question to ask is not 'what caused war in 1914?' but 'what had stopped war until 1914, and no longer could?' Throughout the nineteenth century, the peace had been kept by a shared political culture based on mutual assurances and restraints. It was when it was abandoned in the pursuit of world policy that the threat of a general war, not seen in Europe since 1815, returned.

So devastating were the consequences that it is tempting to seek evidence of a malaise stretching back deep into the nineteenth century. It is a temptation which has powerful attractions. All six authors of the chapters in this volume find dark sides to a period usually associated with material and cultural progress. For example, Tony Hopkins contrasts the sunlit world of Daniel Defoe's *Robinson Crusoe* (1719), whose eponymous hero is the archetypal practical optimist, with Joseph Conrad's *Heart of Darkness* (1902), whose central character dies in the Congo with the cry 'The horror! The horror!'. Niall Ferguson quotes Fontane's great novel *Der Stechlin* (1899), in which the Prussian Junker von Stechlin laments that the local glass factory is producing stills that will be used to create corrosive acids and thus 'the tools for the great general world conflagration'. James Sheehan directs us to George Gissing's hymn of hatred to science, which he branded 'the remorseless enemy of mankind'. Of course counter-examples could be found in equal measure, brimful with the belief that all was for the best in the best of all possible centuries, and we shall indeed return to its bright side in the conclusion. However, as a warning against apostrophizing the period as 'the Age of Improvement' or 'the Age of Progress' (the titles of two standard accounts), it may be permitted to end this introduction on a sombre note by quoting from Matthew Arnold's poem 'The Scholar Gypsy' the stanza from which Sheehan takes the second line:

> Thou waitest for the spark from heaven! and we,
> Light half-believers of our casual creeds,
> Who never deeply felt, nor clearly willed,
> Whose insight never has borne fruit in deeds,
> Whose vague resolves never have been fulfilled;
> For whom each year we see
> Breeds new beginnings, disappointments new;
> Who hesitate and falter life away,
> And lose tomorrow the ground won today—
> Ah! do not we, Wanderer, await it too?

1

Politics

Robert Tombs

The triumph of liberalism

Politics, in its modern sense of institutionalized public bargaining for power and advantage, was essentially an invention of the nineteenth century. The ideas and customs that shaped it—including the Judaeo-Christian tradition, feudalism, kingship, justice, rights—were much older. But their reformulation into ideologies and programmes happened quickly: as James J. Sheehan demonstrates in Chapter 5, this was the great age of intellectual systems. The invention of an international political vocabulary traces the process: the 'isms' were born mainly in the 1820s and 1830s: 'liberalism' (in France, 1820s), 'socialism' (in France and Britain, 1830s, possibly taken from Italian), 'conservatism' (in Britain, 1830s), 'communism' (in Britain and France, 1840s). The means through which politics works—bureaucracies, constitutions, parliaments, newspapers, elections—though already functioning in some parts of Europe, such as Britain and Sweden, during the eighteenth century or earlier, became universal during the nineteenth. So did the practices of increasingly professional politicians: 'screwed-up smiles and laboured courtesy, the mock geniality, the hearty shake of the filthy hand, the chuckling reply that must be made to the coarse joke, the loathsome choking compliment that must be paid to the grimy wife and sluttish daughter, the indispensable flattery of the vilest religious prejudices.' Lord Cranborne's 1859 lament would have commanded rueful agreement across much of Europe at the time, and doubtless since.

Similarities leap to the eye when we look across nineteenth-century Europe and its overseas offshoots, from one of which, the United States, it learned many political techniques. Constitutions and parties shared common models. Influential individuals corresponded and met. Cataclysmic events in one country had repercussions elsewhere. Less dramatic issues often came up in several countries. Old age pensions, for example, were adopted in Britain in 1908 and in France in 1910. French parliamentary salaries, static since 1848, increased substantially in 1906, while British MPs began to receive payment in 1911—results of a comparable process of professionalization. Women's suffrage became a significant issue in much of Europe in the 1900s.

Such similarities are signs of shared beliefs, similar problems, and conscious study and emulation of practice abroad. Whether they applauded or deplored it, contemporaries agreed that 'progress' was espousing common forms. In the 1830s, the aristocratic French thinker Alexis de Tocqueville argued, to widespread assent, that equality and democracy on the American pattern was the inevitable future. After 1860, the trend across Europe was to widen the male electorate and enfranchise women for local elections. Even Russia adopted a constitution with an elected parliament in 1905.

Different itineraries thus seemed to be leading to a common destination. France, Italy, Spain, and Portugal reached constitutional liberalism through repeated civil wars and revolutions; but Britain and Scandinavia had experienced only minor tremors. In Germany, great political change was made possible by military victories; whereas in Austria and Russia, it was forced by military defeats. What French political historians have called 'sinistrism'—a general shift to the Left, with ideas of democracy, human rights, and social justice, once extreme, becoming commonplace—can be seen across Europe. As the British liberal Sir William Harcourt remarked ironically in 1888, 'we are all socialists now.' Historicist theories supposing a common 'progressive' path from archaism to modernity were in such circumstances plausible. English 'Whig history', celebrating 'freedom broadening down from precedent to precedent', had analogies on the continent: French Republican history, for example, depicted a liberal parliamentary Republic as the predestined culmination of the French revolutionary saga. Marxism, especially in its popularized versions, charted an inevitable 'scientific' progression from feudalism, via capitalism, to a classless socialist utopia.

Yet behind this appearance of common progress there lurked huge, ever-increasing differences. In west European states and their self-governing colonies in North America and Australasia, political institutions became broadly representative of civil society; elected politicians secured influence over the exercise of power; government became relatively open, and civil liberties were respected. Elsewhere, most obviously in Russia and Austria-Hungary, and to a lesser extent in Germany, there remained what one German liberal politician called 'absolutism tricked out with parliamentary decoration and naïve trifling with pseudoconstitutionalism'. In Spain and her former American colonies, in Italy and in the Balkans, constitutional appearances barely concealed older forms of power-broking, factionalism, and conflict. Hence, the history of nineteenth-century politics can as easily be told as the survival and adaptation of 'old regimes', their institutions, and élites, who even in the most liberal countries retained important positions of power. It would be imprudent to write them off as doomed archaic survivals. The twentieth century shows that powerful interventionist states and manipulative ruling élites had at least as much of a future as liberals who preached self-limiting government by rational debate among public-spirited citizens. Whose politics were more 'modern': those of Guizot and Gladstone, or those of Bismarck and Napoleon III?

Similarities and differences structure this chapter. The first part looks at the broad common political chronology of the continent, at shared fundamental issues, at common social and cultural changes, and at the convergence of ideologies and institutions. The second part summarizes differences between individual states and societies, and their contrasting geopolitical circumstances.

Landmarks

Similar developments in European politics owed much to a broadly shared chronology caused by events on a continental or global scale. These gave rise to consciously similar responses, with commentators, politicians, and people looking abroad for lessons and theories.

The first phase, covering the first decades of the century, was the aftermath of the French Revolution. An ancient political order based on dynastic sovereignty, noble privilege, and corporate rights had been disrupted as whole populations became involved in politics and war, from Ireland to Russia. Monarchies fighting for their lives—in Britain, Prussia, Austria, even Russia—had permitted or encouraged patriotic political participation: passive 'subjects' had become active 'citizens'. Taxation and debt had risen to unprecedented levels. Whole regions had been economically ruined, and others enriched. Churches in France, Spain, Germany, and Italy had been persecuted and expropriated; the Pope himself was imprisoned, and, in France alone, 2,000–3,000 priests and nuns were executed. But in some ways churches emerged stronger as popular leaders and pillars of resistance to invasion. Ancient sovereignties such as the Holy Roman Empire and the Venetian Republic were destroyed: nearly 60 per cent of Germans changed rulers during the Revolution. New states fought for legitimacy, territory, and survival. When war ended, hordes of soldiers were demobilized and war industries slumped. Servants of the revolutionary and Napoleonic regimes and their collaborators were sacked. The general consequence of the turmoil was that from 1814 until at least 1848, Europe was struggling to rebuild viable political systems in the face of hatreds, jealousies, fears of further upheaval, hopes of new revolutionary triumphs, and divided loyalties between rival authorities and ideologies. As we shall see later, this was particularly marked in the core area most disrupted before 1814, which was again severely shaken by revolution in 1830.

The second great shared event, at the tail end of the aftershocks of the French Revolution, was the economic crisis of the later 1840s. Depressions had happened before, and even recently—the post-war slump in 1815–16, agricultural depression in the mid-1820s. But 1845–7 saw something new: the simultaneous shock of one of the last great agricultural crises caused by weather and disease (the potato crop was ravaged by blight) resulting in famine and mass migration; and the new kind of financial crash linked to investment cycles, credit, and confidence. The consequences were deep economic disruption, destitution, bankruptcies, foreclosures, evictions, mass unemployment, and hunger. This did not lead everywhere to revolutionary turmoil. Mass starvation in Ireland may have made such a reaction impossible there. But neither was there major revolt in the most developed areas of Britain or the Low Countries (where thousands starved)—or, in contrast, in backward Russia. But throughout the politically fragile parts of the continent, political systems collapsed like a row of dominoes in February and March 1848 as news of revolution followed the main communication routes: from Naples to Paris (the decisive event); then to Munich and Vienna; and from there within five days to Budapest, Venice, Cracow, Milan, and Berlin. Democracy, republicanism, socialism, and nationalism inter-reacted in one of the greatest popular movements in European history. But counter-revolution was no less contagious: repression of the June 1848 workers' insurrection in Paris and the victory of the Austrian General Radetzky in Italy emboldened conservatives everywhere, and the rest of 1848 and 1849 saw them victorious in Germany, Austria, Hungary, and Italy.

The third great shared episode was also economic in origin: the so-called Great Depression, a long period of economic slowdown that began with stockmarket crises in Berlin, Vienna, and New York in 1873. They were set off by the financial repercussions of the Franco-Prussian War, by a slump in railway shares, and also by structural changes in the world economy. In particular, imported foodstuffs from the Americas, Australia, and eastern Europe caused a long-drawn-out depression in agricultural prices, which in turn affected industry. The political repercussions were extensive, just at the time when mass schooling, cheap newspapers, and extensions of the franchise were altering the political game. Liberalism, seemingly in the ascendant across Europe, suffered. Its free-trade theory, espoused by most progressive opinion, seemed to be at the heart of the crisis, and liberal parties lost power or influence in Germany, Austria, and Britain. Farmers and manufacturers demanded protection from imports, and mobilized politically to force governments to introduce tariffs. Political parties and the electorate were divided. As these 'food taxes' raised living costs for workers already hit by joblessness, support increased for radical and socialist parties, and for more militant, even violent, trade unions. Revolution was again in the air in the 1880s and 1890s. Anarchists threw bombs into the French parliament, and assassinated the Russian tsar, the French president, the Austrian empress, the Spanish prime minister, and the Italian king. Even London's West End saw riots on a (not very) 'Bloody Sunday' in 1887. Governments tried to defuse social unrest by introducing welfare reforms and old age pensions. Small businessmen, fearing the rise of socialism and taxes, also began to organize. Many were attracted to new radical nationalist movements, which burst into politics in Germany, Italy, and France, disrupted the British House of Commons and made the Habsburg Empire almost ungovernable. Political anti-

Semitism appeared as socialists, conservatives, and nationalists attacked Jews as the epitome of rapacious capitalism. Anti-Semitic riots occurred from Brittany to the Black Sea. In France, the political world was convulsed by the Dreyfus Affair (1894–8), when a Jewish officer was wrongly accused of treason. In Vienna, an anti-Semitic populist, Karl Lueger, became mayor in 1897 after the emperor had three times refused to endorse his election. The return of economic dynamism in the late 1890s did not bring calm. Growth encouraged labour militancy, which in several countries intimidated governments into widening the franchise and contributed to growing electoral support for parliamentary socialism: by 1912, the socialist party was the largest party in Germany and the second largest in France. In short, though on the surface constitutional parliamentary politics had become the norm, much of Europe was in a state of political uncertainty. In Germany conservatives muttered about a *coup d'état*. In Austria, parliament effectively ceased to operate. In Russia, the recently granted constitution soon became a dead letter.

The political bedrock

Crises came and went, but three universal and enduring issues brought people into politics and defined their solidarities and conflicts: the state, the land, and religion.

Politics are essentially about influencing the state. As the state impinged increasingly and more efficiently on everyday life, politics mattered to more people. States had raised their demands in the eighteenth and early nineteenth centuries. The stimulus was war, and the men and money it consumed. By 1810 this had reached an unprecedented peak, affecting the whole of society, with inevitable political consequences. Although contemporaries throughout the nineteenth century were acutely aware of state expansion, in financial terms it levelled off or declined after Waterloo, as spending and conscription were reduced to head off political unrest and demands for popular representation. This low expenditure was a fundamental factor in the relative success with which most states coped with the social and economic strains of the century. As Michael Mann has argued, quarrels over taxation are the great generator of class conflict.

Relatively peaceful and parsimonious states suffered fewer political upheavals, for cheap government was a basic popular demand across the progressive spectrum from Gladstone to the Paris Communards. So states remained limited in their peacetime ambitions. In Britain, state expenditure as a percentage of GNP fell throughout the century. Even in France, archetype of state activism, the main concerns throughout the century remained the traditional ones of public order, military power, and prestige. It was essential to maintain peace if taxation was to be limited and political tranquillity preserved. Conversely, war and taxation fuelled political change, most significantly in the continental great powers France, Austria, Prussia, and Russia. Financially fragile states such as Austria were caught in an insoluble dilemma: preserving internal and external security required money for the army; but spending that money meant higher taxes, which would require political concessions; so Austrian conservatives could never afford to defend themselves adequately against internal rebellion or foreign attack. The military effort of all the large states increased during the period of warfare between 1854 and 1871, and during the arms race before 1914, when taxation and conscription again became causes of major political conflict, leading to spectacular expansion of radical and socialist support. Even so, state spending in Europe averaged merely 10 per cent of national income as late as 1913. Only in the late twentieth century, boosted by two world wars, did state spending rise towards 50 per cent, making the economic and fiscal policies of states the supreme political issue.

Although nineteenth-century states curbed their appetites for money and men once Napoleon I had been defeated in 1815, they still extended their peacetime activities. Intent on revenue, efficiency, and obedience, from the late eighteenth century onwards they took over the regulatory, educational, and welfare functions of old autonomous bodies, such as guilds, municipal corporations, provincial estates, universities, religious orders, and charities. The French Revolution had made a clean sweep of these corporate rights, which it condemned as 'privileges', and claimed for the state alone the right to direct society in the name of the common good. Napoleon had created in 1800 a uniform, centralized, hierarchical administration intended to transmit the Emperor's will 'with the speed of an electric fluid'. His successors had no intention of abolishing it, and it was later to be copied in other new or reconstructed states, including

Belgium, Spain, and Italy. Many local oligarchies and miniature sovereignties, especially in the old Holy Roman Empire, had been overthrown, and were replaced by new or greatly extended post-revolutionary states such as Prussia and Bavaria, which had to assert authority over new territories and peoples. Everywhere the instrument was a growing professional 'bureaucracy'.

From the 1840s, states also grew by embracing expanding economic activities considered politically or strategically important. Railways, for moving troops, and posts, for controlling the communication of opinions, are obvious examples. Economic modernization, while promising buoyant tax revenue, also created unrest: so states tried to set rules, protect sensitive interests, and maintain public order. Education, an economic necessity, could also shape how people thought; so, as one French minister put it in the 1880s, 'never shall we accept that the education of the people should be a private industry'. In many countries, therefore, railwaymen, postmen, and teachers were civil servants. The extent of state control corresponded to assessment of the need to defend the state from internal or external threat. It did not depend on the formal characteristics of the state—monarchy or republic, constitutional or authoritarian. Thus, for example, the (relatively threatened) French Third Republic exercised more extensive control than the (secure) British monarchy.

Whatever the extent of and motive for state expansion, it meant jobs, prestige, power, and profit. The number of civilians employed by states soared: during the last third of the century, it rose in Germany from 210,000 to 405,000; in Britain from 99,000 to 395,000; in France from 224,000 to 304,000. Landed and urban élites sought office as prefects, governors, magistrates, and mayors. In constitutional states, they stood for elected office, and used their influence over voters to bargain for favours with central government. As one French prime minister instructed his officials, 'While you owe justice to everyone, you keep your favours for those who have proved their fidelity.' This was a symbiotic relationship: central government needed the support of local élites who could exercise their economic and social authority in the state's interest as well as their own. To influence and benefit from—and sometimes to resist or even attack—the state became the inescapable concern of ever more individuals, communities, and interest groups, who began to organize, making their voices heard through meetings, petitions, and the press. Early political parties, workers' associations, pressure groups, and clandestine movements emerged throughout Europe during the 1810s–1840s, often with links to the various ideological tendencies that had emerged during the French revolutionary or Napoleonic periods. Elections to local, regional, and national assemblies, where they existed, became the focus of politics. Hence, in France in 1848, when manhood suffrage was conceded, 80 or 90 per cent of men voted, many of them illiterate, and living in remote villages. Sometimes this was a sign of touching faith in democracy; often of frank bargaining: 'You can nominate a horse as deputy if we get a railway.' Votes were paid for in favours from the state's cornucopia, or by individual candidates in cash or 'refreshments'. Nowhere were parties and elections free from more or less oppressive interference from state officials and powerful notables. This gave rise to continuing struggles for political liberties, which punctuate all European politics throughout the century.

The second great universal issue was the land: ownership, tenure, the dues to be paid for its use, and the power derived from its possession. Until mid-century, most people in every country except Britain and Belgium tilled the soil; in the most agricultural countries, up to 80 per cent depended on farming or forestry. The land was the centre of their existence, however great the spectrum of economic and social differences. These ranged from the big enclosed farms of East Anglia or Flanders at one extreme, via the specialist vineyards and market gardens of Bordeaux or Holland, the hand-to-mouth smallholdings of Gascony, Ireland, or western Germany, the 'feudal' latifundia of Andalusia and Hungary, to the lower depths of serfdom (even slavery in the Danubian principalities) that remained until mid-century in eastern Europe and parts of Scandinavia. Everywhere, struggles over the land, whether peaceful or violent, shaped political attitudes. What was new in the nineteenth century was that economic change was sweeping away the traditional relationships between people and land, just as political changes were threatening the traditional authority of landowning élites. Bitter disputes over traditional use of forests or common grazing land set rural communities against modernizing landowners and the state. Serfdom and remaining labour obligations were a source of peasant unrest during the first half of the century.

Land remained the most potent source of political power. Landowners expected their tenants and labourers to be loyal, or at least obedient; and this could be enforced by legal restrictions on movement, fines, and even corporal punishment—in some countries until the 1900s. When in the second half of the century peasants began to secure the vote—first in France in 1848, in Germany in 1871, in Britain in 1884, in Spain in 1890, in the Habsburg Monarchy in 1907, in Italy in 1912—landlords in local and national politics expected support at the polls. Where necessary, it was enforced by bribery or coercion: the ballot was public in Austria and Prussia, for example, and not effectively secret in Britain or France. Peasants were often mustered by priest or bailiff to vote in a body. One German landlord distributed completed ballot papers to his peasants in sealed envelopes. A curious voter started to open his to see how he was voting, and received a smack on the head from the outraged bailiff: 'It's a secret ballot, you swine!' In the British context, the term 'deference' is often used: a fairly voluntary acceptance of political leadership by the landed élite, which meant that still in the 1880s some 170 House of Commons seats were occupied by sons of peers or baronets. In France, too, landowners dominated parliament until the 1880s. At election time they often gave unvarnished orders, which might be backed up both by threats of eviction and by rewards for loyalty. In eastern and southern Europe, when peasants received the vote, 'deference' could be enforced by cruder means, including violence. Whether by carrot or by stick, poor rural areas often became the electoral fiefs of conservative landowners or government nominees. But oppression could have the opposite result. Peasants and labourers from as early as 1849 gave unexpected support to supposedly 'proletarian' socialist and anarchist movements in much of southern Europe. With the spread of commercial farming in the later decades of the century, agricultural trade unions, peasant parties (one held the majority in the Danish lower house from 1872), and a huge number of cooperatives (for example, for producing wine, butter, or bacon or providing loans) became significant social and political forces. Rural politics affected the whole system, because not only was the rural population so large, it was also over-represented in parliaments to neutralize the radicalism of the cities.

A viable land settlement was therefore essential for political stability. The 1848 peasant uprisings, coming at the time of maximum rural population and agricultural crisis, forced the abolition of the remnants of serfdom in central Europe. Free peasants or paid labourers, however poor, proved thereafter a less explosive political force, as a disdainful Karl Marx observed—though the vast numbers forced off the land to seek jobs in towns or overseas colonies often became a radical element there. In England and northern France commercial tenant farming created, not equality and fraternity, but at least social stability that tended towards political conservatism. In Denmark, serfdom—completely abolished only in 1861—was replaced by successful peasant landownership. But failure to create a viable land settlement was politically perilous. Poland provides a dramatic example: when nationalist nobles rebelled against Austrian rule in Galicia in 1846 the serfs sided with the Austrians, killing several hundred noble rebels and handing in heads for reward. In Ireland, relatively prosperous tenant farmers kept up an often violent and finally victorious war against large landowners seen as alien, forcing government-funded expropriation of large estates from the 1880s onwards—still not enough to placate what became the bedrock of Irish nationalism, which finally split up Europe's richest and most successful state. The consequences were most dire in Russia, whose government abolished serfdom in fear and trembling in 1861, but left most freed serfs in a state of subjection, poverty, and rumbling discontent. Peasant land-hunger contributed to the collapse of the tsarist state and its liberal successor amid the strains of war in 1917, and helped the rise of the Bolsheviks with their slogan 'All land to the peasants'.

The third universal issue was religion, which created identities and drew still-tangible boundaries from Londonderry to Sarajevo. Religious differences had long contributed to 'national' identities—for example, in Spain, Britain, Russia, and Holland. They were still essential in reviving or creating a sense of nationhood among subject peoples. Within established states, religion was an essential ingredient of political allegiance, even when new ideologies purported to replace it. This religious element in politics could be explicit and formal, as in the case of the German Catholic Centre Party. Or it could create a broader affinity, such as the strong Nonconformist element in the British Liberal Party, the widespread tendency of Jewish and Protestant minorities to support parties of the Left, or the identification of the French Right with Catholicism.

Churches were the main—often the only—social, cultural, educational, and charitable institutions, especially in small communities.

Only the clergy exerted constant ideological influence on the masses—at least until the second half of the century, when in certain countries they found rivals in state-employed schoolteachers. States needed the clergy to communicate instructions, to educate, to urge obedience to the law, and even to vouch for the legitimacy of society and the state. The ironical English summary, 'God bless the squire and his relations, and keep us in our proper stations', had its more political counterpart in the insistence of successive French regimes that after Sunday Mass all priests should intone 'God save our King'—or 'Emperor' or 'Republic'. All governments tried to control churches, and ideally promote an 'established' state church as a source of order. Especially in Protestant countries, their clergy often possessed considerable coercive powers. Many Church of England clergy were magistrates, and, in Germany, men condemned by the Church for immorality could be punished with conscription into the army; Calvinist or Lutheran ministers in Scotland and Scandinavia enjoyed crushing moral authority. Ruthless and cynical new regimes, such as that of Napoleon, whose 1801 Concordat with the Vatican aimed to turn the French clergy into 'gendarmes in cassocks', were as eager to co-opt the churches as were older governments such as that of Frederick William III of Prussia, who in 1822 decreed the amalgamation of the Lutheran and Calvinist churches to make them a more efficient instrument of state. Church authorities were usually eager to be so co-opted, in return for recognition of their social and cultural importance.

Political dissidence, therefore, usually involved religious dissidence too. This could mean anticlericalism or atheism, common on the Left after 1848 throughout Catholic southern Europe, and sometimes violent: for example, three Paris bishops were killed in the 1848 and 1871 insurrections. Or it could mean adherence to non-established religions: opposition to the state was strengthened if it had a religious ally to organize and inspire its followers. It is not always clear which impulse came first, the religious or the political. There were even French villages that converted collectively from Catholicism to Protestantism in the 1850s because they rejected the conservative political influence of the parish priest. On the other hand, many political attitudes had prior religious roots. In any case, the spiritual and temporal were mutually reinforcing. Opposition parties won support from religious minorities by condemning the tithe-gathering and administrative powers of unpopular state churches—a perennial source of literally 'anti-Establishment' attitudes in the Celtic fringes of Britain, for example. In France, where the Revolution had abolished the tithe and sold huge Church estates in the 1790s, for generations the horde of lucky buyers opposed conservatives who might try to restore the Church's old rights—a basic source of political division. French socialists tried, with some success, to create their own religions in the 1830s and 1840s, and used the slogan 'Jesus the First Communist' to win recruits; radical priests responded by inventing Christianized versions of socialism. Many ethnic or nationalist movements depended heavily on—some were even invented by—the clergy, for example, in Greece, Bulgaria, Poland, Romania, Ireland, and Croatia. States retaliated by penalizing churches that were a focus of political opposition. Many refused full equality to adherents of minority religions until well into the century. In England, the University Tests Act (limiting membership of Oxford and Cambridge to Anglicans) survived till 1871. Some governments took more aggressive action. Germany's *Kulturkampf* against the Catholic Church in the 1870s, on the grounds that Catholics were 'enemies of the Reich', and the anticlerical policy of French republican governments after the 1880s, who similarly decided that 'le cléricalisme, voilà l'ennemi!', led to closure of schools, confiscation of property, and even imprisonment of clergy.

Far from dying out over the century, religious questions were given greater importance by political innovation. Democracy gave a voice to the church-going masses, and hence influence to those who taught and preached to them. Nationalism often espoused religion, and vice versa. Compulsory education raised the momentous question of whether the churches would control the new schools and their teaching. Demands for women's political rights offered churches the possibility of greater political influence because women were more religious than men—the reason why the Left in Catholic countries opposed women's suffrage. New social concerns—for example, the sufferings of urban workers—rejuvenated traditional Christian charitable activity. Traditional Christian ideas such as the sinfulness of usury took on new relevance as a critique of capitalism. Consequently, Christian social organizations, political priests, and confessional parties—including the Belgian Catholic Party (1863), the Dutch Protestant Anti-Revolutionary Party (1878), the Austrian

Christian Social Party (1891)—became one of the characteristic and enduring features of the European political landscape.

Politics and change

The nineteenth century was aware, even exaggeratedly aware, of change. Political revolution, industrial revolution, religious decline and revival, and ideological invention created a swirling social and cultural melting pot. Pessimists lamented the collapse of old values: honour displaced by ambition; mutual obligations ignored for profit. Optimists praised economic and intellectual progress; some were impatient to build an ideal society through social revolution or moral transformation. All the new political ideas of the century were responses to this sense of change. All its new political activities were shaped by two spectacular changes: urbanization and communication.

Cities, of course, were not new—in 1800 the biggest on the continent after Paris was ancient Naples—but their sudden expansion was: London, Paris, St Petersburg, Birmingham, Berlin, and many others doubled or tripled in fifty years. This caused misgivings among the political and intellectual élites, who saw urbanization as ugly and degrading. Cities seemed anarchic, lacking the controlling influence of lord and priest, their anonymous 'masses' dehumanized and dangerous: 'The barbarians who threaten society' wrote a French journal in 1831, 'are not in the steppes of Tartary, but on the outskirts of our manufacturing towns'. To conservatives—and not only conservatives—democracy, revolution, and socialism really meant the urban mob on the rampage. Revolutionaries concentrated on the cities too: the cobblestone barricade became the icon of revolution. In 1847–9 the great spasm happened, and, as we have seen, revolt gripped the cities. But the moment passed, stamped out by military jackboots in Paris, Vienna, Berlin, Prague, Venice, and Rome. Two decades later, in May 1871, the era of urban revolution in western Europe ended where it had begun, in Paris. The Paris Commune, the greatest popular uprising of the century, was mercilessly crushed: 'in Paris in flames', concludes François Furet, 'the French Revolution bade farewell to history'.

As it turned out, cities were rarely as turbulent as contemporaries feared or hoped. They were less violent than the countryside, and less prone to revolt. After the first disorderly decades of growth and immigration from the 1840s to the 1870s, they integrated their populations through schools, social and sports clubs, trade unions, churches, and political parties. The 'proletariat' mostly turned towards peaceful industrial action and constitutional politics during the last quarter of the century. So towns proved the centre and dynamo not of anarchy and revolution, but of modern mass politics. Commerce and the professions produced a political personnel able to challenge the monopoly of the landowning gentry. Factory-owners often commanded deference from their workers similar to that of landowners from their tenants, and with the reforms of the second half of the century this could be expressed through the ballot box. Popular leaders—journalists, lawyers, doctors, teachers, trade-union officials, town councillors, writers, professors—could sometimes acquire an influence as great as the old aristocracy. These groups, whom the French republican Léon Gambetta defined in 1875 as 'the new social strata', became the ferment of radical republicanism in France after 1880, and ran radical and socialist movements elsewhere too. Gambetta, a lawyer and son of a grocer, blazed a brilliant trail by leading France against Germany in 1870 at the age of 32. Across the Channel he was followed in the 1880s with only a little less brilliance by the radical manufacturer Joseph Chamberlain, who emerged in his early 40s as a leading political figure in Britain after being a reforming mayor of Birmingham. The charismatic Karl Lueger, reformer and anti-Semite, forced the reluctant Habsburgs to accept him after being elected four times mayor of Vienna. The vehicles of such men were the organizations that urban society both required and made possible: philanthropic and religious societies crusading for temperance, morality, and sanitation; pressure groups for commerce and industry; cooperative and friendly societies providing cheaper groceries, modest insurance against illness and a decent funeral; trade unions, legalized in Britain in 1824 and in France in 1881, but widely existing in semi-clandestinity everywhere. And not least political parties, which changed from informal private clubs into large permanent organizations between the 1870s and the 1900s, with Britain and Germany first to copy the American example.

Communication (discussed by Niall Ferguson in Chapter 3) was the second great change that made all this possible: roads, railways, migration, commerce, literacy, postal services, newspapers, cheap literature. The volume of communication and internal movement increased hugely: in France in 1840, there were six million train journeys per year; in 1900, 430 million. Nineteenth-century politics believed in the motive power of words: in pamphlets, articles, proclamations, even poems, and above all speeches. Politicians began to write in newspapers and even travel the country to influence 'public opinion' directly. Organized campaigns showed how large numbers—including women and other non-electors—could now be mobilized. In Britain, campaigns in the 1820s against the slave trade and in the 1840s against the corn laws involved millions of people and forced government action. This was rarely paralleled. In Germany in 1832, 20,000–30,000 liberal nationalists met at Hambach—a high point of activity. In France in 1847–8 a 'banquet campaign' (political dinners at which politicians proposed 'toasts'—a way of evading laws forbidding public meetings) involved some 20,000 people. Politicians of national standing began addressing public mass meetings only in the 1870s and 1880s—one of many political practices copied from America. In France, Gambetta appointed himself 'travelling salesman of democracy' in the mid-1870s. In Britain, the liberal leader W. E. Gladstone initiated the first modern general election with his Midlothian campaign in 1879: 'imagine', tut-tutted *The Times*, 'a Pitt or a Castlereagh stumping the provinces, and taking into his confidence, not merely a handful of electors, but any crowd he could collect.' And crowds came. Ideology and 'opinion'—which, wrote Balzac, 'was manufactured with ink and paper'—was disseminated ever more widely, mainly in the form of newspapers, across and between states by postal subscription and by mutual copying of reports. Governments tried to restrain and censor—a losing battle. Reading rooms opened for people who could not afford books or newspapers (expensive until the commercial and technological innovations of the 1880s); in clubs and cafés they were read aloud. In England, 1 in 20 adults read Sunday newspapers in 1850; by 1900, 1 in 3.

The profoundest political effect of mass communication was the consolidation of what Benedict Anderson terms 'imagined communities', which exist in the minds of their members. Nations are the most important of these. Liah Greenfeld has argued that 'it is nationalism which has made our world, politically, what it is'. But even in old-established states such as France or England, a sense of common belonging was relatively weak during the eighteenth century. What one French politician called in 1789 'a miscellaneous collection of disaggregated peoples' spoke half-a-dozen languages and dozens of dialects. Local and regional identities mattered more than membership of the abstract 'nation'. Nineteenth-century developments affected this everywhere. Mobility required and promoted a common language, making the 'national culture' essential to modern life and politics. Schools were the main vectors: primary education became practically universal in most countries in the third quarter of the century, and even secondary education multiplied—Germany, the leader, had one million secondary school places by 1900. Literature, textbooks, and newspapers created at least an illusion of shared experience. Symbols—from maps and pictures on schoolroom walls to war memorials and museums—propounded the idea of territorial and historical identity. Parades, festivals, elections, wars, revolutions, even sports events, contributed to a common 'memory' both embroidered and expurgated. As the French philosopher Ernest Renan declared in a famous lecture in 1882, if a nation required 'the common possession of a rich heritage of memories', it also had to forget what was unhelpful to its cohesion. These developments increased the sense of unity within culturally homogenous states, and were exploited by governments to that end; but they also created bitter rivalry between ethnic groups in multinational states. A good example is the Bohemian capital Prague, when Czech-speakers, originally rural immigrants, demanded equal language rights with the Germans—implying equal, or superior, access to jobs. Nationalism thus became the vehicle for a wide range of ambitions and resentments. The theme of defending and advancing the 'national interest' became a crucial element of political discourse, and, with mass military conscription becoming the norm in the last quarter of the century, part of the experience of millions of men.

The nation was not the only imagined community. The development of 'identities' is discussed by Colin Heywood in Chapter 2. 'Class consciousness', especially the sense of belonging to a national or international 'proletariat', has similar features, with shared symbols, congresses, songs (most famously the Internationale), myths, and memories. The Catholic Church, with its increasingly ultramontane culture, including veneration of the Pope as an individual and the appearance of modern international centres of pilgrimage such as Lourdes, similarly became a more genuinely united body rather than an association of largely independent regional churches. The same mechanisms of mobility and communication, through which broader national or international identities supplemented, clashed with, or even replaced older narrower loyalties of clan, parish, or region, underpinned the whole range of ideologies and parties.

Yet this century of change did not displace the old élites. Rarely if ever did the 'new social strata' form common political cause against them (the British Anti-Corn Law League is the exception that proves the rule). Few businessmen went in for full time politics. The new rich were generally integrated into the nobility by marriage and titles. The latter proved at least as adept at using modern political organization and communications as their opponents: the first nineteenth-century election based on manhood suffrage, in France in April 1848, was a conservative victory, with many nobles and priests being elected. Louis-Napoleon Bonaparte proved in 1848–51 in France that a mass electorate could support conservative, indeed authoritarian government. In the more decorous atmosphere of 1880s Britain the 'new social strata' were equally conservative: 'Villa Toryism' was born, and the Conservative Primrose League, with two million members one of the largest organizations in Europe, loyally supported a party run largely by noblemen. So not only in the authoritarian and still rural societies of eastern Europe, but also in the most urban industrial states, the nobility and the established professional bourgeoisie retained a prominent position in government and politics. Often critical of capitalism and contemptuous of the new middle classes, the gentry provided most of the prophets of socialism too, including Blanqui, Bakunin, Tolstoy, and Lenin. At a milder level, the first British Marxist leader, H. M. Hyndman, was educated at Trinity College, Cambridge, and played cricket for Sussex, and the greatest French parliamentary socialist, Jean Jaurès, was a professor of classics and the brother of an admiral.

In short, governing a changing society proved less fraught with danger than commentators in the 1830s and 1840s had predicted. The cities did not become morasses of barbarity. Revolutions proved a damp squib, as the most modern parts of Europe made themselves the most stable. The respectable artisan who attended chapel in his

Sunday best and ran a friendly society in his spare time was a more important and emblematic figure of modernity than the wild-eyed revolutionary with flaming torch. The old élites were quick to organize their own political support, built on popular deference and fear of upheaval, and so aspects of the 'Old Regime' continued, often in rejuvenated form, until 1914 and beyond.

Ideologies and institutions

These too show how Europe was converging, as people looked across borders for models to follow or avoid. This was not new, but was greatly encouraged by common experiences of the French Revolution and the 'Industrial Revolution', a term coined in 1820s France. Certain countries—Britain, by its political liberty, stability, and economic dynamism; America, by its democracy and social mobility; and France, by its revolutionary tradition and cultural prestige—seemed to embody possible futures. Whether admired or detested, they were undeniably significant. The lessons were expounded in an increasingly elaborate international body of ideology, formulated between about 1770 and 1870 by an intelligentsia whose leading figures were famous throughout Europe. The Irishman Edmund Burke and the Savoyard Joseph de Maistre were founding fathers of conservatism; the Scotsman Adam Smith, the Frenchman Alexis de Tocqueville, and the Englishman John Stuart Mill were renowned as liberal theorists; the Frenchman Henri de Saint-Simon, the Welshman Robert Owen, and the Prussian Karl Marx were the most seminal of a host of socialist visionaries; the Pole Adam Mickiewicz, the Irishman Daniel O'Connell, the Italian Giuseppe Mazzini were perhaps the most celebrated prophets of nationalism. What they and many others had in common during these vital creative decades was a perception of Europe in a state of flux that required new ideas and institutions.

Constitutions demonstrate the processes of emulation and convergence. The American and French revolutions had both adopted written constitutions, modelled on a contract between equal citizens. This inspiring fiction became the core of debate in continental Europe before 1848. Were kings or peoples sovereign? Did power belong to governments, or was it conditionally lent by their citizens?

In France, Louis XVIII was in reality forced to concede a constitution in 1814, though it was nominally a royal charter freely 'granted'. For traditional rulers the very concept was anathema: as Frederick William IV put it, never would he let 'a piece of paper' come between him and his subjects. In Spain (whose uncharacteristically liberal 1812 constitution was a model for revolutionaries for a generation), Italy, Germany, and eastern Europe, governments conceded constitutions at times of crisis, such as during the 1830 revolutionary period, and withdrew them when they felt strong enough. Constitutions were not demanded only by revolutionaries and liberals, however. Especially in Germany, they were discreetly supported by modernizing bureaucrats, who saw them as an aid to efficient government by controlling the caprices of monarchs and courtiers. After the 1848 revolutions, most continental states had conceded constitutions, and the question was formally closed, though the Habsburgs suspended theirs in 1851 after the revolutionaries had been safely defeated. The main exceptions were Russia—whose government refused a constitution until forced by the 1905 revolution—and Britain, constitutional in practice, but which in this period underwent no political breakdown that made a codified constitution necessary.

Constitutions necessarily recognized a right of representation. To have representative bodies at all was a great step; after that, their form, powers, and means of election were crucial. What should be represented: the divergent 'interests' within society, or some 'general will' of all? Was the aim to defend existing society, or change it? Monarchs commonly strove to have no more than estates or diets, traditional in form and with a merely advisory role, representing regions and classes rather than a single 'nation' of citizens. Such were hesitantly adopted in most of Germany between 1815 and the 1860s. Liberal reformers wanted national assemblies on the British or French model, with public debates, a voice in legislation, the power to question ministers and influence their appointment and dismissal, and control over the budget, always the crucial lever of power. Democrats and revolutionaries demanded single-chamber parliaments, frequent elections, and salaries for members to make parliaments responsive to popular demands. But after the frightening experience of the French Revolutionary Convention (1792–5), liberals and conservatives wanted second chambers, loosely modelled on the British House of Lords, to restrain potentially radical lower houses. Over the century, many patterns were tried, but by the first years of the twentieth century every large state—even Russia after 1905—had a two-chamber parliament, the upper chamber usually recruited from senior bureaucrats, noble landowners, clergy, and soldiers.

Even the weakest parliaments could harass ministers, and election defeats would embarrass regimes that claimed to enjoy the loyalty of their subjects. So electoral systems and their manipulation became a perpetual tug of war. Who could vote and how? Should the electoral system reflect the social hierarchy as it was, or be a means of changing society? For most of the century, over most of Europe, 'universal' (meaning male) suffrage seemed reckless folly, not least to liberals who stressed the need for rationality and moderation. Only responsible citizens should vote, not the ignorant and suggestible. This meant those owning substantial property and paying direct taxes, especially on land, or sometimes having educational or professional qualifications. Practice varied hugely. In Britain after the 1832 Great Reform Act a jumble of property and traditional qualifications created 650,000 electors, increased by further reforms in 1867 and 1884 to nearly six million—over 60 per cent of adult men. France, after 1848, was the first and for decades the only country to give 'universal' suffrage to nine million men. Napoleon III's success as a vote-winner between 1848 and 1870 suggested to some conservatives that well-managed democracy was not their enemy, because loyal or docile peasants—what Bismarck called 'the healthy elements that constitute the core and the mass of the people'—would outvote turbulent middle- and working-class radicals. But few politicians had the nerve to tread this path.

So even near the end of the century there remained vast differences in the proportion of the population with the vote, even in liberal countries that often retained property or literacy qualifications: in 1890, 27.1 per cent had the vote in France, 23.2 per cent in Greece, 21.7 per cent in Germany, 16.3 per cent in Britain, 13.9 per cent in Denmark, 9.7 per cent in Italy, and 9.1 per cent in Norway. During the 1890s several countries introduced manhood suffrage at least in theory; women, however, if they could vote at all, were generally restricted to local elections. Only in Finland (1906) and Norway (1907) could they vote in national elections. In most of Catholic Europe they had no voting rights whatever: clerical conservatives opposed it for reasons of principle, and the Left for reasons of practice. Moreover, widening the male electorate indirectly set women's rights back and removed the property-based franchise some women had previously possessed.

But the size of the electorate was not the only issue. In pseudo-liberal or authoritarian states such as Prussia, Austria, Romania, and Russia, the electorate (even when nominally 'universal') was divided into 'classes' or 'curials' according to the taxes they paid. So in Prussia, the highest 4 per cent of taxpayers had the same voting power as the lowest 84 per cent; in Austria, it took only sixty-four noblemen to elect a deputy to the lower chamber, but 10,760 peasants. Moreover, the lower curials voted indirectly, via delegates.

However limited the electorate, skewed the rules, or toothless the parliament, elections were still worth winning. New electors often took an admirably serious interest in politics, struggling through long newspaper articles and straining their ears at public meetings. But there was another side to the coin: bribery (in England particularly crude and uproarious, with corruption—usually torrents of free beer—in up to half the boroughs in the early 1880s), manipulation of constituency boundaries, intimidation (for example, by police harassing opposition supporters), barefaced cheating, and a range of carrots and sticks. As a typical French mayor reported in 1889, 'I told them often enough that there would be no compensation [for flood damage] if the commune did not produce a republican majority.' In rural areas where local notables and the clergy and sometimes government officials too, were all supporting the same candidates—as, for example, in rural Austria, Ireland, Spain, and Prussia—the result was foregone even without cheating, and many elections were uncontested. But larger urban electorates required subtler and more expensive treatment, especially propaganda through bribed or subsidized newspapers, canvassing, rallies, leaflets, and posters. Techniques were copied from America—for example, by the French Baron Mackau, who plastered Paris with a reputed two million posters for an election in 1889. This required labour and money, hence more elaborate party organization and often shady methods of fund-raising.

During the century, organized political parties emerged as the main channels of political activity. They had several origins. There were conspiratorial networks aiming at insurrection or mutiny, such as the Italian *Carbonari* of the 1800s and the French Society of the Rights of Man of the 1830s. There were electoral organizations such as the French *Aide-toi le ciel t'aidera*, founded in 1827 to counter official gerrymandering. There were early campaigning organizations in the 1820s aiming to exert influence through propaganda and mobilizing opinion, such as the Anti-Slavery Society or the French *Amis de la Presse*. There were élite parliamentary clubs, whose prototypes were the British Whigs and Tories, which, with the arrival of a mass electorate, began to establish electoral agents and party workers in the constituencies. During the middle decades of the century, political parties appeared in every country, and by the 1900s they adhered to a broadly similar pattern, which tended to absorb all but the furthest extremes of conservatism and socialism: they were legal organizations with distinct ideological tendencies, recognized leaders, permanent officials, newspapers, conferences, and manifestos, aimed above all at winning elections.

By the end of the century, then, constitutions, parliaments, and party politics had become the norm across Europe. But paradoxically, behind this façade of convergence, divergence was greater than in 1815. The significant division was not between monarchies and republics, or even between broad and narrow electoral systems, but between (increasingly stable) liberal parliamentary regimes and (increasingly precarious) authoritarian bureaucracies able to bypass parliament. In western Europe, parliaments controlled governments. In central and eastern Europe they did not. In the German Empire after 1871, the Habsburg Monarchy (after a brief liberal excursion after 1867), and the Russian empire even after the 1905 constitution, power remained with professional officials, nominally dependent on monarchical authority. While Austria and Russia blundered into their systems through a series of disasters and changes of direction, the German constitution had been carefully designed by Bismarck, Prussian Prime Minister then first Chancellor of Germany, to maintain the power of the crown, the army, and the nobility. In brief, the democratic element—the Reichstag, elected by direct manhood suffrage—could not dismiss the imperial chancellor, withhold the imperial budget, or control the federal state governments, notably Prussia, which retained its undemocratic three-class electoral system. Administration was headed by the chancellor, appointed by the king of Prussia as German emperor, and much legislative power rested with the upper chamber, the Bundesrat, composed of officials nominated by the federal states but controlled in practice by Prussia.

Moreover, the armed forces remained largely outside civilian control. In Austria and Russia, constitutions and elected parliaments had similarly little effect on the real exercise of power.

Diverging paths

How can this difference between the steady liberalization of some states and the continuing authoritarianism of others be explained? Historians tend to study countries in isolation, partly for practical reasons, partly because of an assumption that internal social, economic, or cultural conditions are sufficient explanation of a state's political processes. A brief survey of Europe's four most powerful states—Germany, Britain, France, and Russia—will show how divergent their political experience was. But we should not assume too easily that they were unique.

Germany historiography has been particularly introspective. A 'special path' (*Sonderweg*) to modernity, contrasting with the supposedly normal historical progression represented by Britain and France, has been diagnosed as the root of a malaise culminating in the Nazi catastrophe. Germany, in this analysis, did not experience a normal 'bourgeois revolution', as in Britain in the seventeenth century or France in the eighteenth. Although pressure for political change, especially in the name of nationalism and liberalism, had been growing over the previous generation, popular revolution failed in 1848 when the absolutist monarchies reimposed their authority by force. Subsequently, Bismarck emasculated liberalism by successfully uniting Germany, thus fulfilling the ambitions of liberal nationalists who acquiesced in his 'blood-and-iron' methods—wars against Denmark, Austria, and France. The new Reich, established in 1871 by a revolution from above, maintained the power of the old élites behind a constitutional façade. The 'special-path' hypothesis concludes that this created fundamental tension between the modernity of the German economy and society and the reactionary nature of its government, which used increasingly dangerous methods at home and abroad to maintain its power. While the outlines of the story are indisputable, the conclusions of the 'special-path' view are contestable. How 'special' was Germany, whether in comparison with the supposedly 'normal' Britain and France (each very different), with its eastern neighbours Austria and Russia, which also maintained authoritarian monarchies amid social and economic modernization, or indeed with its northern Scandinavian neighbours, which also avoided revolution but yet became democracies?

Yet even if we abandon the view that Germany was unique because of a missing 'bourgeois revolution' (a dubious concept anyway), Germany did face particular political problems. The 1871 Reich was established by the German princes, not the people. It contained important disaffected groups, particularly Catholics and workers, who formed Germany's first mass political parties the Catholic Centre and the Social Democrats, and who were treated as 'enemies of the state'. Important reforms were introduced from above—most notably Bismarck's social-security measures (medical and accident insurance) introduced in 1881–6, far earlier than comparable measures by any democratic or liberal state—with the intention of neutralizing workers' support for socialism. But political opposition was never overcome: indeed, the Catholic and Socialist parties grew. More importantly, the Reich's political system became unmanageable and chaotic. Parties were allowed to compete over legislation and sectional advantages, but never bore the responsibility of government. After the accession of the unstable William II and Bismarck's dismissal in 1890, a succession of imperial appointees as chancellor presided over an uncoordinated and directionless system, without any strategic vision to replace Bismarck's ruthless absolutism.

Britain was, and often still is, used as a yardstick to judge continental states. Its most celebrated characteristic, to contemporaries and to many non-British historians today, was its ability to change gradually and relatively peacefully—this was the version celebrated, and later criticized, as 'Whig history'. But was Britain the norm, the right path to 'modernity'? Or was it an oddity, semi-detached from Europe, preserving elements of the 'Old Regime' into the twentieth century and haphazardly transforming an archaic parliamentary system into a vehicle of managed popular acquiescence? Its history in the early part of the century can be told as a succession of crises averted or postponed by a mixture of concession and repression by a powerful and confident ruling élite united in its determination to defend the system against democratic disruption. Catholic emancipation (1829) averted major strife in Ireland; the Great Reform Act (1832) defused unrest in England by widening parliamentary representation without altering the fundamentals; the repeal of the Corn Laws (1846) defused middle-class radicalism at the cost of temporarily wrecking the Tory party; but the popular radicalism of the Chartists was firmly resisted. From mid-century, British politics—unique in being relatively free from financial crises and invulnerable to external threats—became an absorbing game to win power. Hence many historians analyse it through the élite rivalries of 'high politics' rather than as ideological struggle or social conflict. Gradual democratization, partly the result of this political jockeying for electoral advantage, required the political establishment to be willing to accommodate popular pressure, and the newly enfranchised to be willing to accept existing rules. Similar pragmatic democratization of parliamentary systems can be seen in Scandinavia, Belgium, and Holland. Significantly, reform never solved the problem of Ireland, where it faced sterner disaffection comparable with that in other multinational states, Austria, Germany, and Russia.

France represents a very different 'path' from either Germany or Britain. Revolution bequeathed not peace and normality, but at least a century of division and instability. This cannot be explained in terms of unusual social and economic strains, because France, with wide property ownership, low population growth, and slow economic change, experienced less social disruption than did its neighbours. The answer lies within its political culture. The Revolution bequeathed the idea that politics could transform existence, and that the state should not merely defend and administer society, but shape and lead it. But there was no agreement over the form the state should take or the aims it should pursue. As a nineteenth-century writer put it, 'the Revolution has founded a society but is still seeking a government'. A deeply divided political class nourished a range of conflicting and often utopian ideological goals. Until at least the 1880s—arguably even until the 1980s—there was no consensus over the rules of politics, and chronic division over ideology. Thus, if the British consensus was to contain conflict within the constitutional system, in France the ultimate aim of political opposition was to change it. So every political crisis became a constitutional crisis; violence was never far away. But successive changes of regime—in 1814, 1815, 1830, 1848, 1851, 1870—satisfied only one party, and could never for long command general acceptance or win unquestioned legitimacy. These regimes represented incompatible ideological visions: the Catholic paternalism of the Bourbon Restoration; the élitist liberalism of the July Monarchy; the utopian democracy of the Second Republic; the authoritarian populism of the Second Empire; the democratic liberalism of the Third Republic.

Nevertheless, there was broad agreement that some form of parliamentary representation was the inevitable modern solution. After a chequered history during the Revolution and First Empire, parliamentary prerogatives developed rapidly between 1814 and 1830. The adoption of 'universal' (male) suffrage in 1848 through the revolutionary action of the Parisian crowd proved that democracy could benefit conservatives: a lesson thoroughly applied by Napoleon III, and swiftly learned by Bismarck and the British Tory leader Benjamin Disraeli, who both acted to widen their electorates in 1867. Political freedom was crushed under Napoleon III's authoritarian rule in the 1850s, and progressively won back in the 1860s as what the liberal leader Thiers called 'the necessary liberties'. The Third Republic, which came after Napoleon's fall in 1870, was a compromise, 'the government that divides us least': a democratic republic but with a constitution (1875) designed by monarchists to include a conservative senate, a powerful centralized administration, and an electoral system favouring small rural constituencies. Thus, the republic had as much in common with modern constitutional monarchies such as Belgium and Italy as with older federal republics such as Switzerland or the United States, or the liberal 'Old Regime' of Britain with which it was often compared. The Third Republic's political characteristics as they turned out in practice—marked by fear of a return to dictatorship—were a weak executive, a strong parliament, and loose party organization. This meant rapidly changing ministries, legislative chaos, a stress on local interests and issues, and at election times rhetorical appeals to rally round great ideological principles. This appealed, said one commentator, to the tastes, habits, and even weaknesses of the French people.

Russia was different from all other European societies and polities, even if in appearance it had Westernized features such as an emperor comparable with those of Germany and Austria, and eventually a parliament, the Duma, modelled on Austrian and Prussian practices. It was, of course, an overwhelmingly rural society throughout our period, which meant that many of the changes in political conditions outlined earlier—communication, urbanization, literacy—came later than in the West. Did these conditions determine its politics? We could object that Russia was little more rural than Hungary or Spain. It retained serfdom only about a decade longer than most of central Europe, and abolished it before the United States or Brazil abolished slavery. It underwent rapid economic modernization from the 1890s onwards that made it Europe's third industrial economy by 1913. But it did not manage to stabilize the land question—as argued above, a fundamental political issue. It was undergoing in the 1900s those strains of industrialization and urbanization that Western countries had suffered in the 1840s. Most importantly, the tsarist regime was essentially different from its Western neighbours, for it had developed from a 'proprietary state' in which the tsar was considered the owner of the country and its people. Unlike the West, where feudalism had entrenched the idea of the rule of law and of rights, the tsars' subjects traditionally had no rights and no legal protection. There were no great territorial magnates to provide a political counterweight to the Autocrat, as in Britain in the seventeenth century or France in the eighteenth. There were no ancient provincial assemblies, which had been the cradle of politics in France, Germany, and Austria; no autonomous corporations; no 'bourgeoisie'; no 'civil society'. It was more like a colonial empire than like the post-feudal structures of Austria and Germany, which always recognized certain rights of at least some of their subjects.

Progressive reform proved particularly difficult. In the 1860s serfdom was abolished, a judicial system was introduced, and local government bodies, *zemstva*, were established. But the *zemstva* clashed with the bureaucracy. Alienated intellectuals, usually drawn from the administrative élite (most famously Lenin, son of an ennobled school inspector), were denied most means of political expression. Hence they were not absorbed into constitutional reformism like most radicals and socialists in western Europe during the last quarter of the century. Some gravitated to terrorist groups, which, though small, disrupted grudging reform initiatives that depended on the wavering resolve and fickle sentiments of monarchs and courtiers. Most notoriously, they assassinated the 'tsar liberator' Alexander II in 1881, which halted political reform. His successors resisted devolving power to elected bodies. The last tsar, Nicholas II, and his counsellors subverted the constitution forced on them by the 1905 revolution, and neutralized the Duma by making its Prussian-style electoral system even more undemocratic.

Nevertheless, liberal, nationalist, and revolutionary socialist parties emerged during the 1900s. As in Germany and Austria, imperial ministers tried to control the political system by bargaining, propaganda, repression, and reform from above, plus a Russian invention, police-sponsored demagoguery. Finance Minister Sergei Witte (1893–1903) and Prime Minister Pyotr Stolypin (1906–11) embarked on economic growth and land reform to increase the power of the state and weaken political opposition, but Witte's dismissal and Stolypin's assassination by a right-wing extremist shows the impasse the regime had reached. Autocratic monarchy, in which the tsar was meant to direct and coordinate policy, could not function in a large and modernizing state. In practice it meant factionalism, irresolution, and bureaucratic infighting. The question of whether the regime could either have liberalized itself or strengthened its grip on power if war had not come in 1914 can never be answered with certainty, but the possibility seems slim. In Russian history, the only means of resisting the government had been by peasant insurrection or palace revolution by courtiers and soldiers, like the failed 1825 Decembrist rising by guards officers. The 1917 Bolshevik Revolution combined both these traditions.

As these summaries show, divergent political development can be explained in large part by internal peculiarities: historical, cultural, social, economic; and not least by the deliberate political acts of rulers and peoples. But Europe was not simply a patchwork of juxtaposed states; in important ways it was a system, and its political developments followed certain patterns. Those patterns do not conform to the most obvious hypotheses. There is no clear line between traditionally Catholic and Protestant Europe: Protestant Prussia turned out politically very different from Protestant Holland, and Catholic France very different from Catholic Austria. Having had a revolution was no guarantee of subsequent stability—as in France or Spain; but nor was it necessarily a cause of chronic instability—see Belgium. The richest, most 'modern' countries, such as Germany, were not necessarily the most politically stable or democratic; nor were the poorest necessarily the most troubled. Sharp and sudden changes of political direction show that the political development of states was not running along social, cultural, or economic tramlines. Yet politics is not merely random contingency. As Marx noted, men make history, but not under the conditions they choose.

Geopolitics

Crucial conditions were imposed by the relations between states. There are obvious examples. French political history cannot be explained without reference to the rest of Europe: momentous political changes—in 1789, 1799, 1814–15, 1870, 1940, 1944, 1958—are all intimately connected with war or defeat. Russia's serf emancipation was precipitated by defeat in the Crimea, and its revolutions of 1905 and 1917 were also consequences of defeat. The internal politics of Germany and the Habsburg Empire are similarly punctuated by war. This is not necessarily to assert the 'primacy of external policy'. External policy is often undertaken for domestic reasons, and is always subject to domestic constraints. On the other hand, domestic politics are worked out in conditions set by international power. Less obvious examples than those of the largest states may illustrate the point better. Belgium, like France (of which it had formed a part between 1795 and 1814), underwent revolution in 1830, and experienced comparable turbulence during the years following. But this ended in the late 1830s, and Belgium—unlike France—kept its monarchical form of government thereafter. The determining change is international: guaranteed neutrality and protection from external intervention. Even the most improbable Old Regime remnants—Luxembourg, Liechtenstein, Monaco—survived when protected from outside interference. An example of a different kind is Schleswig-Holstein: in the part annexed to Prussia in 1864–6, farmers voted heavily for Nazis in the 1930s, while those over the border in Denmark voted socialist. Here political development is shaped by frontiers, not by socio-economic structures or cultural traditions. From this perspective, we can divide Europe broadly into four zones: first, the French revolutionary war zone; second, the zone of struggle for mastery between 1850–71; third, the protected zone; fourth, the Russian zone.

We have already noted the devastating social, economic, and political consequences of the French revolutionary wars (1792–1815) but not their geographical dimension. Though all of Europe from Ireland to the Urals was affected, the heart of the continent had to be completely reconstructed after 1814, while the two superpowers, Britain and Russia, held sway on its western and eastern periphery. Germany, its old political mosaic swept away, had to be rebuilt. To be able to resist possible French resurgence, its larger states, notably Prussia and Bavaria, extended into the debris of western Germany, and Austria into northern Italy, which had similarly to be reconstructed after its transformation into a succession of French puppet states and partial annexation by Napoleon. The Bourbon monarchy was restored in France, like its Bourbon cousins in Spain and Naples. Much of central and southern Europe, in short, was under new and uncertain management. Newly acquired subjects had to give loyalty, or at least acquiescence. But thousands of people had been left damaged, displaced, and bitter by the Revolution and its defeat. No one knew whether the new or restored governments were permanent. Would-be revolutionaries hoped that the French Revolution had been only temporarily defeated, and that revolution throughout Europe could be reignited: Poles, Belgians, Spaniards, and Italians were confident that a revolutionary France would march to their aid. Hence, revolution in France in 1830 and 1848 set off turmoil across the continent.

The same expectation of revolutionary contagion underlay the hypersensitive repression of political opinion between 1818 and 1848 by the German great powers, Austria and Prussia, which saw themselves as preserving German and European security against another devastating upheaval. This is the context throughout the 1820s and 1830s for military revolutions in Spain and Naples, liberal and nationalist stirrings and their repression in Germany and Austria, and sporadic unrest in France, Belgium, Poland, the Balkans, and even western Russia. Nowhere in this zone could political life develop free of the prospect of external interference, whether revolutionary or counter-revolutionary. Revolution in France in February 1848 brought the whole of central Europe tumbling into chaos, not least because of a collapse of self-confidence among conservative rulers: 'Eh bien, mon cher,' sighed the Austrian chancellor Metternich, 'tout est fini'. Only when the 1848 revolutions had been crushed did the political instability bequeathed by the French Revolution ebb in this zone of Europe. It is significant that nowhere else was seriously affected by revolution in 1848.

The second zone (which broadly speaking is the core of this first zone after 1848) is that of the struggle for mastery in central Europe between Prussia, Austria, and France, which was fought out with durable political consequences between 1850 and 1871. That struggle is analysed by Paul Schroeder in Chapter 5; it is its internal consequences that concern us here. Violent great-power rivalry in central Europe was, of course, nothing new, but a shared desire to prevent another descent into a catastrophe like the revolutionary wars caused self-restraint between states from 1814 until mid-century. But the sweeping away of the Metternich generation in 1848—who had often pessimistically thought of themselves as merely 'holding on as long as we can'—brought to power over the next few years men prepared to exploit new historical forces, including democracy and nationalism. As Napoleon III put it: 'March at the head of the ideas of your century, and they will sustain you . . . march against them and they will overthrow you.' And Bismarck, more tersely: 'If there has to be revolution, we would rather make it than suffer it.'

Napoleon III hoped to reorder Europe in French interests, Bismarck, to dominate Germany in those of Prussia. Both intended their success to strengthen the political order: to perpetuate Bonapartist rule, and that of the Prussian crown and nobility respectively. Thus, Napoleon's 1859 war to throw Austria out of Italy was intended both to gain France primacy in Europe and to win nationalist support in France: it was partly successful. Bismarck's 1866 war against Austria and the other German states was fought to win for Prussia dominance of Germany and to emasculate the opposition of liberals at home by fulfilling their own nationalist ambitions: it was wholly successful. This political strategy has been called 'Caesarism'—summed up by one historian as 'active authority and passive democracy'. Both Napoleon and Bismarck embraced universal suffrage. Both promoted state-led economic and social reforms, again to sideline opposition and consolidate mass support. The final round in their struggle was the war of 1870. This destroyed Caesarism in France, which then deliberately embarked in the opposite direction of parliamentary liberalism, as we have seen, but consolidated it in Germany for decades.

The other participants in this struggle—Italy and Austria—were also deeply affected. Italy, united as a by-product of the struggles of

France, Austria, and Prussia, faced enduring political problems, for much of its population felt little loyalty for the new nation state. Unification failed to remedy the economic backwardness of the south, and even exacerbated it. Parliamentary politics were corrupted by the exigencies of working the new system: as one politician put it, 'if you make a suit for a hunchback, you have to make a hunchback suit'. Austria was transformed by its defeats in 1859 by France and in 1866 by Prussia. The Hungarians seized the opportunity to reverse their own 1849 defeat and forced partitition in 1867 into a 'dual monarchy' of Austria-Hungary, each with its own government. This was a defeat for dynastic conservatism, but it led to a future of incessant conflict among ethnic groups, not least because of Hungarian oppression of their Romanian and Slav minorities, denied cultural and political equality and subject to blatant electoral gerrymandering. In the Austrian half, parliament was paralysed by multiple ethnic parties. If British politicians failed to cope with Ireland, Austria-Hungary was 'nothing but Irelands'.

The third zone is the protected zone: mainly Britain, the Low Countries, and Scandinavia; to a lesser extent all the maritime fringes of Europe; also some smaller countries, notably Switzerland. It was 'protected'—very unevenly—by British power (most effective of course at sea), by international agreements, and not least by geography. Most of these countries had been cockpits of conflict up to and including the French revolutionary wars, in which they were deeply and damagingly involved; and they experienced tension and sometimes revolution for at least a generation after 1814. Thereafter their political paths showed no single direction. Spain and Portugal in particular underwent a long ordeal of civil violence and political instability. Scandinavia, the Low Countries, and Britain saw struggles between privileged orders and democratic forces similar to those elsewhere in Europe, but they usually ended in compromise; even the acrimonious separation of Norway and Sweden in 1905 was managed without violence. What the countries in this zone had in common was that no external block was put on their political self-determination, and they were generally shielded from the struggles for mastery of the continent after 1848. It seems evident that this increased the likelihood that they would create political stability. We can see the opposite in the cases of Spain (whose internal problems were aggravated by low-key meddling from France and Britain in the

1840s) and Italy (a cockpit for Franco-Austrian rivalry from 1815 to 1866).

The most effectively protected zone was north-western Europe, accepted as the British sphere after 1814. Belgium and Holland—the United Kingdom of the Netherlands—split amid revolution and war in 1830. Their protected position meant first that the revolutionary break-up was allowed to happen without the counter-revolutionary interventions experienced in Germany, Poland, Spain, and Italy, and, secondly, the great powers forcibly settled the conflict in 1839 by the Treaty of London guaranteeing Belgian neutrality and independence. The Belgians and Dutch were thereafter left free to sort out their own problems, but not to fight each other. Their constitutions (from 1831 and 1848) essentially still survive. Faced, like the rest of Europe, with economic disaster in the late 1840s, Belgium, Holland, Britain, and the Scandinavian countries deliberately limited conflict by political concessions: their governments neither overreacted in the face of insurrection and foreign threat, nor surrendered in despair. Denmark was protected by Britain and Russia from German nationalist aggression in 1848, though not from Austro-Prussian attack in 1864. Switzerland, until 1848 a turbulent buffer zone between France and Austria that burst into civil war in 1847, thereafter became truly neutralized and followed a similar path of internal compromise. Constitutional monarchy and parliamentary politics broadly on the British model became accepted in the Low Countries and Scandinavia, which underwent remarkable economic growth, benefiting from peace and free and secure access to the vast British market. The Scandinavian monarchies were transformed from poor and rather backward societies into prosperous agricultural democracies. After 1860, Denmark and Sweden probably had the highest sustained economic growth in Europe in a virtuous circle of stability and prosperity.

Our fourth zone is Russia and its sphere, including semi-autonomous Finland, the later Baltic states, Russian Poland, the Ukraine, and, informally, the eastern Balkans; even Hungary, as noted earlier, was returned to Habsburg rule by Russian troops in 1849. Russia was the second hegemonic power in 1814, but a perceived vulnerability—cultural, political, and later even military—affected its relations with the rest of Europe, and hence its political development. Its rulers feared that Western ideas and practices would be corrupting and destabilizing—a view confirmed by unrest among former soldiers and serving officers during the decade after 1815. Even when rulers lamented Russia's 'backwardness', they also asserted the superior values of its traditions, and feared anyway that change was impossible without disaster. Their victory over Napoleon in 1812, based on formidable if crude military power, and the insulating effect of social and economic primitiveness (Russia had only 1,000 miles of railway in 1860—less than Spain or Belgium), meant that they were able to stay outside the mainstream of European political developments. No outside power tried to interfere. None obstructed their repression of Polish revolt in 1830 and 1863. But Russia was shaken in 1854 by defeat by Britain and France in the Crimean War.

Exposure of the weakness and archaic nature of state and society brought a push to modernize, both to catch up militarily with the West, and to stave off political unrest among the mass of serfs, aware of their rulers' weakness. But then there followed nearly half a century of cautious semi-detachment from European conflicts, notably from the struggle for dominance in central Europe in the 1860s. Wars against Turkey and in Asia did not affect the state's ability to maintain itself, so fundamental reform of the system was abandoned. However, a desire for industrial modernization, primarily for military purposes, brought about from the 1880s a crash programme of railway building and industrialization, which meant heavy peasant taxation and increased urbanization and literacy, bringing inevitable social and political unrest. Opposition was repressed until the unsuccessful 1905 war against Japan. Like the Crimean defeat it had domestic political repercussions, precipitating revolution in the cities and the countryside. Hasty granting of a constitution helped to calm opposition, but the concessions were in practice revoked when the war was ended and the immediate crisis passed.

This is reminiscent of the vacillating policies of conservative states in the 1820s and 1830s, before Napoleon III and Bismarck had shown that democracy could be used. But the tsars had not learnt that lesson, or believed that it did not apply to Russia. War again in 1914, and failure to conduct it successfully, finally destroyed both tsarist prestige and the regime's ability to crush opposition: by 1917 it was beyond saving. The survival of tsarist autocracy throughout our period demanded assertion of power at home and in its 'near abroad': neighbours and subjects respected it only when it seemed invincible. Peace abroad and democratization at home therefore seemed too risky to generations of tsars and their officials: but the alternative, war and repression, ultimately proved fatal. Only when the Russian empire collapsed did Poland, the Baltic states, the Balkans, and much of central Europe have a few years' breathing space to follow their own political paths.

Conclusion

The 'long nineteenth century' begins and ends in a cataclysm of war and revolution. This gives the intervening years, for all their variety, a certain unity as an era of relative peace and of economic, social, cultural, and not least political construction. The primary character-istic is surely inventiveness: of ideologies, discourses, and images; of 'imagined communities' of nation, class, and party; of institutions of rule, representation, and negotiation. This was done, in Disraeli's famous phrase, as 'a leap in the dark', for, though there were recog-nized models for progress and modernity, the political future was nevertheless largely unpredictable and often frightening.

How could so much have been done? The relative infrequency of war meant that states were making lighter demands on their peoples than in the eighteenth or the twentieth centuries. So they had resources to maintain public order, by force if necessary, but also by concession, conciliation, and reform. This was facilitated by a charac-teristic 'Victorian' moral and intellectual earnestness among politi-cians and ordinary people. It is most famously epitomized by Gladstonian liberalism, but is evident to some degree in all countries: a mixture of religion, deference, self-improvement, philanthropy, sci-ence, and progressive optimism, fuelled by the desire to avoid revolu-tion and social chaos. But there were weaknesses too. The appearance of progress and growing consensus was often superficial, concealing an unstable mix of barely compatible ideas, groups, and institutions, such as monarchy and democracy, authority and liberalism, nation and class. This is clearly seen in Germany, a volatile construction attempting to contain democracy within absolutism, and use nation-alism to neutralize class; also in Russia, where an archaic monarchy tried to increase its power by building a modern industrial economy. Across Europe there were unsatisfied groups and unresolved conflicts, most seriously in multinational states and those where genuine political representation was still denied. After 1914 the nineteenth century's most successful political creations—state, nation, political party, integrated citizenry—became devastating weapons of international and internal strife. It would take nearly all the twentieth century to exhaust these conflicts, at unprecedented cost in life and suffering. The most influential of nineteenth-century political inventions, liberal democracy, was left with a pyrrhic victory.

2

Society

Colin Heywood

Conceptualizing change

To live in nineteenth-century Europe was to witness social change on a scale that was both exhilarating and disturbing. It was exhilarating in that the developments associated with the Industrial and French revolutions encouraged hopes of conquering some of the age-old scourges of humanity, such as food shortages, ignorance, and oppression. At the same time, it was disturbing, in that these same revolutionary forces appeared to threaten the whole fabric of society. The nineteenth century was self-consciously an age of improvement, but it was also haunted by the 'social question' (the plight of the rural and urban poor). Frédéric Ozanam (1818–53), the liberal Catholic founder of the Society of Saint Vincent de Paul in France, wrote in 1837:

The question which divides men in our day is no longer a question of political forms, it is a social question—that of deciding whether the spirit of selfishness or the spirit of sacrifice is to carry the day; whether society is to be a huge traffic for the benefit of the strongest, or the consecration of each for the benefit of all, and above all for the protection of the weak.

He feared a terrible struggle between rich and poor, 'the power of gold' and 'the power of despair'. Reactions to social change could range from the warm embrace of a liberal industrialist like Friedrich Harkort in Westphalia, to the utter repulsion of a reactionary figure like Joseph de Maistre. Most contemporaries probably felt some form of ambivalence to the 'progress' around them.

How have historians conceptualized this transformation of the old social order in Europe? They began by depicting it as a shift from a hierarchically organized society of orders (such as the French *Ancien Régime*, with its three Estates) to a more fluid one of classes. Briefly stated, this involved an industrial revolution sooner or later transforming the social structure of each nation, paving the way for a 'bourgeois revolution'. With the old aristocratic order swept away, in the western part of Europe at least, the industrial bourgeoisie was ready to confront a newly emerging working class. During the late twentieth century, however, historians have become dissatisfied with this essentially Marxist account. In the first place, recent findings in economic history tend to undermine some of its key assumptions. They indicate that, even in Britain, industrialization was such a gradual and fragmented process that it would have been unable to produce a clear-cut polarization of society into a dominant bourgeoisie and a subordinate working class. The notion of a 'bourgeois revolution', whether if the dramatic type that convulsed France in 1789, or the 'silent' version at work in Spain during the early nineteenth century, becomes difficult to sustain. In its place there is evidence of some form of fusion or accommodation between landed and commercial interests.

A more radical critique of the established view calls into question the whole 'base-superstructure' model of social change associated with Marxism, and its assumption that economic forces ultimately determine the political and cultural life of a society. The recent tendency has been to 'unhook' political from socio-economic change. Historians now give more weight to what is perceived to be relatively autonomous change in the political and cultural sphere. Above all, for those who have taken the 'linguistic turn', the way language shapes our perception of the world is a major preoccupation. They argue that language produces 'reality', rather than simply reflecting it. From this perspective, it is not simply the experience of exploitation or wealth that leads to different forms of class consciousness, but, to quote Gareth Stedman Jones, 'a particular linguistic ordering of experience'. The task of the historian is then to focus on 'the making of meaning as a central human activity' (Patrick Joyce). The upshot, in the wake of post-structuralism, is a move to abandon relatively fixed and stable notions of classes and social structures in favour of 'mobile, fractured and contradictory' *identities*. These can be understood only in their particular historical contexts. Instead of envisaging, say, a working class taking its final form under capitalism and seeking its political expression in the form of socialism, we are invited to consider a 'working class' that is a social construct, serving to unite various groups at particular periods and places (such as Europe in the late nineteenth and early twentieth centuries) for political purposes. People might well consider themselves to be workers, therefore, but at the same time (and, in many cases, more importantly) they would act as parents, inhabitants of a neighbourhood, members of a church, enthusiasts of a sport or a hobby, and so on. In true 'postmodern' fashion, all such identities are thought to be overlapping, indeterminate, and unstable, since they cannot be tied to a material base in the economy. Even society becomes 'society', discursively constructed in the early nineteenth century as an object to be studied and reformed.

What emerges from all this is a 'new social history' left in some disarray, as political and cultural history invades much of its territory, and an orthodox view of nineteenth-century social change severely mauled by historians who have taken the 'linguistic turn'. A remnant of the older view remains in the general consensus among historians that there was a shift from the *language* of orders to the *language* of classes. On the one hand, during the eighteenth century, people in most parts of Europe still talked in terms of a society divided into three (or occasionally four) estates: those who fought, those who prayed, and those who worked with their hands, for example. On the other hand, from around the 1750s, they referred more and more to class, such as the familiar triptych of higher, middle, and lower class. Karl Marx (1818–53), lining up bourgeois and proletarians in his *Communist Manifesto* of 1848, famously declared that 'the history of all hitherto existing society is the history of class struggle'. This shift occurred more rapidly in western Europe than in the east. Russians were accustomed to using a system of four estates (*sosloviia*) to describe their society throughout the nineteenth century, though latterly they had to recognize anomalies such as the 'working class' (*rabochii klass*). However, throughout Europe, many contemporaries used the old and the new terminology interchangeably for much of the period, suggesting that their understanding of class might be different from our own. They also made use of other, moral-cum-political divisions when discussing their society, such as the industrious and the privileged idle, or the People and its oppressors.

More damagingly still for the older orthodoxy, historians have come to realize that its implicit assumption that a class was a 'coherent, homogenized, anthropomorphized actor', or, as E. P. Thompson witheringly put it, a 'thing', is now scarcely tenable. In other words, they are reluctant to suggest that classes were composed of people with similar social backgrounds who could act like an individual to defend their interests, with expressions such as 'the bourgeoisie realized the danger' or 'the working class was suspicious of this policy'. Instead they emphasize the varied nature of people's identities, with gender in particular looming large. There remains the contentious issue of deciding the relationship between the 'social' and the 'linguistic'. In principle, everyone agrees, it should be reciprocal, but in practice historians leave themselves open to charges of 'socio-economic reductionism' or 'linguistic determinism'. If, on the one side, reading politics directly from the social structure appears all too simple, on the other, focusing exclusively on language leaves little scope for explaining much social and political change.

This chapter will seek to convey a sense of this more complex, and in some ways more intriguing, account of social change in nineteenth-century Europe. It is structured around contemporary representations of what would now be called the 'good society'. Such representations would, of course, have been legion, and so the focus is on some of the more influential ones, which have been grouped under the three headings of liberal, socialist, and conservative. The Marxist influence caused many scholars to assert that such ideologies promoted the interests of, respectively, the middle, working, and upper classes. There is a grain of truth here, but we are all now too conscious of middle-class socialists, Tory workers, and the like, to pursue this line uncritically. The material will, therefore, be reworked to explore the constituencies, real or 'imagined', to which these competing visions of society appealed, the constant process of formation and reformation of collective identities, and the mingling of hope and disillusionment associated with the pursuit of an ideal. The pervading impression conveyed by the nineteenth-century sources is of a yearning for social harmony in the midst of change, and a certain unease about the direction in which industrial society was moving.

Liberalism, the 'middling strata', and the competitive society

At first sight, nineteenth-century liberalism appears an unlikely path to social harmony. The main priorities for liberals were in the political and economic spheres. They campaigned above all for some form of representative government in place of absolutism, and a *laissez-faire* regime in place of bureaucratic regulation of the economy. In these respects, their influence was of course enormous, particularly in the western part of Europe. Like the Thatcherites and Reaganites of the 1980s, they can be accused of some indifference to 'social' affairs, meaning that they often had little sympathy for the predicament of the poor. Liberals were inclined to blame poverty on the moral failings of the poor themselves, the Spanish poet Ramón de Campoamor, for example, asserting that it was 'the product of laziness, vice and ineptitude'. The hard line among liberals was that, under a *laissez-faire* regime, material progress would eventually benefit all members of society. The answer to poverty, therefore, lay in the realm of economic policy. John Prince Smith was a notable apologist for *Manchestertum* in Germany, insisting during the 1840s that the poor had an 'aversion to labour' that poor-relief schemes would only encourage. Other liberals were more compassionate, proposing various measures to help people help themselves, such as savings banks and adult education classes, and even a limited amount of state intervention, to protect child labour, for example.

Certainly, the individual stood at the centre of the liberal theory of progress: in principle at least, they would oppose anything that interfered with individual freedom. This could lead to a rather narrow view of social relations. During the 1820s, for example, Harriet Martineau (1802–76) envisaged society as nothing more than an 'aggregate of individuals'. What they hoped to create was a bracing environment in which education, talent, and hard work would be rewarded, at the expense of aristocratic privilege. Such competitive individualism was not to everyone's taste. Critics dismissed it as producing an 'atomized' form of society, based on the principle of 'everyone for himself, and all . . . for riches, nothing for the poor', as the French socialist Pierre Leroux (1797–1871) put it during the early

1830s. Was liberalism, then, simply a weapon for the new middle class in its struggle against the aristocracy? Did it have any sense of a broader good society? And how far were its ideals for society realized over the course of the century?

In the long term, the liberal ideal implied a classless society of free and equal individuals. In the short term, though, liberalism appealed quite unashamedly to the 'middling strata' of society. On the one hand, this involved denigrating those above and below them: the aristocracy and the 'lower orders'. For example, the former were depicted in a number of German novels of the 1850s and 1860s as too effete, devious, and ignorant to cope with the modern world. The latter were always considered too dependent on employers and charitable institutions for full citizenship. On the other hand, those in between were idealized in various ways. For this to happen, it is important to realize, they had to be defined in moral and political terms, as much as in the economic ones we conventionally associate with class.

Dror Wahrman has recently argued that commercial and industrial development provided the backdrop in both England and France for the narrative of a rising middle class, yet in neither country had it proceeded far enough by the 1820s to provide a compelling reason for such a conceptualization. The most pressing forces intervening were, for him, political ones: the need for French *doctrinaires* to stake a claim against an embattled aristocracy, and for English Whigs to come to terms with another supposedly 'post-aristocratic society' after 1832. He depicts these liberals conjuring up an 'imagined constituency', the 'middle-class', which was wooed with assertions of its intelligence and independence, making it eminently suitable to represent the interests of society as a whole. In 1831 Lord Brougham famously declared: 'By the People, I mean the middle classes, the wealth and intelligence of the country, the glory of the British name.' Similarly, in the German states, liberals defined their social identity in terms of a conveniently vague *Mittelstand* or *Mittelklasse*. There was the claim once again that this group amounted to something more than an intermediate level of society. Friedrich Dahlmann, writing in 1847, called it the 'core of the nation', which managed to combine the wisdom of the old clerical estate with the wealth and power of the old nobility. Where the middling strata were thin on the ground, as in Spain or Hungary, liberalism could take on a strong aristocratic tinge.

Generally, though, these groups provided the bulk of liberal support during the first half of the century. In Germany, for example, liberalism attracted the odd aristocrat and a few skilled workers, but mostly it was a cause for government officials, members of the professions, businessmen, craftsmen, and independent farmers.

Indeed, it might be said that the ideal society for the liberals was one that would be classless, because most people would be middle class. Social harmony would be guaranteed by avoiding substantial differences in the ownership of property. Benjamin Constant (1767–1830), in Restoration France, looked forward to a nation of independent property-owners, with the 'rich and hard-working bourgeoisie' accounting for 99 per cent of the population. Liberals were firm believers in progress, but, being solid members of the 'respectable' part of society, were determined to keep as tight a rein on change as was possible. In the political sphere, before 1848 the majority favoured the *juste milieu* of a constitutional monarchy and some form of restricted suffrage. However, there was also a radical wing to liberalism, which eventually blended into socialism. Politically it might be committed to republicanism or democracy, and, unlike orthodox liberals, it was prepared to countenance state intervention in such areas as primary education and progressive income tax. Yet it remained faithful to the vision of a society of small property-owners. Republican leaders in Paris during the 1840s idealized a democratic and fiercely egalitarian society, revolving around independent peasants, shopkeepers, and small workshop masters. At the same period, Chartists in England floated a Land Plan, which would have allowed some of the population at least the independence of a life on a small farm. This project proved extremely popular in the factory districts of northern England, anticipating later working-class support for Liberalism and the commitment to land reform.

There were other variations on the liberal 'good society' that took account of local circumstances, especially the preponderance of either industry or agriculture. In the north of England, a wealthy élite promoted the vision of an industrial community described by the historian R. J. Morris as 'a society of independent, hard-working, self-disciplined owners of small units of property'. At the extreme, there was the logic of a competitive industrial society producing an élite of savants and industrialists, and a mass of labourers doomed to a rather grim existence—as foreseen by Charles Dunoyer in 1825. However, most liberals were not interested in industrial society: at mid-century they still yearned for a world of small-scale enterprise in agriculture and the handicraft trades. In the southern and western states of Germany, for example, liberals remained committed to the old trade guilds, on the grounds that they helped preserve small, independent workshop masters.

Fundamental to the existence of any form of liberal vision for society was a thriving 'public sphere'. This is defined by Jürgen Habermas as a sphere where private individuals, ideally independent of influence from the family and business on one side, and the state on the other, come together in various institutions to form public opinion. Habermas links its formation during the eighteenth century to the rise of a capitalist economy and a 'bourgeoisie' of merchants, bankers, entrepreneurs, and manufacturers. However, as his critics have pointed out, the 'public sphere' can also be seen as an arena where various types of identity, by no means exclusively 'bourgeois', could be forged. The outstanding institutional change facilitating this process was the mushrooming of voluntary associations in western Europe during the late eighteenth and nineteenth centuries. Their activities included poor relief, popular education, moral reform, thrift, scientific investigation, and leisure. In Marburg, a small university town in Hesse, the early nineteenth century witnessed a flurry of foundations, from the socially exclusive social circle *Sonntagsgesellschaft* to more popular clubs involved with gymnastics, shooting, and music. Similarly, Manchester had its Subscription Library, its Literary and Philosophical Society, its Royal Manchester Institute, and its Billiard Club, to name but a few of its institutions. Such associations undoubtedly offered solutions to pressing problems for property-owners in the towns that the state was failing to address—notably, public order and poverty. They sponsored 'rational' leisure pursuits (reading, as opposed to drinking, for example), and facilitated control of charitable initiatives. They also enabled those with sufficient leisure and affluence to relax in the company of their own kind. The diary of J. W. Shorthouse, the son of a Quaker manufacturer in Birmingham, revealed a remarkably sociable existence during the 1850s, including sports, reading, lectures, concerts, and travel.

Some historians have asserted that the voluntary associations had the function of encouraging middle-class consciousness in the face of some very obvious material and ideological differences. However, this seems unduly dogmatic, there being little evidence that class was a focus of their interests. The associations might well pander to feelings of exclusiveness in the highly status-conscious societies of Europe. At the same time, it is worth emphasizing that the liberals prized debate and dissent in their social order. The 'public sphere' had the scope to form a whole series of collective identities, some of which competed, whilst others overlapped. People might see themselves as, say, aristocrats or middle class, Catholics or Protestants, monarchists or republicans, members of a town choir, supporters of a gymnastic club, part of a scientific community, or devotees of various charities. Take belonging to a church. This could be an important part of an individual's identity, given the time and effort required, and the loyalties generated by rivalry with other denominations. The example of Bradford reveals the established Anglican church struggling to come to terms with the new urban and industrial society, whilst three Nonconformist sects—the Baptists, the Congregationalists, and the Methodists—went from strength to strength. The historian Theodore Koditschek has shown how even the busiest entrepreneurs were prepared to become deacons or lay readers in their congregations, and to work with Sunday schools, bible societies, and charities. The snuff-maker William Whitaker even went bankrupt in 1860 after making excessive contributions to his Wesleyan Methodist church. In Lille, a small group of employers in the Association catholique des patrons du Nord worked hard to defend the Catholic faith—without a great deal of success, it must be said. The other camp in France was the anticlerical one, which also had its share of crusaders. The stock character here is Monsieur Homais, the chemist in Flaubert's *Madame Bovary*, who laboured tirelessly to defend his principles: 'My God is the God of Socrates, of Franklin, Voltaire and Béranger! I am for the *Savoyard Curate's Confession of Faith* and the immortal principles of '89!'

Women were not entirely excluded from these voluntary associations, being particularly involved in charitable activities such as visiting the poor and setting up soup kitchens. In principle, such associations should have formed part of a liberal project for society more favourable to the emancipation of women than a conservative one. Liberals did, after all, have in common with feminists a commitment to individual liberties and to educational reform.

However, in practice, the realities of existing power relations between the sexes intervened, and it is difficult to avoid the conclusion that nineteenth-century liberalism did more to empower men than women. Liberals took for granted what they considered to be the 'natural' and eternal inequality of women, rarely offering them the vote in the nineteenth century, or even legal equality with men. At the heart of their thinking was the age-old notion of 'separate spheres' for men and women: a 'public' world of business and politics for the former, and a 'private' one revolving around the home and child-rearing for the latter. Whether the 'domestic ideology' that under-pinned this sexual division of labour within the family should be particularly associated with the middle class is a matter of some debate. What is clear is that most women from this background committed themselves to home and hearth (though not necessarily to idleness, of course) rather than to a career—helped by the relative affluence of their husbands, and the employment of a domestic ser-vant. Conversely, there was a tendency for married women to be excluded over the course of the century from direct involvement in the running of the larger farms and businesses. The context here was the more pressing need for some kind of scientific or technical train-ing. In the French town of Roubaix, for example, during the earlier part of the century, women like Pauline Motte-Brédart (1795–1871) could establish a reputation as shrewd business operators, as they shuttled back and forth between their homes and the family cotton mill. From mid-century onwards, this option was effectively closed to them, as they were expected to devote all their energy to domesticity. Bonnie Smith asserts that these women were eventually alienated from the values of industrial society, being drawn into perceiving the social order as a static and hierarchical construct. This did not pre-vent women from being important sources of capital in family firms: indeed, to quote Ute Frevert on marriages, 'a match at the right time and place could write off debts, win over loyal members of a firm, create business relationships and cement political coalitions'.

Yet there was always a certain tension between the very particular type of femininity imposed by the 'domestic ideology', and the reality of many women's aspirations in the later part of the century. Even when they operated within the general framework of a mothering role, seeking the opportunity for a broader secondary education and careers in caring professions such as teaching or medicine, they encountered fierce opposition from defenders of the status quo. Pilar Tauregui, one of the first women to attend a medical school in Spain, had stones thrown at her by her classmates in 1881. Male teachers in Germany tried around 1900 to prove that there was no advantage in employing (cheaper) females on the grounds that the women took more sick leave and had more nervous breakdowns than they did! In the end, the gains made by women in education and the professions before 1914 were very limited, leaving the impression of seething discontent in various quarters.

This leads to the question of how far the pleasing vision from the 1830s and 1840s of a society of hard-working, independent property-owners survived into the latter part of the century. The answer must be that it was steadily forced into retreat everywhere in Europe. Even the 'middle class' itself was increasingly pulled apart by competing status groups and economic interests. At the very top, a small number of merchants, industrialists, and, above all, bankers increasingly distanced themselves from their peers. The Industrial Revolution had thrown up a new figure in the form of the self-made man: someone who had risen from rags to riches on the basis of sheer hard work and technical competence. He was, in truth, something of a myth, given that most of the very wealthy in business came from anything but humble backgrounds. None the less, huge fortunes could be made in business, and the occasional *parvenu* managed to impose himself, such as Titus Salt, who built up a huge woollen spinning empire in Bradford, or August Borsig, who began his career as a carpenter and ended it as a manufacturer of locomotives in Berlin. By the late nineteenth century, new forms of wealth were beginning to rival, and even surpass, the old. In Britain, businessmen (predominantly in the financial sector rather than in industry) began to overtake land-owners from around 1880. According to W. D. Rubinstein, of the 100 millionaires who died in Britain during the period 1900–14, seventy-two had a business background. In France, studies of wealth in several major cities reveal the growing weight of big business from the Second Empire period onwards: in Paris, it was merchants and bankers who took the lead, in Lyons and Lille, manufacturers.

These wealthy bourgeois bought landed estates, established their own exclusive social networks, and sought honours such as a place in the British House of Lords or membership of the German reserve officer corps. Some of them established contacts with the traditional landed élites, though these took different forms across the continent. In Russia, the Romanovs managed to co-opt the embryonic middle class into a late version of the society of orders, granting them privileges and establishing a special *chin* (rank) for merchants and industrialists in the Table of Ranks. Meanwhile German businessmen were held at arm's length by the landed élite. A big armaments' manufacturer like F. A. Krupp might have his Villa Hügel, invite members of the old élite to dine with him, and appear in court circles, but most other top businessmen had to be content with an opulent lifestyle without the titled connections. In Britain, by contrast, a long tradition of younger sons of the gentry going into trade and the professions helped lower the barriers between the two sides a little, the integration through marriage of merchant bankers from the City of London and landed aristocrats being particularly striking. In Naples, too, a new commercial oligarchy managed to intermarry with the lower reaches of the local aristocracy, helped by the proliferation of minor titles. In these various ways, a new plutocracy was emerging in western Europe during the late nineteenth century, composed of aristocratic and bourgeois elements, which compromised the original liberal ideal.

Meanwhile, what might be called the foot soldiers of that particular vision, the *petite bourgeoisie* of master artisans and shopkeepers, faced an increasingly hostile environment. Their numbers may have expanded, above all on the retail side, but in general they fared relatively poorly as societies became wealthier during the nineteenth century. In Paris, for example, Adeline Daumard estimates that they owned 20 per cent of the total wealth in 1820, but only 3 per cent in 1911. The independence that they prized above all else was always threatened by their need to solicit contracts and credit from merchant wholesalers. Some were more vulnerable than others: one can distinguish a core of well-established craftsmen and shopkeepers, and a more peripheral group of men and women who were short of both capital and training, and who drifted in and out of the trades more rapidly. In Bremen, during the years 1890–1914, one-third of all shops ceased trading within their first six years. At the same period the Parisian handicraft trades had both a 'luxury' and a 'current' branch. The former relied on an élite of highly trained artisans, who flourished in the manufacture of such luxuries as fine furniture, jewellery, and artistic bronzes. The latter, by contrast, spawned an army of more specialized (and less skilled) craftsmen, typified by the ubiquitous tailors and shoemakers, who worked with cheaper materials and were subject to a more extensive division of labour. One can also note, as David Blackbourn has done in the case of imperial Germany, divergences between artisans and retailers on the issue of free trade, and between this 'old' section and a newer one composed of white-collar workers in the public sector.

Early signs of disgruntlement were registered in England at mid-century by Samuel Smiles (1812–1904). According to the historian R. J. Morris, the famous work *Self Help* (1859), far from being a celebration of material success, was a desperate effort by the *petite bourgeoisie* to assert itself when caught between a selfish and violent ruling class and a poverty-stricken and no less violent working class. In the end, small masters and shopkeepers continued to be thought of as part of a larger middle class in Britain. Their counterparts on the continent were perceived more clearly as a small business group, identified by the German term *Mittelstand* or the French *classe moyenne*. Whereas members of the British *petite bourgeoisie* remained faithful to the Liberal Party and the individualist ideal, their neighbours were sometimes tempted by political associations such as the Allgemeiner deutscher Handwerkerbund (General Union of German Artisans), founded in 1882, or the Belgian Association nationale de la petite bourgeoisie, established in 1900. This did not rule out many from this milieu having close links with workers in their neighbourhoods, though there was always the potential for conflict over credit and price levels.

A further distinction within the 'middle class' can be made between business and professional interests, particularly in those countries that were latecomers to industrialization. In Germany the *Wirtschaftsbürgertum* of entrepreneurs, managers, and *rentiers* stood further apart from the *Bildungsbürgertum* of lawyers, judges, university-educated civil servants, journalists, and so on, than was the case in Britain and France. The business interest in Germany was relatively slow to materialize during the nineteenth century, while the state bureaucracy remained exceptionally large and prestigious. Sons of businessmen generally attended a *Realgymnasium* and a technical university, leaving the *Gymnasien* and law or philosophy faculties to the sons of officials. Intermarriage between the two wings was rare, and, if those with a business background sometimes entered the professions, movement in the other direction was most exceptional. Similarly, in Italy the professional *borghesia* of the state bureaucracy had become something of a caste by the end of the century, able to rival the power of a newly emerging industrial interest. A more gradual process of industrialization in other parts of western Europe encouraged an intermingling of families with different occupational backgrounds. French *lycées* and British public schools allowed some scope for a common secondary education, and marriage barriers were less in evidence. The Heywoods, a wealthy banking family in Manchester, had family links with local industrial and commercial interests, the Church of England (a Bishop of Winchester), and the legal profession (two barristers with landed estates in Bedfordshire and Cornwall). Even so, some tension remained, as the historian Harold Perkin emphasized, with his struggle in England between the 'entrepreneurial' and the 'professional' ideal.

In sum, the 'middle class', as Dror Wahrman observes in the British case, turned out to be more middle than class. There were many appeals for middle-class support in the political arena of nineteenth-century Europe. It may be that the *Bürgertum* of continental Europe (which excluded the lower middle class) was a more coherent and self-conscious status group than the British or American middle class. More in evidence, though, was a constant process of formation and reformation. As the threat from absolutism and aristocratic patronage eased in the West, so various sectional interests came to prevail. 'Monopoly capitalism' began to supplant the original competitive form, and the professions fought hard to enhance their status, doctors and lawyers leading the way with specialist organizations. All this was a long way from the spirit of harmony that the liberal version of the 'good society' hoped for among the 'middling sort'. No less importantly, liberal hopes that the ownership of property in various forms would become generalized as the economy developed proved hopelessly optimistic. Doubtless many people did manage to enjoy a measure of independence because of their property and education, but gross inequalities persisted through the century. By the final third of the century, it was becoming clear that classic liberal 'philanthropic' initiatives to help the poor could not eliminate the impoverished 'residuum' obstinately floundering in the midst of plenty. The original liberal vision of society was well and truly blighted by this persistence of the 'social question', which called into question its faith in progress, social harmony, and a 'civil society' free from state inter-ference. In the French case, Jacques Donzelot has traced the invention of 'the social' after 1848, provoked by the declining faith in individual responsibility so dear to the liberals, and the corresponding willing-ness of the Republican state to begin shouldering the burden of some of the hazards of daily life. This development arguably laid the foun-dations for social legislation covering problems such as accidents at work, unemployment, and old age.

Socialism, the workers, and the cooperative society

Various critiques of liberalism and its alleged consequences for social relations appeared almost from the beginning. Whether radicals or conservatives, they all seized on mass pauperization as the Achilles' heel of a project dedicated to progress. Already by the 1830s and 1840s, they had established in a flood of pamphlets and articles the stock image of a labour force demoralized by long working hours, low wages, and poor housing. A French journalist warned in 1831 that 'the barbarians who threaten society are not in the Caucasus or the steppes of Tartary; they are in the *faubourgs* of our manufacturing towns'. Whereas liberals saw harsh conditions as a test of character, which some would pass and others fail, their opponents considered them an indictment of liberal political economy. The early socialists were vehement in their condemnation of the competitive society: Louis Blanc (1811–82), for example, described it as 'a system of extermination', which he held responsible for a long list of evils, from poverty and moral degradation to crime and industrial crises. They also came up with a rich crop of socialist versions of the 'good soci-ety', elaborated in far more detail than any proposed by the liberals. But what did the 'barbarians' themselves have to say? In other words, is there space for something between the well-known socialist doc-trines of Marx, Proudhon, and company, on the one hand, and the catalogue of harsh living and working conditions repeatedly docu-mented by contemporaries and history books on the other? Recent work by historians concerned with the cultural dimension to the Industrial Revolution has made this possible. For evidence, they have turned to the writings of people who were often only marginally involved with the day-to-day life of the proletariat, but whose exceptional talents gave them considerable authority in their communities: above all, militants in the labour movement, worker-poets, and contributors to working-class newspapers. What this section will investigate is how workers viewed their plight, what their vision of the 'good society' might have been, the role of 'artisans' among them, and how they responded to socialist appeals to act as a 'working class'.

Needless to say, workers (that is to say, manual labour dependent on wages) resented being written off as 'barbarians', 'slaves', or any other type of subhuman. The Parisian tailor Grignon admitted in 1833 that his comrades might have to work for fourteen to eighteen hours a day, and that they had little time for education. However, he blamed this on a government that favoured the rich over the poor, denying workers their human dignity. In emphasizing the political causes of social problems, he was typical of his milieu: 'advanced' opinion among workers pinned great faith on winning the vote, achieving a republic, securing lower taxes, and so on, as the way forward. Otherwise, workers were particularly critical of the way their independence was being undermined by the wage system. They frequently complained that they were being deprived of the enjoyment of the fruits of their labour. They were rather less impressed than the liberals with the new middle classes, seeing most of them as useless intermediaries: 'a crowd of traffickers, merchants, commission-agents, trustees, traders, dealers, etc.', as the weaver Charles Noiret put it in 1840. While these usurpers wheedled their way in between producers and consumers to take their cut, unrestrained competition was forcing down wages to unbearable levels. The 'social question', then, was a matter of a new 'financial aristocracy' expanding far beyond its proper role in trading and lending, upsetting what Grignon called the 'relationships of independence and equality' between masters and men. Workers looked back with some nostalgia to a time when communities had not been undermined by individualism: to the 'cottage economy' of handloom weavers, for example, so dear to operatives in the Lancashire cotton mills.

'Association' was the key to the 'good society' for the early socialists during the 1830s and 1840s. They emphasized the benefits of cooperation within a free and voluntary association, in contrast to the competition between workers and the oppressive discipline of the workshops imposed by capitalism. To some extent, workers owed the idea to the detailed schemes proposed by middle-class theorists such as Robert Owen (1771–1858) and Charles Fourier (1772–1837). The famous *phalanstères* dreamed up by Fourier were to operate like vast hotels, lodging around 1,600 people, and, at the same time, serve as units of production. To solve the problem of making work both attractive and productive, it would be rewarded with a system of dividends instead of wages, and be performed among groups of friends. Some of these 'utopian' socialists, such as Fourier and Wilhelm Weitling (1808–71), virtually ignored industrial machinery, whilst others, notably Owen at New Lanark and Étienne Cabet (1788–1856) in his *Icaria*, welcomed it. The majority were suspicious of the state, but Louis Blanc gave it a pivotal role in establishing his social workshops. There were diverse approaches to private property, with Fourier defending it, but Cabet and Owen inclining more towards communism. Finally, they all assumed that their communities would be based on some form of religion, Cabet contending that communism was really Christianity in practice. The idea of association also emerged among workers themselves, particularly in a political hothouse like Paris, as part of their struggle against exploitation by employers. During a strike against the masters, it was tempting to think about doing without them entirely. The early phase of the 1848 Revolution provoked a flurry of associations dedicated to the emancipation of labour, Parisian building workers, for example, asserting that they wished to escape from 'bondage', so that henceforth they would work only for themselves and their families.

Such gentle visions of community and cooperation barely survived the violent denouement to 1848, and the harsh political climate that followed. During the second half of the century, it became increasingly clear that the capitalist system was firmly established in western Europe. None the less, there were many continuities right down to the First World War period. A number of socialist groups, particularly on the continent, maintained their faith in producers' cooperatives as a means of emancipating trades from the wage system. There were also echoes of the old search for relationships of mutual respect between masters and skilled labour, evident among trade unionists in the engineering and shipbuilding trades on Tyneside. Towards the end of the century, the various socialist groups talked increasingly in terms of class and class struggle, and envisaged relying more on the state to help the poor and disadvantaged. For some, the 'good society' would have to await apocalyptic revolutionary change, leading to the classless society dreamed of by Marxists, or the collectivism of the anarchists. For others, perhaps the majority of socialists in Europe at this period, the ideal was closer to existing conditions, a series of reforms to promote the interests of workers being sufficient to achieve their aims. A survey of German workers on the eve of the First World War found many hankering after a simple rural life. A young miner hoped for plenty of food, a little beer, and a good night's sleep after work, and added, 'I'd build myself a nice house so that I could live in something *I* owned.' Similarly, a metal-fitter in the Central Industrial Region of Russia idealized for the engineer F. P. Pavlov a glassworks where he had once worked, in which each family had a hut, a little barn for cattle, a vegetable garden, and access to grazing for its cattle.

The leaders of the early 'Utopian' forms of socialism hoped to rally support from most parts of the social spectrum. In the end, most of their followers came from the ranks of skilled craftsmen. Almost four-fifths of Cabet's Icarians, perhaps 50,000 strong in France during the 1840s, were employed in the handicraft trades, tailors and shoemakers being particularly prominent. Historians have often been tempted to link 'Utopian' socialism with the preoccupations of the 'artisan'. John Breuilly has gone as far as to suggest that the ideas of Weitling, himself a tailor, were based completely upon a vision of craft production in small workshops. The assumption has been that 'artisans' played a prominent role in the early labour movement because, on the one hand, their status as skilled workers was under threat from capitalist forces, and, on the other, they had the capability to mount a spirited resistance. Christopher Johnson was influential in pursuing this line of argument, using the history of the tailors in Paris as a case study. He attributed their militancy during the 1830s and 1840s to the precarious position of skilled males in the bespoke tailoring trade once *confection* (the production of ready-made clothing) took a hold. Tailoring risked becoming a typically 'sweated' trade, relying on cheap, mainly female labour for the bulk of its output. The tailors retaliated with well-organized militancy, fortified by their pride in a skilled trade. There were indeed many communities of urban artisans across Europe, whose solidarity rested on men living, working, and relaxing together in a particular neighbourhood. Perhaps the most notorious at mid-century were the *canuts* (silk-weavers) of Lyons. Their uprising in 1831 sent a tremor throughout the continent, as they took over their city and swore 'to live working or die fighting'. The 'radical-artisan' model is therefore a compelling one.

However, there are two main drawbacks to it. In the first place, it suffers from a narrow focus: it tells us a good deal about the plight of skilled males during the early stages of industrialization, but very little about other workers, women in particular. Some of the early socialists, notably Owen, Fourier, and the Saint-Simonians, were, by the standards of the time, outstanding feminists. Fourier asserted that 'the best nations have always been those which concede the greatest amount of liberty to women'. On these grounds, for what it is worth, he thought the French 'the foremost civilized nation', the Spanish 'the least indulgent towards the fair sex'. In his *phalanstères* he proposed that women work on equal terms to men, and that they be freed from the constraints of marriage. However, there were signs of a certain divergence of male and female visions within the socialist camp. Joan Scott has highlighted these in a study of skilled labour in the Parisian garment trades during the 1830s and 1840s. The tailors, while not denying women the right to work for wages, favoured a clear separation between home and work, allowing the trade to be dominated by teams of skilled males in the workshops. The seamstresses, by contrast, would accept both workshop and household forms of organization, seeing their interests better served by measures to regulate piece rates in their trade. Underlying their stance was a Saint-Simonian vision of a social republic in which women could obtain a divorce, control their own wages, refuse the domination of a selfish husband, and combine childcare with the 'right to work'. In the words of *La Voix des femmes* in 1848: 'The working woman will contribute her share to her family income and we, who have demanded the right to work for all, will dare also to believe in equality, the religious and fraternal expression of the two sexes.' Unfortunately for women, their male colleagues all too often failed to share their enthusiasm for equality. Sally Alexander noted the way that radicalism in Britain during the early nineteenth century spoke the language of its leaders: small master craftsmen, displaced domestic workers, artisans, and skilled factory workers. These men looked back to the eighteenth century for their vision of a new social order. They took it for granted that work for women should merely involve 'assisting' skilled male workers, and that a woman's place in the family should be one of subordination to a male head of household.

A further drawback to the 'radical-artisan' thesis is its focus on shoemaking and tailoring. Jacques Rancière asks why these two trades featured so prominently among radical movements when they were the least respected of all trades in the community. He cites the worker-poet Hilbey, who admitted that he worked only on children's clothes because they required a minimum of care and intelligence: 'Let those who want nicely stitched and fashioned clothes make them for themselves, if they like. I, for my part, intend to brutalize myself as little as possible.' So much for pride in the craft! It may be that militancy in these two trades can be attributed to the very weakness of their trade solidarity, encouraging them to rally to values external to the trade—such as republicanism or utopianism.

A number of historians have therefore moved on to seek the source of collective identities among workers in the cultural sphere. They have noted the influence of the past on nineteenth-century categories. The brotherhood of Christianity became the solidarity of workers, for example, or the bourgeois Third Estate of the *Ancien Régime* was complemented by the Fourth Estate of 'the people'. For the socialist leader Alexander Herzen (1812–70), the peasant commune in Russia, the *mir* or *obshchina*, would form the basis for an anarchist system of small, self-governing units of production. The historian William Sewell has pursued this line in some depth, arguing that artisans in France took the lead in class-consciousness activity up to 1848 largely under the influence of an ethos inherited from the ancient guild system. The guilds, he argued, defended the material interests of a trade, but also created a 'moral community' held together by oaths of loyalty and devotion to a patron saint. The workers' movement of the early nineteenth century persisted with notions of the trade as an ordered moral and spiritual community, since they bolstered its opposition to competitive individualism. It also updated its political and organizational language to account for the French Revolution: manual labourers became 'the people', for example, and the corporation became a free and voluntary association. The story ends in the spring of 1848, with workers in Paris struggling to construct an entire, new social order based on labour. In this way, the responses of workers to the challenge of the new industrial system were shaped by 'pre-existing values, assumptions, practices, expectations, and sentiments'.

Jacques Rancière has gone even further in cutting the workers' dreams of the 1830s and 1840s from their experiences in the workshops. In his view, the past gives way to a small band of eccentric workers as the pivotal influence. These men were more interested in ideas than in the dreary routines of manual labour. Their 'contradictory relations' with Saint-Simonians, Icarians, and other prophets of the new world were what forged the discourse of worker identity. Although ignored by the masses in normal circumstances, they came to the fore during periods of struggle. In 1833 the striking tailors turned to André Troncin, 'a man who divided his free time between the student cafés and his reading of the great thinkers'. In 1848 the house-painters sought their plan of action from 'their bizarre colleague Confais the café-keeper, who ordinarily bored them to death with his Fourierist harmonies and his phrenological experiments'.

Later versions of socialism often appealed to an explicitly proletarian constituency. Yet socialists were to discover that the 'working class' was as fragmented as any 'middle class'. Even as they worked to forge a solidarity among workers, their own prejudices served to exclude some potential members. A close look at socialist visions for the future reveals that they were generally skewed towards the aspirations of skilled male labour in the workshops and factories: of mule-spinners, metalworkers, engineers, railwaymen, building-workers, and the like. British historians in particular have debated whether this type of worker constituted an 'aristocracy of labour', bribed by good wages, authority over others, and a certain amount of control over their work into accepting the existing social order. Socialist leaders could certainly reveal themselves to be every bit as suspicious of casual and unskilled labour as the bourgeoisie. The world of the militant was perhaps too austere and work-oriented for the taste of those whose lives were dominated by bouts of unemployment, violence, and petty crime. Socialists sometimes tried to accommodate peasant interests, but without much success. The Populist movement was an early experiment in bringing socialism to the peasantry, peculiar to Russia, that failed to arouse much of a response. From the late 1860s onwards, Spanish and Italian anarchists were able to harness to their cause massive discontent among landless agricultural labourers, on the huge *latifundia* of western Andalusia and in the Po valley respectively. Other militants sought to channel the collectivist traditions of rural communities to socialism, the French Parti Ouvrier, for example, making some headway among small peasant-proprietors in Provence during the early twentieth century. In general, though, the socialists were reluctant to countenance any redistribution of land, holding to the initial Marxist view that the peasantry was doomed to disappear under capitalism.

The militants also continued to struggle with the general socialist commitment to advance the cause of women workers. Later socialist theorists were usually vaguer on women's issues than the 'Utopians', Marx, for example, confining himself to the prediction that the 'bourgeois' family would vanish along with capitalism. The German August Bebel (1840–1913) was something of an exception, his *Woman under Socialism* (1879) arguing that an end to 'sex slavery' would be possible only if 'the existing state and social order were radically transformed'. Certainly, many women workers pinned their faith in socialism, from the Owenites and Saint-Simonians of the 1830s, to the Russian 'Amazons' and the German feminists in the Social Democratic Party of the late nineteenth century. Towards the end of the century, certain groups of organized labour began to demand that men be paid a 'family wage' that would allow them to support their families without the need for their wives or children to engage in paid work. In the French case, this was particularly marked in trades such as printing and leather-working, where males were threatened by competition from cheaper female labour. Many working women, who were accustomed to operating in both the so-called public and private spheres, were unimpressed. The German feminist Clara Zetkin (1857–1933) had no illusions but that 'work is the indispensable condition for economic independence'.

Even male workers were divided by differences such as those of status, skill, trade, religious affiliation, political ideology, local and regional loyalties, geographical origins, and so on. In the mines and steelworks of the Basque province, employers were able to use strong regional identities among workers to their own advantage during the early twentieth century. The fierce Basque nationalism of the natives, which was heavily tinged with Catholicism and antisocialism, set them apart from immigrants from Galicia, Valencia, and Zamora. Similar divisions between immigrants and natives erupted with the

Irish in Lancashire, Belgians in northern France, and Poles in the Ruhr. Many trades had elaborate hierarchies of status, to which workers were acutely sensitive. Metalworkers in St Petersburg listed over 100 separate occupational categories when replying to a survey of their industry in 1908. One of these men, S. I. Kanatchikov, recalled in his memoirs that skilled patternmakers were contemptuous of peasant workers, not least because they looked different: 'they wore high boots, traditional cotton-print blouses girdled with a sash, had their hair cut "under a pot", and wore beards that were rarely touched by a barber's hand.' Likewise, the established *villauds* of Limoges scorned the *bicanards*, fresh in from the countryside, as dour rustics, still listening for the call of the rooster rather than the factory bell. Sometimes operatives developed loyalties to a particular firm, the family that owned it, and the neighbourhood that they dominated. Patrick Joyce has uncovered the remarkable phenomenon of rival cotton mills voting solidly Conservative or Liberal during the 1868 elections in Blackburn.

The labour movements of the various countries of Europe did, of course, have some success in persuading such disparate groups to act to promote common interests, and perhaps even to think of themselves as a working class. They had to their credit over the course of the century a contribution to reformist measures to improve shop-floor conditions, housing, education, social security, and so on. They also had many failures, as workers chose to support very different versions of the 'good society', such as those of the liberals or conservative Catholics. That the movements never managed to conquer any of the European states before 1914 is hardly surprising. Yet many historians have been inclined to judge each case on the extent to which it approached 'revolutionary consciousness'. It is easy to see the German labour movement, with its huge membership, centralized administration, and ostensible commitment to Marxist doctrines as 'advanced', and its smaller, more reformist British counterpart as 'backward'. But such a teleological approach betrays the residual influence of 'vulgar' Marxism. As the Fox-Genoveses later admitted somewhat ruefully, the luxury enjoyed by Marxist historians until the 1950s was that they knew the end of the story: the accession to power of the working class. Now that this appears an unlikely outcome, historians are freer to consider each national (and indeed regional) labour movement according to its circumstances.

The revolutionary stance of many workers in Russia and Germany might be attributed partly to the disruptive effects of belated but rapid industrialization in these two countries, and partly to the authoritarian character of the state. Conversely, the reformist approach of the British can be linked to a certain willingness among employers to enter into collective bargaining with trade unions, and to the existence of a parliamentary state. There were several versions of the socialist 'good society', it should be remembered, not all of which required a violent political revolution.

Conservatism, the 'upper strata', and the hierarchical society

It might seem perverse to end a survey of the nineteenth century with the ideal of a stable, hierarchical society. Such a vision certainly harked back to the *Ancien Régime* conception of a society of ranks and orders. Traditional images of the Great Chain of Being had suggested a divinely ordained hierarchy, in which, according to the Anglican catechism, each should labour truly 'to do his duty in that state of life to which it shall please God to call him'. During the 1750s Soame Jenyns had drawn out the conservative implications for the social order of this view of the cosmos:

The universe resembles a large and well-regulated family, in which all the officers and servants, and even the domestic animals, are subservient to each other in a proper subordination; each enjoys the privileges and perquisites peculiar to his place, and at the same time contributes, by that just subordination, to the magnificence and happiness of the whole.

By the late eighteenth century, under the influence of the Enlightenment, such notions were beginning to fall out of favour. However, the coming of the French Revolution, and in particular its violent turn during the Terror, provoked a strain of counter-revolutionary thought that would resonate through the nineteenth century. Some thinkers evidently looked to the past for inspiration. Joseph de Maistre (1753–1821) was convinced that the only way people could live in society was through unquestioning obedience to what he admitted to be irrational institutions, such as the hereditary monarchy, the

Catholic Church, and lifelong marriage. He perceived the enemies of the social order in France to include Protestants, lawyers, metaphysicians, journalists, Jews, American revolutionaries, intellectuals, scientists, and critics: anyone who might lead people to criticize existing sources of authority. Social Catholics in France like Armand de Melun also looked back nostalgically to the Bourbon monarchy, though they were no less impressed by the medieval guilds. During the 1840s Melun hoped to resurrect the corporative system in a new form appropriate to nineteenth-century conditions, by bringing together Christian masters and their apprentices in a *patronage*.

The most influential of this counter-revolutionary wave was the Irish-born politician Edmund Burke (1729–97), his *Reflections on the Revolution in France* (1790) arguably laying the foundations for modern conservatism. The 'good society' for Burke approximated to the one around him in late-eighteenth-century Europe. His aim was to ensure that change allowed the organic growth of established institutions to continue. In accepting that societies might progress slowly towards more complex and civilized forms, Burke distanced himself from a purely reactionary position. What he took exception to was the belief that societies could be refashioned according to abstract principles, as the French Revolutionaries had tried to do during the 1790s in the name of liberty and equality. He asserted that each society had its own set of prejudices, which were the basis for harmony: 'we cherish them because they are prejudices, and the longer they have lasted, and the more generally they have prevailed, the more we cherish them.' The wise legislator would build upon these, rather than attempt the hazardous business of attempting to improve them. This led him to defend existing institutions, such as the Church of England (and the Roman Catholic Church in France), and the existing social hierarchy. He, no less than the liberals, thought of property-owners as the backbone of society, though in his case it was the big aristocratic ones who counted most: 'the great Oaks that shade a country.' He accepted inequalities between individuals, anticipating that even in England the majority of the population would remain poor and ignorant. His influence was by no means confined to England; indeed, his most receptive audience was to be found in the German states.

Supporters of the old order were among the most ardent critics of the social consequences of individualism and the new *laissez-faire* economics: the very Catholic and very conservative Comte Alban de Villeneuve-Bargemont in France, say, or the maverick Tory Thomas Carlyle in England. Their general contention was that the 'cash nexus' was destroying the paternal concern of the rich for the poor that had flourished in the traditional organic and hierarchical society. Villeneuve-Bargemont lambasted the new 'English' science of economics during the 1830s, accusing it of breaking the fraternal bonds that linked master and worker, the strong and the weak. On the one hand, to produce goods as cheaply as possible, industry was reducing the wages of its workers to the bare minimum. On the other, to stimulate consumption, it was fostering new tastes and new needs among these same workers. Such a contradictory system, based on 'an insatiable egoism and a profound disdain for human nature', was having a disastrous effect on the moral and material condition of labour. Villeneuve-Bargement was one of the first to detect a shift from the old problem of poverty to the new one of pauperism—a whole class allegedly reduced to indigence by the progress of industry. The debate on the 'social question' raged with no less intensity in central and eastern Europe. Faced with the liberal reforms of the early nineteenth century in Prussia, Ludwig von der Marwitz sounded off in fine style against their chief protagonist, Baron vom Stein:

He . . . began to revolutionize the fatherland. He began the war of the propertyless against property, of industry against agriculture, of the transitory against the stable, of crass materialism against the divinely established order, of imaginary profit against justice, of the present moment against the past and the future, of the individual against the family, of speculators and counting houses against fields and trades, of government bureaucrats against relationships derived from the history of the country, of learning and conceited talent against virtue and honorable character.

During the 1840s, the Prussian king Frederick William IV and his advisers were able to resist demands for a constitution by exploiting liberal weakness in this sphere. Only an autocratic regime, they asserted, could defend the poor and the weak, advance social justice and promote works of Christian charity. (This was a bit rich from a regime so obviously devoted to landed and even business interests!)

The strategy of attempting to forge an alliance between the crown and the proletariat against a liberal bourgeoisie that these Prussian conservatives liked to discuss would have a long history. In 1844, for example, Frederick William helped found the Central Society for the Welfare of the Working Classes in Berlin. Later in the century Bismarck would make his famous bid to tie workers to the fate of the Prussian state by means of social insurance schemes. The key question was always whether those consigned to the lower ranks would accept the legitimacy of a rigidly hierarchical vision of the social order. Evidence on this point is difficult to muster: how far peasants or workers were coerced into submission, and how far they accepted the authority of father figures above them, remains a moot point. It seems likely that in certain circumstances it was possible to secure something more than mere outward signs of deference from the 'lower orders'. Employers in the early textile mills were often conspicuously successful in encouraging a family type of atmosphere among their operatives. They were helped by their daily contacts with their employees on the shop floor, and the relative isolation of their communities: one thinks of the calico-printers Oberkampf at Jouy and Gros-Davillier at Wesserling. The factory districts of Lancashire, so influential in forming the views of Marx and Engels on the nature of capitalism, may, ironically have been the location for one of the most genuinely deferential labour forces in Europe. Patrick Joyce argues that northern employers were skilled in the arts of an élite, with the result that the factory worker of the mid-nineteenth century 'knew his place' in the hierarchy. Large-scale enterprises in mining and metallurgy, such as the Schneiders at Le Creusot or the Krupps at Essen, attempted to adapt this paternalist tradition to their own circumstances. Although they needed to delegate authority more to managers and overseers, they too managed to generate considerable loyalty to their companies by means of an aggressively paternalist regime.

A more common stereotype of the deferential worker would be someone like old Hodge, the English farm labourer. Again, where the landowner was present on his estate, and his farm labour generally isolated from external influence, as in parts of the Midlands, or, in Prussia, in the eastern provinces of Brandenburg and Pomerania, paternalism may have worked. However, even on the land, by the nineteenth century there were too many sources of friction between employers and labourers for this type of loyalty to have been the norm. In central and eastern Europe, the draconian powers exercised by serf-owners and later the fraught process of emancipation caused problems, whilst in England there was the background of enclosure and the New Poor Law of 1834 to sour relations. Robert Berdahl concludes that, on the estates of the Prussian nobility, outward deference concealed an inward 'secret war' against the masters: 'deference was frequently coupled with the mocking laugh behind the master's back, the smirk that undermined the bow.' There was indeed a tradition of 'unbridled passion for litigation' among the peasantry in Prussia, which, as William W. Hagen has argued, bore witness to their determination to emancipate themselves as far as possible from the 'baleful powers' of the Junkers.

This leads to the obvious point that, for all the talk of mutual respect at all levels, any elaborate hierarchy along the lines of a Great Chain was bound to remain, in the words of Arthur Lovejoy, 'more gratifying to the higher than consoling to the lower ranks'. The Prussian Junkers were typical of those who promoted this model of society during the nineteenth century, claiming to run their estates as good 'house-fathers', and attempting to preserve the traditional notion of the three *stände*: the nobility, the peasantry, and the townspeople. Similarly in Russia it was privileged groups such as the gentry, the clergy, and the industrial and commercial élites who attempted to maintain their identities within the *soslovie* system during the upheavals of the early twentieth century. One should be wary of writing off too easily the effectiveness of such attempts at conserving ancient hierarchies. Arno Mayer made a well-documented case to show that the outbreak of war in 1914 was part of a rearguard action by the *anciens régimes* in Europe to resist the rise of industrial capitalism. He asserted that historians have generally underestimated the endurance of old forces and old ideas during the nineteenth and early twentieth centuries, notably those of the peasant economy, the hereditary and privileged nobility, and the Church. The consensus among historians is now that Mayer overplayed a good hand. All the evidence points to new forms of industrial and commercial wealth overhauling landed wealth towards the end of the nineteenth century, as we have already noted. None the less, his emphasis on the capacity of the forces of inertia and resistance to contain a dynamic new industrial society is a useful antidote to much of the literature.

How did the 'old order' manage to survive for so long? Certainly not by simply looking back to a golden age of deference and community. The fact is that many of those who defended the traditional hierarchy also 'bought in' heavily to the new liberal order. Take the strategies of the landowning aristocracy. First, it often profited from a liberalization of the market to increase or at least consolidate its landholdings, even though measures such as disentailment and bans on the sale of land to commoners were directly aimed at its interests. Spanish nobles, for example, accepted the process of *desamortización* during the late eighteenth and early nineteenth centuries, since it recognized their property rights, and compensated them with Treasury obligations for the loss of their feudal dues. Secondly, aristocrats sometimes became 'entrepreneurs of the soil', profiting from the buoyant market for cereals, at least until the Great Depression of 1873–96 made life difficult. The Junkers of eastern Prussia provided the outstanding example here. They took advantage of their large estates, and the feeble position of emancipated serfs, to supply urban markets in western Europe. The Russian nobility attempted to follow suit, but generally found the going harder: the peasant commune proved resistant to change, the climate inhospitable, and communications difficult. Finally, aristocrats diversified beyond their traditional agricultural interests, investing in industry or urban property. Genuinely entrepreneurial noblemen were few and far between: the Prussian Prince Guido Henckel von Donnersmarch sounds an unlikely candidate, but he developed interests in a number of 'new' industries, such as cellulose, wire, chrome, viscose, and paper. More to aristocratic taste was exploiting coal deposits under their land, or collecting rents from urban properties: a few English families such as the Grosvenors and the Russells became fabulously wealthy through their ownership of estates in London. Of course, there was a cost to these strategies: it became increasingly difficult for, say, the Junkers to talk of their paternal concern for *their* peasants on *their* land when estates were being bought and sold for profit. In other words, big landowners probably did as much as anybody else to undermine the type of society they claimed to be defending.

The question remains as to whether there was any coherence to this 'old order': was conservatism a focus for an 'upper class' formed from elements of the old landed aristocracy and a newer élite of outstandingly wealthy landowners, bureaucrats, and businessmen? There is a suggestion of this type of outcome in parts of western Europe, above all in England. However, it is the least convincing of all classes. There was a world of difference in status between, say, the great families of the English peerage and the lower gentry, not to mention the awareness of differences in rank between nobles and commoners. In Paris during the 1840s, according to a gossip columnist, the best families kept themselves apart, the likes of the Polignacs, the Bauffremonts, the Sainte-Aldégondes, the Bondys, the Crillons, the Villoutreys, and the Brissacs meeting regularly in a town house near the Boulevard St Germain.

The 'landed interest' was a possible alternative source of cohesion, typified by the mobilization of German farmers under aristocratic leadership in the Bund der Landwirte following the Great Depression in agriculture (1873–96). But, of course, landowners came in all sizes. In England, the new Domesday Book of 1874–6 revealed that there were one million owners, amongst whom a favoured minority of 7,000 had 80 per cent of the land. In France, the contrast was all too obvious between the big, wealthy holdings of the Paris basin and the poorer ones in the south. East of the Elbe an 'upper class' was even less plausible. The Russian nobility remained aloof from the business élite, and was held in contempt by the intelligentsia. Moreover, there were similar disparities in wealth and status: magnates of the Silesian nobility had little in common with backwoodsmen like the Prussian Junkers. The conclusion must be that elements of the 'organic', hierarchical society idealized by conservatives survived through to 1914. At the same time, the French Revolution of 1789 was an ominous warning of what might lie ahead for the 'old order'. Deference to traditional rank was increasingly difficult to secure, as Marwitz reflected in his memoirs:

In my youth, a man of my standing was considered to be foremost wherever he allowed himself to be seen; people tipped their hats to him, they stepped aside for him. Now, in my old age, I cannot, to be sure, say that my personal presence does not command proper respect, but the Estate [*Stand*] no longer does. One is lost in the crowd, no one steps aside, no one tips his hat, but they will run over you if you don't get out of the way.

Conclusion

The nineteenth-century concern to study and reform an abstract 'society' resulted in vast numbers of competing conceptions of the ideal. These ranged from detailed blueprints for a new social order to supposedly pragmatic defences of the existing one. If it was potentially subversive ideas along liberal and socialist lines that made much of the running over the course of the century, one should not forget the continuing influence of faith in the old hierarchies. Such a conflict of ideas on the 'good society' gives a hint of the complex, pluralistic nature of the social order in Europe. Can one say anything more precise about it? Past generalizations based on class terminology, such as a 'bourgeois society', or a bourgeois one compromised by feudal influences, or even a surviving *ancien régime*, now find little favour among historians. The classes involved appear too monolithic, the frame of reference too limiting. Instead, the recent historiography depicts a more variegated and less stable pattern of identities, in which class is merely one among many forms. It invites us to think in terms of various communities that formed and reformed, partly as people moved from the country to the town, found new jobs, developed new leisure interests, and so on, and partly as they reflected on the meaning of their experiences. These communities might be large-scale 'imagined' ones, such as a nation or a class, or small-scale, face-to-face ones, such as a neighbourhood or a sports club. The way is open to avoid some of the resounding abstractions of the past on 'industrial society' or 'the bourgeoisie'. Instead, historians can give a more subtle view of the institutions and relationships in which people lived, and the ways in which they constructed their identities.

3

The European economy, 1815–1914

Niall Ferguson

Apocalyptic visions

Though it is no longer fashionable to do so, it is possible to interpret Richard Wagner's monumental tetralogical cycle, *The Ring of the Nibelung (Der Ring des Nibelungen)*, as an allegory of nineteenth-century economic development. Its central argument, as the Rhine-maiden Wellgunde tells the dwarf Alberich in the very first scene of *Rheingold*, is that money—to be precise, gold that has been mined and worked—is power: 'He that would fashion from the Rhinegold the ring / that would confer on him immeasurable might / could win the world's wealth for his own.' But there is a catch: 'Only he who forswears love's power, / only he who forfeits love's delight, / only he can attain the magic / to fashion the gold into a ring.' In other words, the acquisition of wealth and emotional fulfilment are mutually exclusive. His lecherous advances having been mockingly rebuffed by the Rhine maidens, Alberich has little difficulty in opting for the former: significantly, the first act of capital accumulation in *The Ring* is his theft of the gold.

This is not the only economic symbolism in *Rhinegold*. The next scene is dominated by a contractual dispute between the god Wotan and the giants Fafner and Fasolt, who have just completed the construction of a new fortress, Valhalla. It is the third scene, however, that contains the most explicit economics. Here we see Alberich in his new incarnation as the heartless master of Nibelheim, mercilessly sweating his fellow dwarfs, the Nibelungs, in an immense gold factory. As his wretched brother Mime explains, his people were once 'carefree smiths' who 'created / ornaments for our women, wondrous trinkets, / dainty trifles for Nibelungs, / and lightly laughed out our work. / Now this villain compels us / to creep into our caverns / and ever toil for him alone ... without pause or peace.' The relentless pace of work demanded by Alberich is memorably evoked by the sound of hammers rhythmically striking anvils. It is a sound we hear again later in the cycle—in *Siegfried*, Act I, Scene iii—when the eponymous hero reforges his father's shattered sword Notung: perhaps the only example of a breakthrough in arms manufacturing set to music.

Of course, few serious Wagnerians nowadays would wish to overplay the economic theme in *The Ring*. (The recent production that dressed Alberich in a top hat and Siegfried in a worker's blue overalls illustrated the dangers of such overemphasis.) In any case, Wagner himself was inclined to see the cycle in rather different terms, especially after he had read Schopenhauer. On the other hand, it was Wagner himself who compared London with Nibelheim. Nor is it without significance that he conceived the cycle in the revolutionary year 1848, shortly before taking to the barricades of Dresden alongside the anarchist Mikhail Bakunin. By the time the completed *Ring* was given its first performance in August 1876, Wagner had certainly moved away from the radical politics of his youth. But to the young Irish writer George Bernard Shaw, who turned 20 that same year, the economic subtext of Wagner's work was still discernible: he was even seen in the Reading Room of the British Museum studying the orchestral score of *Tristan und Isolde* alongside a French translation of Marx's *Das Kapital*. In Shaw's *The Perfect Wagnerite* (1899), *The Ring* is an allegory of the class system: Alberich is a 'poor, rough, vulgar, coarse fellow' who seeks 'to take his part in aristocratic society' but is 'snubbed into the knowledge that only as a millionaire could he ever hope to bring that society to his feet and buy himself a beautiful and refined wife. His choice is forced upon him. He forswears love as thousands forswear it every day; and in a moment the gold is in his grasp.'

The parallel Shaw discerned between Wagner and Marx is less fanciful than might be thought. The crux of *The Ring* is the curse Alberich places on the ring at the moment it is stolen from him by the gods:

> Since its gold gave me measureless might,
> now may its magic bring death to whoever wears it!
>
> .   .   .   .
>
> Whoever possesses it shall be consumed with care,
> and whoever has it not be gnawed with envy!
> Each shall itch to possess it,
> but none shall in it find pleasure!
> Its owner shall guard it profitlessly,
> for through it he shall meet his executioner!

That curse is fulfilled with the death of Siegfried in *Twilight of the Gods*, at the end of which Brünnhilde's suicide on his funeral pyre returns the ring to the Rhine and sets 'Valhalla's vaulting towers' ablaze in an almost unstageable conflagration. It is no coincidence that Marx foresaw a similar end for capitalism in the first volume of his *Capital* (1867)—a work comparable with the *Ring* in scale if not in aesthetic beauty. In chapter 32, Marx gave a memorable sketch of capitalist economic development:

The transformation of the individualized and scattered means of production into socially concentrated means of production, the transformation, therefore, of the dwarf-like property of the many into the giant property of the few and the expropriation of the great mass of the people from the soil, from the means of subsistence and from the instruments of labour . . . forms the pre-history of capital . . . Private property which is personally earned . . . is supplanted by capitalist private property, which rests on the exploitation of alien, but formally free labour.

The imagery of dwarfs and giants is at least suggestive. Moreover, like Wagner, Marx foresaw a day of reckoning:

Along with the constant decrease of the number of capitalist magnates, who usurp and monopolize all the advantages of this process of transformation, the mass of misery, oppression, slavery, degradation and exploitation grows; but with this there also grows the revolt of the working class, a class constantly increasing in numbers, and trained, united and organized by the very mechanism of the capitalist mode of production. The monopoly of capital becomes a fetter upon the mode of production . . . The centralization of the means of production and the socialization of labour reach a point at which they become incompatible with their capitalist integument. This integument is burst asunder. The knell of capitalist private property sounds. The expropriators are expropriated.

A later German Marxist, August Bebel, made the parallel explicit when he prophesied 'the twilight of the gods of the bourgeois world'.

Marx's originality lay in the way he fused Hegel's philosophy with Ricardo's political economy. The least original thing about *Capital*, however, was its prediction that capitalism would go the way of Valhalla. The idea of an approaching cataclysm was, to use another Wagnerian term, one of the great leitmotifs of nineteenth-century culture (in Germany, there was even a satirical magazine called *Kladderadatsch*), and was far from being monopolized by the political Left—or, for that matter, by Germans. At the end of Fyodor Dostoevsky's *Crime and Punishment* (1866), the nihilist murderer Raskolnikov has a feverish and clearly allegorical dream in which 'the whole world . . . suffered a terrible, unprecedented and unparalleled plague':

Those infected were seized immediately and went mad . . . The most ordinary trades were abandoned, because everyone proposed his own ideas, his own criticisms, and they could not agree. Agriculture came to a halt. In some places, knots of people would gather together, reach some agreement, and swear not to separate; no sooner was this accomplished, however, than something quite different from what they had proposed took place. They started accusing each other, fighting each other, and stabbing away. Fires blazed up; hunger set in. Everything and everybody went to wrack and ruin.

For Dostoevsky, it was modern political philosophy rather than capitalism that threatened to plunge mankind into the abyss; but his prophecy of doom was strikingly similar to those of Wagner and Marx.

On a smaller scale, the topos of dissolution as a consequence of modernization recurs throughout nineteenth-century literature. In Dickens's *Dombey and Son* (1846–8), the railways that carve their way through London and transport the merchant Dombey to Bath are sinister agents of destruction and death. In Zola's *L'Argent* (1891), the rise and fall of a bank provides a metaphor for the rottenness of Louis Napoleon's Second Empire. Even in Theodor Fontane's nostalgic *Der Stechlin* (1899), the local glass factory at Globsow symbolizes the impeding collapse of the old rural order in the Mark of Brandenburg. As the old Junker Dubslav von Stechlin laments:

They . . . send [the stills that they manufacture] to other factories and right away they start distilling all kinds of dreadful things in these green balloons:

hydrochloric acid; sulphuric acid; smoking nitric acid ... And each drop burns a hole, whether in linen, or in cloth, or in leather; in everything; everything is burnt and scorched. And when I think that my Globsowers are playing a part, and quite happily supplying the tools for the great general world conflagration [*Generalweltanbrennung*]—ah, *meine Herren*, that gives me pain.

With such selective use of literary sources, then, it would not be difficult to portray nineteenth-century European economic history as a tale of wickedness and wretchedness, culminating in a more or less inevitable *Generalweltanbrennung*. Perhaps that is not surprising: as an occupational group, professional writers have always been conspicuously ungrateful for the benefits conferred by economic progress, not the least of which has been a huge expansion in the market for printed words. (Fontane, Dickens, and Zola were all beneficiaries of that expansion, though Wagner had to rely on the artist's traditional prop of royal patronage, Dostoevsky gambled his money away, and Marx was a financial incompetent: as his mother complained in 1868, 'It's a pity little Karl didn't *make* some capital instead.') The reality is that the period 1815 to 1914 witnessed unprecedented economic growth in Europe, from which the majority of Europeans undoubtedly benefited; and, if the period did end apocalyptically in 1914, it is far from clear that this was the inevitable consequence of the internal contradictions of capitalism.

Quantifying growth

It was another critic of industrial society, Benjamin Disraeli, who coined the famous phrase about 'lies, damned lies and statistics': it is a phrase worth recalling whenever economic historians attempt to estimate GNP, or any other aggregative economic measure unknown to contemporaries. Still, Bairoch's figures for European GNP have the merit of conveying rough orders of magnitude. According to his calculations, per capita GNP—that is, total economic output for every European—increased in real terms by around 120 per cent between 1830 and 1913. That is not to say that every European was more than twice as well off in 1913 than in 1830, for such figures take no account of changes in the distribution of income. The important point is that this increase in average individual income was more rapid than any previous increase. It seems plausible that the average annual rate of growth of per capita GNP averaged no more than 0.3 per cent prior to 1800; the average figure for the period 1830 to 1910, by contrast, was around 0.9 per cent, rising to 1.5 per cent in the 1860s and 1890s. Only in the depressed decade 1870–80 did the growth rate revert to the earlier, sluggish tempo. True, the nineteenth century compares unfavourably with the second half of the twentieth century. In the 1950s and 1960s, European per capita GNP grew at an average annual rate of more than 4.5 per cent. On the other hand, nineteenth-century Europe experienced no economic disruptions to match the First and Second World Wars. This truly was a watershed in European economic history therefore, even if an increase of 0.6 per cent in the average annual rate of per capita GNP appears trifling. Here too—in their seeming smallness—the statistics lie.

Nor is this the only difficulty with a quantitative approach to the economic history of the century after 1815. Until recently, most economic historians followed political historians in writing the history of nation states. Alexander Gerschenkron's classic model of economic development and 'backwardness' distinguished between:

(1) countries with ample private wealth able to finance enterprise (Britain);
(2) countries in which banks were needed to mobilize adequate but more dispersed funds (Germany, Austria, and Italy, with France, Belgium, and Switzerland lying somewhere in between 1 and 2); and
(3) countries in which only the state could do the job (Russia).

This tendency to think in national categories has been encouraged by the simple fact that most (though not all) economic statistics for the period are derived from figures collected by governments. In turn, the economic history of 'Europe' has often been written as the sum of the economic histories of the continent's principal nation states. This approach tends to understate the scale and the nature of economic change. For example, if Bairoch's figures for total (as opposed to per capita) GNP are used to construct 'league tables' of the top ten European economies in 1830 and 1913, there is virtually no change: at the beginning and at the end of the period, Russia comes first, Britain third, Austria–Hungary fifth, Italy sixth, Spain seventh, Belgium eighth, and the Netherlands ninth. The only differences are that France and Germany swap places, the latter rising from fourth to second; Sweden replaces Portugal at the bottom of the chart; and the gap between the top three and the middle four widens. A similar league table for per capita figures is not much more illuminating: Britain, the Netherlands, Belgium, and Switzerland were in the top five in 1830 and in 1913. There are other oddities. The economies that experienced the most pronounced growth in per capita GNP in this period were Denmark, Sweden, and Switzerland; yet in the two Scandinavian countries barely a quarter of the active population were engaged in manufacturing, mining, or building in 1910, compared with more than 40 per cent who were employed in agriculture, forestry, and fishing.

Perhaps the most useful point to emerge from such figures is that there was a downward 'development gradient' as one moved east across the Elbe or south towards the Mediterranean. What is more, the gap between West and East widened during the century. If one compares real GNP per capita in the so-called industrial 'core' (France, Germany, Italy, the Netherlands, Switzerland, and Britain) with the periphery (Russia and Portugal) in 1830, the core was 25 per cent ahead. A similar comparison in 1913 (which adds Austria to the core group and Spain, Bulgaria, Greece, Hungary, Romania, and Serbia to the periphery) reveals a gap of 123 per cent.

There are three different approaches that can be taken. The first is to study economic sectors rather than geographical units. A second approach, championed by Sidney Pollard, is to think of economic change in regional terms. This is important as most major national states included some relatively undeveloped rural regions as well as rapidly growing industrial (and commercial) regions—hence the relatively undramatic national growth rates noted above. The third and most illuminating approach, however, is to understand the economy of the nineteenth century in global terms; perhaps even—at the risk of anachronism—to think of the century 1815–1914 as the first era of 'globalization'. In many ways, as we shall see, it is misleading to think in terms of a distinct and integrated European economy. The true significance of the period before 1914 lies in the dynamic relationship between Europe and the rest of the world.

Explaining growth: labour supply

In a simple supply-side model of growth, an increase in total output is explicable by an increase in the quantity or the quality of land, labour, and/or capital. It is safe to say that, in most of Europe, nineteenth-century growth had little to do with increasing the area of land under cultivation: of far more importance were the other two factors of production. However, in the case of the supply of labour, the apparently straightforward relationship between rising population and rising output turns out to be complex and in some ways contradictory.

Table 3.1 shows estimates for the European population and its rate of increase between 1800 and 1913 (though it is worth noting that the acceleration pre-dated 1800). To set this in perspective, world population rose in the same period from around 906 million to at most 1,608 million: the European percentage, therefore, rose from 23 per cent to 26 per cent, but in absolute terms the population of Asia remained larger, and the population of North America grew more rapidly (for reasons discussed below). Compared with our own world, which has a population more than three times as large, it was an uncrowded age; but by the standards of previous centuries Europe experienced a demographic revolution.

What made population growth revolutionary was that it kept going. In his *Essay on the Principle of Population* (1798), the English clergyman and political economist Thomas Malthus had predicted 'a strong and constantly operating check on population from the difficulty of subsistence', because the production of food could increase

Table 3.1 European population growth, 1800–1913

Year	Population (m.)	Annual rate of increase (%)
1800	205	0.54
1850	275	0.59
1870	320	0.76
1900	414	0.86
1913	481	1.16

only arithmetically, while the production of people could increase geometrically. He regarded an increase in 'misery' (i.e. starvation) and 'vice' (i.e. contraception and abortion) as inevitable consequences of population growth; and he had history on his side. Yet the nineteenth century was not the thirteenth or the sixteenth, and Malthus was confounded.

It is far from easy to identify the causes of this great population increase. It used to be thought that it was due to a decline in the death rate explicable by improved food supply and health, and there is some evidence to support this. In the second half of the century, death rates fell, especially in north-western Europe, from 22.4 per thousand in Britain in 1850 to 14.7 in 1906–10. The equivalent figures for Germany were 26.8 and 17.5. Even in Russia there was a fall from 35.7 per thousand to 29.5 between 1876–80 and 1906–10. Between 1870 and 1910, average male life expectancy rose in most countries: from 48 to 56 in Norway, the healthiest of countries, and from 30 to 41 in Austria, the least. Yet these figures need to be qualified. Everywhere, the real improvement in mortality came late, after around 1880 at the earliest. Famine did not vanish in the course of the nineteenth century: the potato blight of 1845–7 may have caused as many as a million deaths in Ireland and also afflicted some south-west German states, while there was a drought-induced famine in parts of Russia as late as 1891–2 which claimed around 800,000 victims. In both cases, hunger was exacerbated by cholera, though the deadly bacterium vibrio cholerae 01 did its worst damage in crowded and insanitary cities like Hamburg, where it claimed nearly 9,000 lives in 1892. Tuberculosis also spread more readily in urban areas. It is a striking statistic that average male life expectancy was barely 30 in Berlin in 1880, compared with 43 in rural Hanover. And everywhere infant mortality remained high: in 1840, 25 per cent of all children died before their fifth birthday in western Europe and even in 1901 the infant mortality rate was 14 per cent. Women in childbirth were especially vulnerable too. 'What's money, after all? . . . What can it do[?]', little Paul asks his father in *Dombey and Son*. His father replies: 'Money, Paul, can do anything.' 'Why didn't money save me my mamma?', returns the child. 'It isn't cruel is it?' And he too duly expires, after barely a term at school. Good health and long life for the majority are twentieth-century achievements (today the death rate is just 11 per thousand in Britain, infant mortality 8 per thousand and average life expectancy 76).

It has been argued that nineteenth-century demographic change had more to do with fertility than mortality. The classic study of a sample of English and Welsh parish registers by Wrigley and Schofield shows a fall in mean age at first marriage for both men and women from 28.1 (male) and 27.0 (female) in 1700–49 to 26.5 and 24.3 respectively in 1800–49. This translated into a 'baby boom'. Of women who married in Britain in the 1870s, 18 per cent had ten or more live births, while more than half—52 per cent—had six or more. (Again, it is worth comparing this with the end of the twentieth century, when the average number of children per woman is 1.8.) However, there does not seem to have been a comparable tendency in Germany: in Prussia the average age at first marriage was 27.9 even in the late 1860s, though slight increases in marital fertility can be detected in East Prussia, Württemberg, Baden, and Pomerania in the 1850s. True, the eighteenth century had seen a sharp rise in the number of illegitimate births, which continued into the nineteenth century, but infant mortality for children born out of wedlock was 80 per cent higher than for legitimate children. Nor was there a French baby boom: indeed, compared with other west European countries, French population growth was slow—a phenomenon that perturbed contemporaries.

Explaining reduced mortality is easier than explaining increased fertility. Attempts have been made for England to link higher reproductive rates to the increased demand for labour by plotting population growth against rising real wages, but these are unconvincing. (So is David Hackett Fischer's suggestion that the rate of population growth and the absolute price level fluctuated together.) Such simplistic correlations do not explain why fertility began to be curbed in Britain in the last quarter of the nineteenth century, so that by 1905 just 9 per cent of British women had six or more children. The rationale of procreation varies from one social group to another: clearly, there is a trade-off between the cost of bringing up a child and the benefit of having a child as (for example) a cheap source of labour from the age of around 10, a provider when parents can no longer earn, or an heir to whom accumulated capital can be passed. So-called proto-industrialization (rural, household-based manufacturing) in Flanders was itself a response to population pressure; but it also tended to encourage earlier marriage and bigger family size because children could easily do the work involved. However, the effect of this was to drive down incomes, so that proto-industrial areas were vulnerable to food shortage and often had to resort to mass emigration. The typical French peasant household, by contrast, had an incentive to remain small in order to avoid subdividing its landholding between an excessive number of sons, and this strategy allowed any surplus to be invested or consumed. On balance, it seems unlikely that there was a straightforward causal relationship between population growth and economic growth: after all, population grew very rapidly in non-industrializing parts of Europe too. Indeed, rising population may even have been a brake on economic growth, the effects of which were mitigated only by emigration (see below).

Of course, population growth ensured that there were no labour shortages in the nineteenth century. However, plentiful labour is not necessarily a good thing *per se*. The availability of cheap 'hands' can act as a disincentive to invest in labour-saving, productivity-increasing technology. The important point about European labour in the nineteenth century was not that it was plentiful but that it was free and of improving quality. The liberalization of the labour market following the abolition of serfdom in the countryside and the weakening of restrictive urban guilds ushered in a period of unprecedented—and since lost—labour-market flexibility. As so often, it was a process that began in the west: the institution of unfree agricultural labour, long gone in England, was dismantled in France in the 1790s, in the German lands by stages from around 1811 to 1848, and in Russia and Russian Poland in the 1860s. Guilds had already been weakened in most states in the eighteenth century, were further eroded by the development of industries beyond traditional town walls, but were not wholly abolished throughout Germany until 1869 (somnulent Mecklenburg was their last bastion).

Investment in 'human capital'—that is, education—was also economically vital. There is a clear correlation between literacy and growth (though the direction of causation was not all one way). Taking figures for adult male illiteracy (derived from marriage registers) as an indicator, illiteracy in England and Wales fell from 33 per cent in 1840 to 3 per cent in 1900; in France from 32 per cent in 1855 to 3 per cent in 1905 (though with enormous regional variations); in Scotland from 11 per cent in 1855 to 2 per cent in 1900; and in Prussia from 16 per cent in 1825 to zero by 1910. By contrast, the figure for Ireland was still 34 per cent in 1900. In Italy 38 per cent of those over 6 could not read and write as late as 1910, while for Spain the comparable figure was 50 per cent of those over 10. The illiteracy rate was even higher in Portugal, and in Russia it was around 60 per cent (though this was an improvement on the figure of nearly 80 per cent in 1897, reflecting the quadrupling in the number of primary schools between 1878 and 1911). Before building factories, therefore, it was a good idea to build schools. It has sometimes been argued that one reason British industry began to lag behind that of Germany in the later nineteenth century was that the Germans developed a superior system of technical education: the network of craft schools (*Gewerbschulen*) and technical colleges (*technische Hochschulen*).

Capital

As with labour, the role of capital in economic development can be understood in terms of both quantity and quality. Clearly, the nineteenth century saw immense investment—that is to say, expenditure of money on slowly depreciating productive assets. Table 3.2 shows figures for average annual net investment in Prussia in the first half of the century and these suggest a total increase in the level of investment of around 50 per cent, with transport clearly the sector of greatest activity. Between 1851–60 and 1881–90, total annual investment increased by no less than 200 per cent and by 1906–10 investment in Germany as a whole was running at the very high level of 15.7 per cent of national income (compared with just 4 per cent in 1847). Yet such aggregate figures conceal one of the most important points of all about the process of economic change before 1850—namely, the relative cheapness of investment in industry. When August Borsig started up his engineering factory in Berlin in 1837, for example, he

Table 3.2 Average annual net investment in Prussia (million marks, 1913 prices)

Years	Agriculture	Buildings	Transport	Industry	Total
1816–22	86.5	28.7	7.0	2.8	125.0
1840–49	59.9	69.2	73.7	7.0	209.8

needed just 196,500 marks of capital. This was one of the keys to the early industrial revolution: most of the first wave of technological innovations did not cost much to install.

The innovations themselves are, without doubt, the *sine qua non* of the story: it was they—or rather their inventors—who, in David Landes's memorable image, unbound the Prometheus of the world economy. The first half of the nineteenth century saw the dissemination in a relatively small number of west and central European regions of a variety of new technologies that either originated or were first systematically applied in eighteenth-century Britain. The contribution of British entrepreneurs, mechanics, and skilled workmen to this process cannot be qualified exactly, but it was undoubtedly huge; though even with such assistance the transfer of technology proved to be less easy than might have been thought (for example, it took around seventy years to perfect British coke-smelting in France). After around 1860 there was a second wave of more scientifically sophisticated and sometimes more expensive technologies which owed more to Germany and the United States than to Britain.

In its first phase, industrialization meant cheaper and better clothes (mainly made of cotton), cheaper and better metals (pig iron, wrought iron, and steel) and faster travel (mainly by rail). Nearly all the key technological advances in textile production had been made in Britain before 1800 (the only real breakthrough of the nineteenth century was the sewing machine). Cotton-spinning was transformed by Lewis Paul and John Wyatt's spinning machine (1738), James Hargreaves's spinning jenny (1766), which multiplied the productivity of a spinner by a factor of eight, Richard Arkwright's water frame (1769), and Samuel Crompton's mule, a cross between the jenny and the water frame (1779). Weaving was likewise mechanized by John Kay's flying shuttle (early 1730s), Edmund Cartwright's power loom (1787), and Richard Roberts's self-acting mule (1830). The process of transfer to the continent was relatively straightforward. British entrepreneurs either took the new methods across the Channel themselves (as William Cockerill did when he emigrated to Belgium in 1798), or continentals came to Britain and took them back home (as the Alsatian Nicolas Schlumberger did when he returned from Manchester with plans for textile machinery 'sewn in his coat').

It was a similar story with regard to iron. Abraham Darby had introduced coke-smelting in a blast furnace to produce what became known as pig iron (after its oblong shape) as early as 1709, though the next major improvements (Henry Cort's methods of rolling and puddling) did not come until the 1780s. Again, British entrepreneurs exported the new methods (Aaron Manby and Daniel Wilson founded the Charenton ironworks in France) or Frenchmen and Germans copied them (as the Schneider brothers did at the Le Creusot coke-smelting plant). Steel, with its lower carbon content, was much more costly to produce until the Englishman Henry Bessemer developed the idea of a steel converter (1856); but it was the German Friedrich Siemens and the Frenchmen Pierre and Émile Martin who independently invented a process for open-hearth steel production five years later—though this was further improved by Percy Gilchrist and Sidney Thomas in 1878.

The steam engine too was born in eighteenth-century Britain, then exported. Thomas Newcomen built the first engine with a piston in 1705; James Watt introduced the separate condenser, which greatly improved fuel efficiency in 1768; John Wilkinson enhanced perform-ance still further with his smooth piston cylinders in 1776, and Rich-ard Trevithick produced his high-pressure steam engine in 1802. The last great steam breakthrough—the steam turbine—was also a British invention (Charles Parsons, 1884). Here, especially, British know-how was indispensable: the Cockerills in Belgium soon branched out from textile machinery to steam engines and pumps.

At every stage, as economic historians like to say, there were 'for-ward' and 'backward' linkages: steam power could be used in cotton mills, ending their dependence on fast-flowing rivers, while at the same time giving the manufacturers of iron and steel a rapidly grow-ing market. Even the industry that technology did least for benefited to a degree: although men continued throughout the century to hack out coal with rudimentary tools, the introduction of steam pumps made deeper mines possible and machinery made it easier to get coal to the surface.

Nowhere were these linkages more important, however, than in the development of railways. Originally devised to transport coal from mine shafts, iron rails combined with the steam-powered carriage (an early version of which was devised by William Murdock in 1785) to produce the nineteenth century's most important economic phe-nomenon. Here the technology transfer was swift. Within a few years of the opening of the line between Liverpool and Manchester (1830), the Pereire brothers had begun their Paris–St-Germain line, and between 1828 and 1848 around 2,000 kilometres of track were built in France, with peaks of investment in 1841, 1843, and 1846–7. Without British capital and technology, the progress would certainly have been slower. Roughly half the capital invested in French railways by 1847 was British and only a quarter of French locomotives were domestically produced. Yet in the majority of railway-building economies the effect was not just to boost the demand for British industry: the railways acted as a huge stimulus for indigenous coal, iron, and engineering. This illustrates the 'altruistic' effect of Britain's liberal attitude towards trade in both technology and its products. Far from using free trade to inundate the continent with its own cheaper manufactures, Britain facilitated the industrialization of western Europe by 'equipping her rivals while they were in a better position than herself, paying lower wages, to make use of the new technology' (Pollard). Britain exported not finished goods but semi-finished and capital goods to the continent (typically, 61 per cent of all British textile exports to non-Mediterranean Europe took the form of yarn in 1837–42) and then imported increasing quantities of finished goods from Germany and France.

Trade between Britain and the continent naturally depended on good sea transport: here, despite premature dreams of a Channel tunnel, the railways could not help. But the steam engine could. From as early as 1821 there was a packet steamer across the Channel, though the problems of storing bulky coal slowed the obsolescence of sailing boats. The last but not the least of the first wave of major technologies was gas lighting, pioneered in the 1790s by the ingenious William Murdock—one of the many clever Scots who made such a disproportionate contribution to industrialization. Safe and cheap lighting was invaluable in dark north European winters.

Men like Murdock were not trained scientists but skilful tinkerers who learnt on the job. After 1850 formal scientific knowledge began to matter more, though the distinction between tinkering and experimentation should not be too sharply drawn. The discovery that in many ways created the modern chemicals industry was made by a chemistry student, William Henry Perkin, in 1856, when he was trying vainly to synthesize quinine. By chance, he discovered that a vivid mauve dye could be created from naphtha, an ingredient of coaltar. The application of this discovery spelt the end for the madder root and other centuries-old sources of pigmentation, and gave the world a garish array of new colours: fuchsia, magenta, blue de Lyon, aniline yellow, dahlia pink, and alizarin red. Yet British entrepreneurs strikingly failed to exploit Perkin's work. Instead, it was German companies—Hoechst, Badische Anilin u. Soda-Fabrik (BASF), Bayer, and Agfa—that made the running: by 1900 as much as 90 per cent of the world's artificial dyestuffs were 'Made in Germany', a phrase that came to symbolize Britain's relative decline. Britain also lagged behind in the development of early pharmaceuticals and the use of nitrates and phosphates in explosives and fertilizers.

Something similar happened with the commercial exploitation of electricity. It was a British scientist—Humphry Davy—who discovered potassium and sodium and produced the first electric arc light, and his assistant Michael Faraday who first caused a wire carrying an electric current to revolve around a magnetic pole (1831) and demonstrated that electricity could be generated by rotating a copper disc between the poles of a magnet. However, it was a Belgian, Zénobe Gramme, who produced the first dynamo in 1870, and Joseph Swan found himself overshadowed by the American Thomas Edison in marketing the filament lamp, which they both invented at around the same time (1878–9). Nor was there a British firm that could rival the Allgemeine Elektrizitäts Gesellschaft (AEG), which Emil Rathenau established after seeing Edison's electric bulb at the Paris Exhibition of 1881.

In the development of oil as a lubricant, a source of light and an alternative source of fuel to coal, Britain was also slow. James Young first used oil for lubrication in Derbyshire in 1848, and it was Young who first distilled paraffin from coal. But there was little British involvement in the exploitation of these discoveries when oil was discovered in Ploesti in Romania (1857), Baku on the Russian Black Sea (1860), and Boryslaw in Habsburg Galicia (1863). In the Russian fields—which produced half the world's oil by 1900—the key figures were the Swedish Nobel brothers and the French Rothschilds. The development of the four-stroke internal combustion engine as a means of propulsion was principally the achievement of German engineers such as Carl Benz and Gottlieb Daimler (1884), though

Frenchmen devised the gear box (Émile Levassor in 1891) and the pneumatic tyre (André Michelin in the 1890s), without which the motor carriage would have had limited appeal. British innovative genius was also conspicuous by its absence in the infancy of air transport: the first dirigible airship was the German Zeppelin (in 1900), the first mechanized flight the American Wright brothers' (in 1903), and the first airborne Channel crossing by a Frenchman (Louis Blériot in 1909).

The contribution of new technologies should not, of course, be overstated. Attempts to establish the 'social savings' generated by railways (i.e. their contribution to GNP including all linkages) have been made by posing 'counter-factual' questions about how economies would have developed without them. In the case of Britain, for example, it has been argued that 'the maintenance of 1865 freight transport services in the absence of English railways would have required a diversion of 3 to 3.5 per cent of the UK national income' (Hawke). Certainly, we should not forget how much traffic continued to be carried by other means. The French were great believers in roads: there were already some 40,000 kilometres of road in 1800 and new roads were being built at the rate of 1,300 kilometres a year under Louis Philippe. But even after the introduction of John Macadam's road-surfacing method (1827), roads were a far less efficient way of transporting heavy loads (including armies) than railways. Of more economic importance were natural and artificial waterways: no railway could carry as much as the Rhine or the Elbe, and among the greatest feats of European engineering in the nineteenth century were great canals such as the Suez (1869), Panama (1895), and Kiel (1914).

In general, new technologies did not invariably drive out the old, in the way that the power loom made the handloom weavers obsolete. With some exceptions, glass, watches, brick walls, and shoes were made in much the same way in 1900 as they had been in 1800; but industrialization greatly increased the demand for these articles, and those who made them did not want for work.

The spirit of capitalism

Invention is one thing; commercial application another. The question remains: why did some people in some parts of Europe prove so much better than others at entrepreneurship? In his famous essay on 'The Protestant Ethic and the Spirit of Capitalism' (1901) the German sociologist Max Weber ventured an answer. Pointing to the fact that German Catholics had been less economically successful in the nineteenth century than German Protestants, he argued that there was a distinctive ethic that had arisen from Calvinist theology. According to Weber, Calvinists came to see 'the earning of more and more money . . . as an end in itself . . . combined with the strict avoidance of all spontaneous enjoyment of life'. For the inwardly isolated individual that Calvinism created, 'intense worldly activity' became a way of 'prov[ing] one's faith' and attaining confidence in one's membership of the Elect. Thus 'Christian asceticism . . . strode into the market place'. Although Weber occasionally used the phrase 'rational conduct' to describe this behaviour, he drew a distinction between it and the rationalism of the eighteenth-century Enlightenment: for the Calvinist-capitalist 'gets nothing out of his wealth for himself, except the sense of having done his job well'. Thus 'from the viewpoint of personal happiness . . . this sort of life, where a man exists for the sake of his business, instead of the reverse', was 'irrational'.

It is not difficult to find fault with Weber's thesis; but it contains an important truth. Much nineteenth-century economic development clearly *was* driven by men for whom work was an end in itself. In literature, such Calvinist-capitalists appear as grim, even diabolical figures: the *reductio ad absurdum* is Gillespie Strang in J. Macdougall Hay's *Gillespie* (1914), whose individualistic addiction to profit for its own sake destroys not only a small Scottish village community but his own wife and son. The weakness of the Weber argument is the assumption that only Calvinism and its derivative sects could produce what would nowadays be called 'workaholics'. In a passage not often quoted, Weber echoed Marx (and countless anti-Semites) in arguing that 'the Jews stood on the side of the politically and speculatively oriented adventurous capitalism; their ethos was, in a word, that of pariah-capitalism'. (Similar nonsense was given wider currency by another German sociologist, Werner Sombart.) The reality was that Jews were just as capable of producing a work ethic that differed from the Calvinist variant only in its apparent compatibility with a happy family life. Nathan Rothschild was born in the Frankfurt ghetto, paid his dues as a textile merchant in Manchester between 1799 and 1811, made his fortune by financing Wellington's last campaigns against Napoleon, and effectively invented the modern international bond market. 'After dinner', he wrote to his brothers in 1816, 'I usually have nothing to do. I do not read books, I do not play cards, I do not go to the theatre, my only pleasure is my business . . .' His youngest brother James worked no less relentlessly until his death in 1868 at the age of 76. Because the Rothschilds were Jews, jealous contemporaries never tired of alleging that there was something reprehensible—'speculative' rather than 'productive'— about their business; but their contribution to the development of railways in France, Spain, northern Italy, and the Habsburg Empire was huge. Catholics too were capable of generating a work ethic: the economic success of Belgium and northern France is otherwise unintelligible.

Yet, whatever its origin, we should not see the asceticism of the workaholic entrepreneur as the only component of capitalist culture, for an entirely ascetic culture would never have been able to absorb all the products of the industrial age. Despite Say's reassuring 'law', there is no guarantee that supply will always create its own demand. The vital question is what people do with an increase in real income arising from, say, a technological improvement that reduces the cost of living. Do they increase family size by marrying younger? Do they spend it on having masses sung for themselves or their ancestors? Do they simply work less, restoring their income to its old level (the 'leisure preference')? Do they save some of the increment, or invest it themselves in new equipment to improve the efficiency of their own labour? Or do they spend it on cotton and cutlery? Only by spending a significant proportion of their additional income in the last of these ways could people propel the industrial revolution forward. The fact that they did so is as important a phenomenon as Weber's work ethic.

Other sectors

The revolutionary changes were more than industrial, however. Agriculture, commerce, and finance were all transformed, and these changes were the auxiliaries that made industrialization sustainable.

It should never be forgotten that the majority of Europeans were still engaged in agriculture in 1900: Britain was exceptional in that only 9 per cent of the active population was employed in farming, forestry, or fishing. For Belgium, the Netherlands, and Switzerland, the proportion was between a quarter and a third. For Germany, France, Ireland, and Scandinavia, it was between a third and a half. For Italy, Spain, and Austria–Hungary it was between a half and two-thirds. For Russia and Bulgaria, it was 80 per cent. Especially for peasants and landless rural labourers, the weather still mattered more than the business cycle: a very dry year like 1826, or a series of very wet years, as in the mid-1840s, could make the difference between hunger and health.

The divergent rates of employment in agriculture correlate roughly to variations in the forms of land tenure across Europe. Strictly speaking, these differed widely even within quite small regions: tenurial customs, after all, were legacies of the age before integrated markets. Still, it is possible to distinguish roughly between four or five types. In the Netherlands, England, Wales, and parts of Scotland, tenants generally had good-sized holdings and relatively secure tenure. In these areas, serfdom was a distant memory and proximity to commercial centres had encouraged a move from subsistence farming to 'market gardening' from around the sixteenth century. Holland led the way with investment in drainage, new crops, and methods of rotation, techniques soon adopted in Britain. It was in these areas that the land was most productive: yield ratios for seed corn were around 11 or 12 to one in the Netherlands and Britain, compared with 4.4 to one in eastern Europe. In much of France, by contrast, one legacy of revolution in the 1790s was a high proportion of peasant proprietors with relatively modest holdings (though the south had *métayage* or sharecropping). Similar types of tenure could be found in much of western Germany and parts of Scandinavia. Broadly speaking, the further east or south one moved, the greater the power of landowners over those who worked the land. In Bavaria, Austria, but especially in East Elbian (and parts of central) Prussia, as well as Hungary and the Baltic lands, landowners were able to reduce large numbers of their tenants to the status of landless labourers following emancipation. The typical East Elbian *Junker* had almost untrammelled authority over his *Gut*: not only could he run it as a business, producing grain for export in the buoyant decades of the mid-century; he also controlled justice and other administration in his capacity as *Landrat*. However, not every large landowner exploited the opportunities of capitalist agriculture. In large tracts of Spain and southern Italy (as well as in Ireland), large latifundia were left to stagnate by absent or apathetic landlords.

The extreme case of landowner failure was in Russia, where high levels of indebtedness were rarely due to successful agricultural investment. When Alexander II came to emancipate the serfs in 1861, 66 per cent of the 22 million serfs owned by 610,000 landowners were already mortgaged to the state, so that when the government advanced 80 per cent of the serfs' 'redemption' payments to the landowners, it kept two-thirds of the money to liquidate these debts. In Prussia, emancipation was the cue for landowners to work their estates more efficiently; Russian nobles continued to sell off their property, so that between 1870 and 1905 the total proportion of arable land they owned fell by a third to just over a fifth. Ivan Goncharov's *Oblomov* (1859) memorably caricatured the bone-idle provincial landowner: 'Lying down was not for Oblomov a necessity, as it is for a sick man or a man who is sleepy; or a matter of chance, as it is for a man who is tired; or a pleasure, as it is for a lazy man: it was his normal condition.'

On the other hand, the peasants freed by the emancipation edict also proved relatively uninterested in capitalist-style agriculture. Their response to freedom was to procreate and subdivide the land they had now acquired. The average peasant plot at the turn of the century was just 7 acres, though 20 per cent of peasant households had less than 2.7 acres and 7 per cent had none at all. Chekhov's short story 'Peasants' (1897) harrowingly captures the nastiness, brutishness and shortness of life in a village of the time. In many parts of Russia, the style of communal agriculture had more in common with India than with the rest of Europe. Small wonder the tiny élite of educated urban-dwelling Russians were appalled and contemptuous when they encountered this world. In Turgenev's *Fathers and Sons*

(1861), the nihilist student Bazarov—himself from peasant stock—exclaims: 'Even the emancipation of the serfs is not likely to be to [Russia's] advantage, since those peasants of ours are only too glad to rob even themselves to drink themselves silly.'

Still, such strictures should not be overdone. It is a striking fact that by 1894 Russia was exporting 9.7 million tons of grain (though admittedly half the surplus came from a relatively few large and efficient estates). And the evidence for a steady rise in peasant living standards is unmistakable: rising revenues from the taxes on vodka, kerosene, matches, and sugar. Despite the continuing rapid rise in population, per capita incomes were going up. In this respect, Russia was not wholly out of step with the rest of Europe: just slower. For Europe as a whole, wheat production rose 194 per cent between the 1830s and 1909–14. The French statistics for wheat production (Fig. 3.1) show a clear upward trend (though they also show how widely the harvest fluctuated from year to year). In Germany, most of the increase came in the second half of the century: the average wheat yield per acre rose from 100 (1800) to 119 (1848–52) to 201 (1908–12). Nor were the improvements confined to grain production: new crops such as sugar beet, potatoes, maize, turnips, and clover and new breeds of sheep like the merino greatly enhanced the productivity of the farms suited to them. Research by chemists like the Giessen professor Julius von Liebig revealed what could be achieved by fertilizing soil with manure and imported nitrates. Finally, though much less extensively, there was some mechanization of agriculture, beginning with McCormick's horse-drawn reaper and culminating in the petrol-driven tractor (1905).

Despite all these improvements, however, Europe did not feed itself. In the second half of the century, the development of the more fertile plains of North America, Australia, and Argentina created a new source of still cheaper grain: whereas in 1850 these countries accounted for 10 per cent of world wheat production, by the eve of the First World War the figure had risen to 30 per cent. As the technology of food preservation (canning, refrigeration) and transportation improved, the more advanced European economies increased their imports from these areas. Britain was by far the most dependent on imports: foreign wheat as a percentage of total consumption rose from 3 per cent (1811–30) to 13 per cent (1830–51) to 30 per cent (1851–60) and finally to 79 per cent (1891–5). But even Germany, despite the

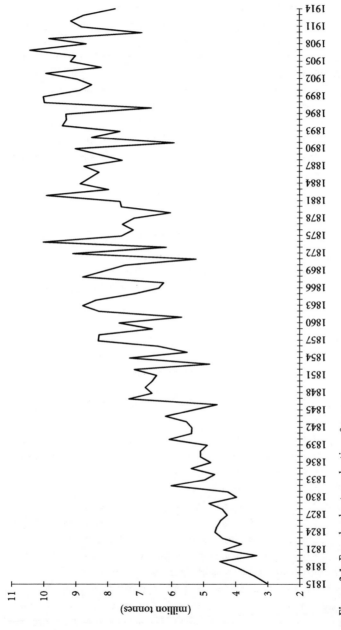

Figure 3.1 French wheat production 1815–1914.

size and strength of its own agriculture, began to import food: by 1890 around a tenth of its wheat came from abroad.

These imports were merely part of a huge and growing volume of international trade (see below). Of course, this was not new: the development of large-scale overseas commerce can be traced back to the seventeenth and eighteenth centuries, when the Dutch, the British, and the French constructed empires to supply themselves with tea, coffee, and sugar. However, trade mattered even more in the nineteenth century. As a proportion of national income for Europe as a whole, exports rose from 9.4 per cent in 1860 to 10.9 per cent in 1870, 12.6 per cent in 1890, and 14 per cent in 1913—a level it has not equalled since. Table 3.3 shows the relative importance of trade for four major economies (note the relatively high proportions for Germany). Behind these figures lay the world of the great commercial ports and the countless small merchant houses that conducted the world's trade. In Thomas Mann's *Buddenbrooks* (1903) that world appears to be on the wane. But Mann's novel is set in declining Lübeck: in neighbouring Hamburg, the families of the *Weltbürgertum* were brimming over with self-confidence at the turn of the century as their overseas business boomed.

Commerce was unusual in continuing throughout the period to be conducted by numerous relatively small (often family-based) firms. In the other service sectors there was a good deal more concentration. After the initial free-for-all, in which numerous small companies competed for railway 'concessions' (the right to build and operate railways for specified periods), there was a sustained process of centralization. In France, the network came to be dominated by a handful of giant companies like the PLM (Paris–Lyons–Marseilles) and the Nord (the most profitable of the big French companies). Even more

Table 3.3 Trade as a percentage of national income, 1885–1913

Country	Imports	Exports
Britain	32	24
Switzerland	40	30
Germany	20	17
Russia	6	9

impressive (and proof that railways integrated international as well as national markets) was the Imperial Lombardo Venetian and Central Italian Railway Company, which connected Austria and Italy in the 1850s. In shipping too there was concentration: by 1913 the Hamburg–America line had a fleet of 175 ocean-going ships (plus a further nineteen under construction) and employed around 29,000 people.

It was not only the transport of goods and people that increased ahead of total economic output: there was also a huge increase in the movement of information. The nineteenth-century communications revolution needs to be considered separately from the Industrial Revolution described above, though the two were certainly inter-dependent. At first, it did not involve much new technology (though the availability of cheaper paper may have encouraged more letter-writing). The development of postal systems was perfectly possible without extensive railway or steamboat services: indeed, the use by businessmen of pigeons as couriers in the first half of the century showed that even horses and sailboats could be dispensed with. Here, as in so many spheres of nineteenth-century life, speed was of the essence: a letter from London could take up to a week to reach Frank-furt in 1817, and the service from Paris to Berlin took nine days. Pigeons were only a provisional solution. The discovery by Karl Frie-drich Gauss and Wilhelm Weber that electric signals could be trans-mitted by means of wire (1832) was the technological breakthrough necessary for the development of the telegraph. Ten years later, a wire was in commercial operation between Paddington and Slough (it was logical for them to follow railway routes); there was a cross-Channel service from 1850, and a transatlantic cable in use from 1865. From then on, the most important diplomatic and business communica-tions took the form of telegrams. The new technologies also trans-formed the well-established newspaper. From 1814 *The Times* was printed on a steam press; from 1850 Julius Reuter was able to supply it and other papers with foreign news through his telegraphic news service; and from the 1870s journalists could type their stories.

Nor did the nineteenth-century communications revolution end there. Alexander Graham Bell's first telephone call in 1876 ushered in the era of ephemeral conversation, though Europeans took to the phone with varying degrees of enthusiasm: by 1912 Germany had four times as many telephones than France, though even in Russia the new means of communication had caught on. When the Chief of the

Russian General Staff wanted to prevent the Tsar from revoking the order for mobilization in 1914, he threatened to smash his own telephone. The Viennese satirist Karl Kraus had a point when he declared that the war had been caused by the combination of 'thrones and telephones'. It was also the nineteenth century that saw the birth of the photograph (Joseph Niepce in 1827 and Louis Daguerre in 1839), sound recording (Thomas Edison, 1876), the moving picture (Louis and Auguste Lumière, 1895) and the wireless radio (Guglielmo Marconi, 1895). It is the conventional wisdom that the twentieth century has witnessed a revolution in communications; that of the nineteenth century was arguably more profound. The time it took to transmit information from one international capital to another was shortened by more between 1800 and 1900 than it has been in the twentieth century. It took twenty days for a letter sent from Paris to reach St Petersburg in 1800. By 1900 the journey time over land had been cut to just thirty hours. By July 1914, judging by the diplomatic records, a telegram between the two capitals was usually recorded as having been received just an hour or two after it had been sent.

No economic sector was more profoundly affected by the improvement in communications than finance. Of all businessmen, bankers probably suffered the most hostile representation in the literature of the period. Balzac's Nucingen was just one of numerous fraudulent financiers in fiction: Dickens's Merdle, Trollope's Melmotte, and Zola's Gundermann were variations on the same theme. Such men existed, of course: Bethel Henry Strousberg, the Romanian railway 'king', was one of several rogues who made their fortunes rapidly in railway finance, only to lose them just as rapidly when their accounting reached the limit of its creativity. Yet the positive contribution of banking to European economic development is undeniable, even if its precise significance continues to be debated. Much has been made of the role of the Pereire brothers' Crédit Mobilier, an investment bank that they founded in 1852 and that spawned a host of imitators. In fact, the difference in approach between such 'new' joint-stock banks and the 'old' private banks (of which the Rothschilds' was the greatest) should not be exaggerated: in France and Austria the private bankers were just as eager to be involved in railway finance. Moreover, the Crédit Mobilier (which raised finance for investment by selling bonds and attracting deposits) proved an unstable model: the Pereires' bank collapsed in 1867. Nevertheless, it was clear by the end of the 1870s, if not earlier, that joint-stock banks were better suited to industrial finance than private banks, if only because of the unprecedented capital requirements of the second wave of industries. Gradually, the next generation of joint-stock banks—banks such as the Midland, the Crédit Lyonnais, and the Deutsche Bank—grew larger in terms of their capital and assets than the private banks—though there were important differences between the way the British joint-stock banks financed industry (by means of overdrafts) and the longer-term investments made by the German 'great banks', which became major industrial shareholders. It is also worth noting that, at the time of the dissolution of their international partnership (c.1905), the three Rothschild banks in London, Paris, and Vienna still constituted the biggest bank in the world in terms of capital. It cannot be without significance that the biggest family fortune of the nineteenth century—at its zenith in 1899 the partners' capital totalled £41 million—was financial rather than industrial.

The geography of change

The notion that there is a link between economic development and nation-building, and that the nation state is therefore the proper focus for economic history—and was in fact a product *of* economic history—is an old and resilient one. In his *National System of Political Economy* (1841), Friedrich List described his projected German railway network as 'a tonic for the national spirit' and 'a tight belt around the loins of the German nation' that—in conjuction with the Prussian customs union (*Zollverein*) established in 1834 and a measure of tariff protection for German industry—would bring about the 'internal unification' of Germany. Economics could thus help the state and the state could help economic development. The extent to which this happened in practice remains controversial. There is no doubt that many governments thought in consciously developmental terms, most obviously Leopold I's in Belgium, Napoleon III's in France, and Count Witte's in Russia. Sometimes governments merely continued policies that had originated in the previous century: the Prussian state had owned mines and factories then, so that its acquisition of further productive assets in the nineteenth century was not a major departure. Nor was it strictly speaking novel for the Tsarist government to plough money into Western-style armaments. However, the extent to which European states directly involved themselves in railway construction had no real precedent. Almost nowhere in Europe was the British practice imitated of leaving railways entirely to the private sector. In France the state subsidized the various private railway companies in a variety of ways: from 1840 until 1849 around 7.2 million francs were spent annually on railways by the new Ministry for Public Works, between a fifth and a quarter of annual average gross investment. Elsewhere—in Belgium, Hanover, Baden, and Prussia—the state built the railways itself. In Russia the state's role was even greater (see below).

Yet the classical liberal view that government intervention was either superfluous or harmful remains influential. In support of the liberal view, it is clear that the role of the state in nineteenth-century Europe was small compared with its role in the eighteenth or twentieth centuries. As a proportion of net national product (NNP), central government expenditure in Britain fell from around 18 per cent in 1820–4 to 8.2 per cent in 1910–13; the comparable figures for Germany are 20 per cent and 6.6 per cent. The main contribution the state made in most European countries was, therefore, to get out of the way of economic development. It did this not only by holding expenditure down below the average rate of growth, but also by removing legal obstacles: the liberalization of the labour market was part of this process; as was the rather slower liberalization of the capital market, which allowed joint-stock companies to be formed with limited liability (a crucial but contentious reform, given the consequence that an individual could preserve his private fortune in the event of his company going bust). Of particular importance, it has often been argued, was the liberalization of trade. This began with the creation of a series of single markets (i.e., regions without internal customs barriers): the Prussian *Zollverein*, which grew steadily from 1834, the Austro-Hungarian customs union (1850), the Russo-Polish (1851), and the Italian single market, which was a direct consequence of Italian unification. The zenith of free trade came in the 1860s, when France and then Germany effectively adopted the British system.

In this light, the role of the state was primarily parisitical rather than developmental: it got more from the economy than the economy got from it. Freeing the capital market and trade increased the fiscal strength of states by widening the market for government bonds and (in the case of customs unions) enhancing net revenue from lower and centrally collected duties. Even direct state involvement was often motivated primarily by fiscal considerations. State investment in railways and other assets accounted for substantial shares of public revenue in those countries that undertook it. Prussian income from state enterprises rose from 31 per cent of total revenue in 1847 to 47 per cent in 1867. By 1913 more than half of all the German states' revenue came from publicly owned enterprises. The contrast with the twentieth century, when 'nationalized' industries tended to lose money, is striking.

Nevertheless, the liberal view does need to be qualified. First, there is no evidence that the return to protectionism on the continent after the 1870s was economically harmful. Average tariff rates in Germany in 1913 were 16 per cent, and customs revenue between 1880 and 1913 amounted to 8 per cent of national income, compared with figures of zero and 5 per cent in still liberal Britain. This certainly did not hamper German growth: on the contrary, the German economy grew faster than the British in this period. (Between 1898 and 1913, Germany's NNP rose by 84 per cent, Britain's by just 40 per cent.) Nor did rising tariffs in Europe as a whole (and the United States) impede the growth of trade, which was more rapid in the so-called neo-mercantilist period than in the decades of free trade. Indeed, the trade of those countries that did adopt protectionism grew more rapidly than that of Britain. This was because tariffs were primarily intended to raise revenue and so had to be low enough not to choke off trade. It could also be argued that, as an alternative to direct taxation, tariffs had the economic advantage of encouraging capital accumulation (albeit at the cost of greater inequality). The experience of Britain in the early phase of industrialization, when its infant textile industry was protected from Indian imports, also lends credibility to the view that free trade was not the *sine qua non* of economic success.

The most obvious challenge to the liberal view of economic development is posed by the experience of Russia. There is no question that Russia industrialized rapidly in the three decades before 1914. The average annual growth rate was 3.3 per cent between 1885 and 1913; industrial output rose by between 4.5 and 5 per cent per annum; investment rose from 8 per cent to 10 per cent of national income and capital formation per head rose by 55 per cent between 1890 and 1913. Russian performance in the 'staple' industries was especially strong: the output of pig iron more than doubled between 1898 and 1913, the railway network grew by 57 per cent, and raw cotton consumption by 82 per cent. By almost any measure it was the fastest-growing economy in Europe. It used to be thought, following Gerschenkron, that this achievement owed a great deal to state investment in railways and heavy industry, financed by foreign loans. Russia was also strongly protectionist: revenues from customs accounted for 31 per cent of national income between 1880 and 1913, and by 1913 average tariff rates on dutiable imports were 73 per cent. Critics of Tsarist economic policy, on the other hand, have more recently argued that the state distorted rather than accelerated economic development economy, crowding out private-sector investment and stifling nascent consumer industries for the sake of a bloated military–industrial complex. Yet there is a difficulty with this critique. As a proportion of national income, the government debt burden fell significantly in this period from 65 per cent of NNP in 1887 to 47 per cent in 1913. There is no evidence of crowding out: on the contrary, it seems clear that foreign investors were much more willing to lend to the government than they were to lend to private Russian companies. It is hard to believe that a more liberal policy would have achieved such rapid growth.

Of course, when we speak of 'Russian industrial growth' we are only really concerned with a few isolated regions; and there is a strong case for viewing nineteenth-century economic development in regional rather than national terms. With the possible exception of Belgium, there was certainly not much congruence between economic and political units. By the middle of the century, textile manufacturing similar to that pioneered in Manchester could be found in the north of France (Reims, and the Lille–Tourcoing–Roubaix area), Alsace (Mulhouse), the Massif Central (Lyons, St-Etienne), the Wupper valley (Barmen, Elberfeld), northern Switzerland (Basle), Saxony (Chemnitz), and Catalonia. The main textile centres in eastern Europe were Lodz, Nizhny-Novgorod, and St Petersburg. In the same way, there were distinct coal regions: central Scotland, the north of England and south Wales; the Sambre and Meuse valleys; the French Nord *département* and the upper Loire; from the 1840s, the Ruhr (where the rivers Lippe, Emscher, and Ruhr flow into the Rhine) and later Upper Silesia and the Donets basin near Rostov on Don. Iron and engineering centres were to be found in Luxembourg and Lorraine, the Saar and Upper Silesia, the Ruhr (Essen and Oberhausen), and later Krivoi Rog in the Ukraine, as well as Sweden and the Urals.

An important consequence of this regional pattern of industrialization was a very high level of migration *within* countries. In Prussia between 1816 and 1871, Posen, Pomerania, Brandenburg, Saxony, and Westphalia all lost population; Berlin, Silesia, and the Rhineland all gained. In the next thirty years the united Germany experienced further population movements from the east and south to the west and north. Similar shifts occurred in every country, and perhaps the most striking monuments of the age were the great cities thus created. Urbanization generally built on existing foundations. Many of the great political centres—Paris, Berlin, and Vienna—acquired large industrial belts. So too did some of the inland commercial centres (Cologne and to a lesser extent Frankfurt) and the sea ports (Glasgow, Liverpool, Rotterdam, and Hamburg, where migrants accounted for 58 per cent of the total population increase between 1871 and 1910). But the most striking symbols of the century were the cities that sprang up from next to nothing: Manchester, Birmingham, Middlesbrough, Gelsenkirchen, Oberhausen, Essen. The pace of urbanization should not be overstated, of course: even in 1910 around 40 per cent of Germans lived in villages with fewer than 2,000 inhabitants—double the proportion living in cities with more than 100,000 residents. Still, the largely unplanned and unregulated growth of cities presented governments with perhaps the greatest of all challenges in the period. It was this more than anything else that overwhelmed the liberal 'nightwatchman state'.

Yet the most important point about the nineteenth century was not its regional concentration, but its international extent. We have already seen how important trade was, as measured by its rising share of European national income. Arguably even more important was the immense amount of international migration. Between 1800 and 1845 around 1.5 million Europeans left the continent. In the next thirty years nine million left, with the annual average rising from 250,000 (1846–50) to 428,000 (1854). And between 1871 and 1891 no fewer than 27.6 million emigrated. In the last pre-war decade the annual average was 1.4 million. Some countries experienced a veritable exodus: in the 1880s the Irish emigration rate was nearly 14 per thousand. Even at its peak, the German rate was just half that (see Fig. 3.2). By far the most

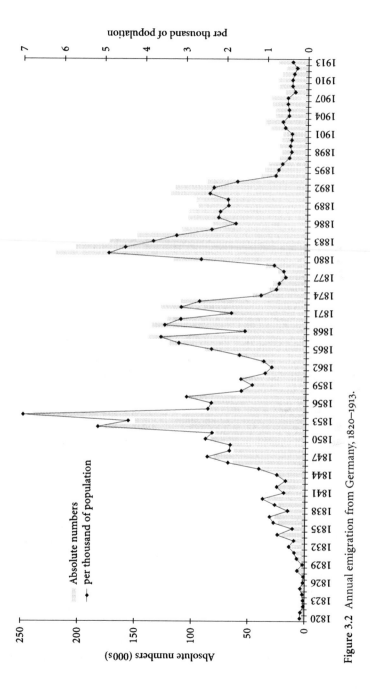

Figure 3.2 Annual emigration from Germany, 1820–1913.

popular destination was, needless to say, the United States. Of some 33.6 million people who went there, 12.7 were from mainland Britain (with Scots over-represented), 4.1 million from Ireland, 7 million from Scandinavia, and 5 million from Germany. Around two million came from Italy, and a further two million from Russia (many of them Jews fleeing state-sanctioned persecution). Many Europeans (some 3.6 million) also went to South America. Two million people left for Australia and New Zealand and 1.5 million (mainly French) settled in North Africa. There was also a huge movement of population from European Russia to the vast Siberian hinterland of the Tsarist Empire—more than two million in the first decade of the twentieth century. No account of European economic development in the nineteenth century can overlook this enormous outflow of people. Though fertility might possibly have been curbed more in the absence of emigration, it is at least arguable that the existence of less densely populated continents outside Europe and the availability of cheap transport to them did as much to disprove Malthus as the improvements in European agriculture described above.

Why did people go? The hero of Dickens's *Martin Chuzzelwit* (1843–4) was untypical in one respect: his decision to leave was impulsive. But his motive was the usual one. His adoring Mary warns him: 'It is a long, long distance; there is a wide ocean to be crossed; illness and want are sad calamities in any place, but in a foreign country dreadful to endure. Have you thought of all this?' But Martin replies: 'You should ask me in the same breath, have I thought of starving at home; have I thought of doing porter's work for a living; have I thought of holding horses in the streets to earn my roll of bread from day to day?' Though some emigrants (especially those who left after 1848) had political reasons for quitting Europe, the majority went to escape unemployment or to take advantage of plentiful cheap land. Not all were as disappointed in American real estate as Dickens's hero, though many—perhaps as many as 30 or 40 per cent—did return home. And Dickens is especially convincing about the wretched conditions experienced by emigrants who travelled in steerage. At mid-century, the average transatlantic voyage lasted between one and a half and three months; on one such voyage, 108 out of 544 German passengers died. Perhaps the greatest beneficiaries of the exodus were the shipping magnates like Albert Ballin, the founder of the Hamburg–Amerika line, who began his business career selling steerage tickets at a discount.

The emigration of people was accompanied—and to some extent facilitated—by the export of capital from Europe. Table 3.4 gives approximate totals for overseas investment on the eve of the First World War. As the figures make clear, Britain led the field by far, but was unusual in that relatively little of its overseas investment was in Europe. France, by contrast, was principally interested in Europe, and particularly in Russia: 27.5 per cent of all French overseas investment was in Russia, of which 90 per cent was in state bonds. In the British case, the process was a cumulative one. By the 1850s British overseas investments already totalled around £200 million. In the second half of the century, however, there were three great waves of capital export. Between 1861 and 1872, net foreign investment rose from just 1.4 per cent of GNP to 7.7 per cent, before dropping back down to 0.8 per cent in 1877. It then rose more or less steadily to 7.3 per cent in 1890, before once again falling down below 1 per cent in 1901. In the third upswing, foreign investment rose to a peak of 9.1 per cent in 1913—a level not subsequently surpassed until the 1990s. The economic significance of this is often misunderstood by historians who see capital export as in some sense a 'drain' on the economy of the British Isles. Although there was clearly an inverse relationship between the cycle of foreign investment and that of domestic fixed investment, the income earned on overseas investments more than matched the export of new capital, just as (when coupled with revenue from 'invisible' earnings) it invariably exceeded the trade deficit. In the 1890s net foreign investment amounted to 3.3 per cent of GNP,

Table 3.4 Overseas investment, 1914

Country	Total (bn. francs)	Of which in Europe (%)
Britain	20.0	5.2
France	9.0	51.9
Germany	5.8	44.0
USA	3.5	20.0
Other	7.1	n.a.
TOTAL	45.4	26.4

Note: n.a. = not applicable.

compared with net property income from abroad of 5.6 per cent. For the next decade the figures were 5.1 and 5.9 respectively.

Why did the British economy behave in this way? The greater part of overseas investment was 'portfolio' rather than 'direct' in nature—in other words, it was mediated by stock exchanges through sales of bonds and shares issued on behalf of foreign governments and companies. According to Edelstein, the explanation for the 'pull' of foreign securities was simply that, even allowing for the higher degree of risk involved, their yields were significantly higher (by around 1.5 percentage points) than those of domestic securities when averaged out over the period 1870–1913. However, this averaging conceals substantial fluctuations. Analyzing the accounts of 482 firms, Davis and Huttenback have shown that domestic rates of return were sometimes higher than foreign—in the 1890s for example. Their work also quantifies the importance of imperialism, as rates of return on investments in the Empire were significantly different from those on investments in foreign territories not politically controlled by Britain: as much as 67 per cent higher in the period before 1884, but 40 per cent lower thereafter. Yet the imperial share of new issues rose from 35 per cent in 1870–89 to 43 per cent between 1890 and 1914. Arguably, then, the rising level of British investment abroad was an economically irrational product of imperialism—a case of capital following the flag rather than maximum returns. On the other hand, imperial possessions were not the main destination of British investment taken as a whole: for the period between 1865 and 1914, only around 25 per cent of investment went to the Empire, compared with 30 per cent for the British economy itself and 45 per cent for foreign economies.

One of the vital preconditions for these high levels of capital export was the relative stability of the international monetary system. As Table 3.5 shows, it is an oversimplification to regard the nineteenth century as the age of the gold standard. As late as 1868, only Britain and its economic dependency Portugal were on the gold standard, in the technical sense that only gold was treated as a reserve metal by the note-issuing bank, and its notes were convertible into gold on demand. The other European countries were either on a pure silver standard or on a bimetallic (gold and silver) system. By 1908, however, silver had effectively been demonetized in Europe, and, although a number of countries could not offer full convertibility, in practice exchange rates were fixed in gold terms. The triumph of gold was due

Table 3.5 The emergence of the gold standard, 1868–1908

Country	1868		1908	
	Standard	Convertibility	Standard	Convertibility
UK	Gold	Yes	Gold	Yes
France	Bimetallic	Yes	Gold	Yes
Belgium	Bimetallic	Yes	Gold	Yes
Switzerland	Bimetallic	Yes	Gold	Yes
Italy	Bimetallic	No	Gold	No
Germany	Silver[a]	Yes	Gold	Yes
Netherlands	Silver	Yes	Gold	Yes
Denmark	Silver	Yes	Gold	Yes
Norway	Silver	Yes	Gold	Yes
Sweden	Silver	Yes	Gold	Yes
Austria	Silver	No	Gold	No
Russia	Bimetallic	No	Gold	Yes
Greece	Bimetallic	No	Gold	Yes[b]
Spain	Bimetallic	No	Gold	No
Portugal	Gold[c]	Yes	Gold	No
Romania	Bimetallic	No	Gold	Yes
Ottoman Empire	Gold	No	Gold exchange	Yes

[a] Except Bremen.

[b] 1910.

[c] 1854.

partly to British commercial primacy. It also owed much to the discovery of gold in California (1848), Australia (1851), and later South Africa: without those discoveries, tying currencies to gold would have imposed an intolerable deflation. The fact that silver was mined in even greater quantities explains the decline of its price in silver terms, which also diminished its appeal. The gold standard was also part of a wider trend towards international cooperation: like the International Telegraph Union (1875), the World Postal Union (1878), and the Central Bureau for Railway Traffic (1890), the transition to gold was debated at international conferences, and the functioning of the system relied on collaboration between the major central banks.

Economic historians have since shown that the practice of the gold standard did not always conform to the rules of 'bullionism—the British doctrine that the domestic circulation of paper money should be automatically linked to the balance of payments *via* the issuing bank's gold reserve and discount rate. Nevertheless, the key contribution of the system was price stability over the medium and long term. As Fig. 3.3 shows (using the example of Germany), the period 1815–1914 was flanked by two periods of price instability due to the fiscal and monetary strains caused by the wars. In the century between Waterloo and the Marne, however, prices were strikingly stable. To be precise: there was a period of post-war deflation (1818–24), then a period of fluctuation around an unchanged mean (with peaks in 1847, 1856, and 1873), then a deflationary period (1874–1886), then stability until around 1896, followed by gentle inflation to 1914.

Economists continue to debate the economic costs and benefits of low inflation. One important argument in favour is that expectations of price stability in the medium to long term caused interest rates to fall, as illustrated by Fig. 3.4 (showing the yields on the benchmark bonds of three major European powers). Comparing the nineteenth century with the period after 1914, there would appear to be a correlation between price stability, low interest rates, and high levels of investment.

It is nevertheless important to emphasize that, in the *short* term, prices tended to *fluctuate* quite rapidly. Moreover—and this is a point no composite index can show—technological change led to substantial changes in relative prices (for example, the dramatic fall in the price of cotton goods at the beginning of the period). Fig. 3.5 illustrates this point by showing how iron and non-animal agricultural prices fluctuated in Germany at the time of the so-called Great Depression. This shows clearly that the price of iron fell much further than the price of farm produce after 1873, which helps to explain why heavy industrialists were willing to join forces with agrarians in support of protective tariffs.

Given the restrictions on politically induced monetary expansion, price fluctuations provide a reasonable proxy for economic activity for most of the nineteenth century. They remind us of a vital point about the period—easily forgotten by those devoted to aggregates and averages—namely, the erratic nature of growth. As a rule, contemporaries are more struck by short-range fluctuations in economic activity than by a long-run upward trend: these fluctuations were more pronounced in the nineteenth century than in the second half of the twentieth century because since 1945 governments have been more willing and able to smooth the economic cycle by adjusting

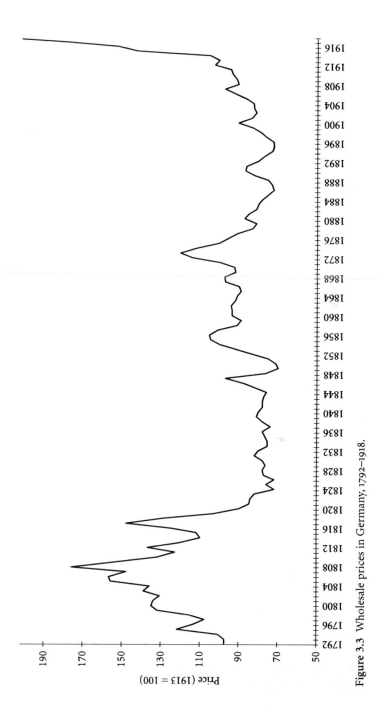

Figure 3.3 Wholesale prices in Germany, 1792–1918.

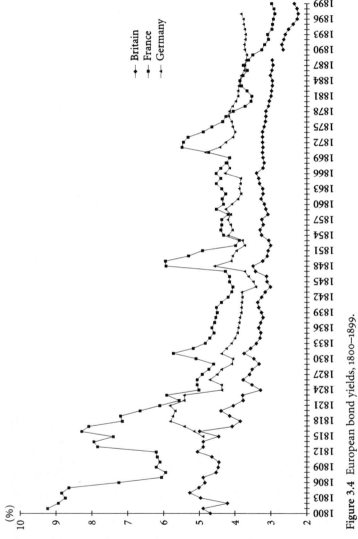

Figure 3.4 European bond yields, 1800–1899.

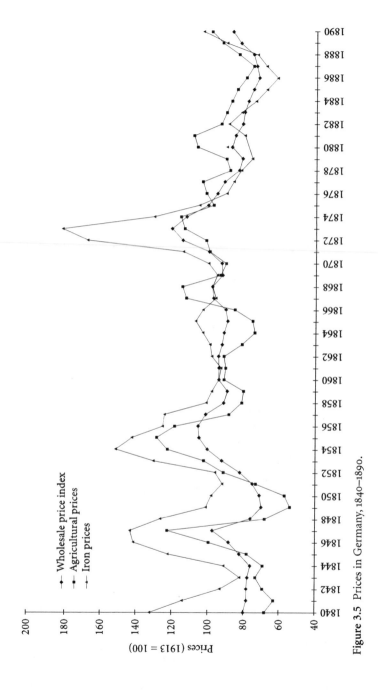

Figure 3.5 Prices in Germany, 1840–1890.

Prices (1913 = 100)

Wholesale price index
Agricultural prices
Iron prices

monetary and fiscal policies. The idea of counter-cyclical policy was anathema to the Victorians. Admittedly, Bairoch's figures for GNP suggest that the variance in annual growth rates became smaller in the course of the century, largely because of the decrease in the relative importance of inherently volatile agricultural production. Nevertheless, the trade cycle's booms and busts continued to be the most important economic events in the lives of contemporaries. As prices of assets and goods fell, companies cut their dividends, their production, their employees' wages, and their payrolls, delayed payment of their creditors, and—if all else failed—went bankrupt (a last resort that then, unlike today, carried a stigma so dreadful that it frequently drove men to suicide). As today, the focal points of economic volatility were stock markets—London, Paris, Vienna, Berlin, and New York were the most important—where the bonds and shares issued to finance joint-stock companies were traded. Fig. 3.6 illustrates the ups and downs of the British stock market, showing that the secular trend of asset prices was upwards, but that the market was subject to substantial fluctuations in the short and medium term. Thus monthly falls in share prices of more than 5 per cent occurred in 1822, 1825, 1826, 1828, 1836, 1841, 1866, and 1903. The crucial point (obvious from the figure, is that, despite the image of the trade 'cycle', the stock market did not fluctuate in a regular and predictable way. To the many investors who saw their savings wiped out in an unexpected crash, it was tempting to attribute its apparently random movements to the machinations of sinister speculators. Vivid descriptions of the social effects of such crises can be found in Dickens's *Little Dorritt*, Trollope's *The Way We Live Now*, and Zola's *L'Argent*. Yet no amount of criticism of stock markets deterred investors from returning to them when share prices showed signs of resuming their long upswing.

Consequences

The social, political, and international consequences of the nineteenth century's great economic metamorphosis are dealt with in detail elsewhere in this volume. It is nevertheless worth asking here how far the rise and fall of classes, political parties, and states were

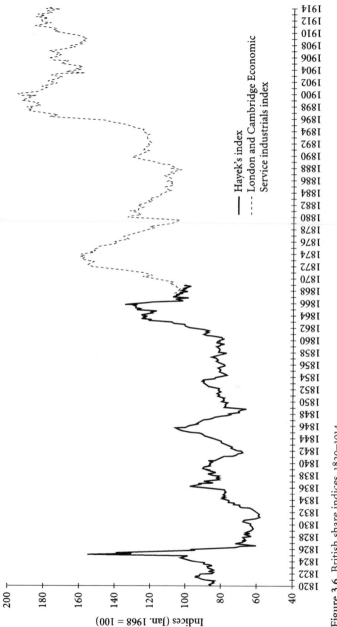

Figure 3.6 British share indices, 1820–1914.

influenced—perhaps even caused—by economic factors. After all, with the possible exception of Darwin's theory of natural selection, no nineteenth-century idea has been more influential than Marx's economic determinism.

It is certainly arguable that it was economics—the need to earn money—that shaped people's lives more than anything else. To take the case of one not untypical city, Hamburg in 1907, 73 per cent of all men aged between 16 and 60 were in employment, as were 38 per cent of all men over 70 and 33 per cent of unmarried women. Mostly that meant manual work: nearly two-thirds of the working population worked with their hands, including the 11 per cent who were domestic servants. The hours were long: up to 82 hours per week in some occupations. And the lion's share of the money thus earned went on renting flats that were cramped and often insanitary (when the great Prussian bacteriologist Robert Koch saw the Alley Quarters of the old town in 1892, his comment was: 'I forget I am in Europe'). This, then, was the lot of 'the masses'. Zola memorably described in *L'Assommoir* (1877) how the workers led the social cavalcade that began every day at 6 a.m. in the Boulevard de la Chapelle, near the Gare du Nord:

You could tell the locksmiths by their blue overalls, masons by their white jackets, painters by their coats with long smocks showing underneath. From a distance this crowd looked a uniformly nondescript plaster colour, a neutral tone made up chiefly of faded blue and dirty grey. Now and again some workman would stop to light his pipe, but the others tramped on round him with never a smile, never a word to a mate, pasty faces all turned towards Paris, which swallowed them one by one . . .

By 8 o'clock, however, the scene had changed:

After the workmen came the workgirls—polishers, dressmakers, florists, huddled up in their thin dresses, tap-tapping along the outer boulevards in threes and fours, chattering away and giggling, darting keen glances about them . . . Next the office workers passed along, blowing on their fingers and munching their penny rolls as they walked; lean young men in suits a size too small . . . or little old men with toddling gait and faces tired and pale from long hours at the desk, looking at their watches to regulate their speed within a second or two. And finally . . . the local well-to-do . . . taking their stroll in the sun.

The seriously rich—like the family that had financed the construction of the Gare du Nord itself, the Rothschilds—would rarely have been seen in such a quarter.) The old question bears repeating: how could such an unequal society survive? Why did it not succumb long before the great crisis of 1917–18—to the revolutions promised by Marx?

One narrowly economic answer to that question is that, by a number of measures, the sustained increase in inequality predicted by Marx did not take place. True, Adeline Daumard calculated that, whereas in 1820 merchants, industrialists, proprietors, and rentiers held 53 per cent of all wealth in Paris, by 1911 the figure was 81 per cent. Lindert and Williamson also concluded that income distribution became more unequal in England and Wales between 1801–3 and 1867, with the top 5 or 10 per cent benefiting at the expense of those in the middle. However, it seems that this trend probably reversed itself between 1867 and 1913. According to one estimate, the proportion of total income going to the top 5 per cent of earners fell from 48 per cent in 1880 to 43 per cent in 1913. Evidence for other countries is mixed: the share of income going to the top 5 per cent also fell in Denmark from 37 per cent (1870) to 30 per cent (1908), but in Saxony it was static at around 33 per cent, while in Prussia it rose from 28 per cent (1873–5) to 31 per cent (1911–13). For Germany as a whole, on the other hand, the proportion of national income attributable to wages rose from 47 per cent in the 1870s to 53 per cent in 1910–14. This seems consistent with other evidence of falling returns to capital, stable rents, and rising real wages. In other words, if industrialization led to an increase in inequality in the first half of the period 1815–1914, this seems to have been 'corrected' thereafter. Not much of this correction can be attributed to redistributive taxation (the main source of income levelling in the post-1914 period). Capitalism, *pace* Marx, was able to redistribute income by increasing incomes across the social spectrum and enabling more people to save and accumulate wealth.

The political implications of economic change also continue to loom large in modern historiography. A central question remains the one posed by many radicals following the disappointments of 1849–52: why did the bourgeoisie prefer authoritarian, aristocratic regimes to workers' and artisans' movements with which they could (in theory) have made common cause? Yet this question understates the fundamental conflict that seemed to exist between liberalism and democracy: to most liberals, it was axiomatic that liberalism depended on a restriction of political representation to those with 'property' and 'education' (i.e. income above a certain threshold). Those franchise qualifications were one of the most visible ways in which politics and economics intersected during the period. No one thought more cynically about these matters than Bismarck (who had himself studied economic history as a young man). 'The bourgeoisie has always been the curatrix of revolution,' he reasoned, 'while below the three thaler line nine-tenths of the population are conservative.' It was on this basis that he adopted universal male suffrage for the German parliament—one of the great political miscalculations of modern times. Bismarck was nearer the mark, however, when he declared in 1878: 'The predominance of economic issues in internal affairs is making inexorable progress . . . The parties would emerge as sharply defined communities of interests on which one could count and which would pursue tit-for-tat policies.' The trouble was that the policies adopted by his successors to forge a parliamentary bloc of agrarian Conservatives, business Liberals, and (sometimes) peasant Catholics created unforeseen countervailing pressures. The combination of tariffs on grain—'dear bread'—and rising expenditure on the navy and the army—'militarism'—paved the way for the Social Democrats' electoral triumph in 1912.

The fact of the First World War, of course, remains the strongest piece of evidence that the capitalist system was—just as Marx and Dubslav von Stechlin had prophecied—bound to culminate in a *Generalweltanbrennung*. One modern argument relates the international conflict that broke out in 1914 to long-run economic tendencies by suggesting that differential rates of industrial growth undermined the stability of the 'balance of power'. Table 3.6 shows the changing

Table 3.6 Relative shares of world manufacturing output (%)

	1800	1860	1900
Europe	28.1	53.2	62.0
UK	4.3	19.9	18.5
Germany	3.5	4.9	13.2
Russia	5.6	7.0	8.8
France	4.2	7.9	6.8
Habsburg Empire	3.2	4.2	4.7
Italy	2.5	2.5	2.5

industrial balance of power in the period. Clearly, the biggest change within Europe was the rise of Germany to a position not far behind Britain. This has suggested to some historians an almost inevitable 'rise of Anglo-German antagonism', climaxing in a German 'bid for world power' in 1914. Such arguments have been reinforced by another economically deterministic argument: that Germany's aggressive foreign policy was the result of internal social conflict. According to the posthumously influential German historian Eckart Kehr, the explanation for Wilhelmine Germany's ultimately suicidal commitment to a two-front war lay in the Prussian agrarians' desire for tariffs, which antagonized Russia, the heavy industrialists' desire for naval orders, which antagonized Britain, and their combined desire to combat the advance of Social Democracy by a strategy of 'social imperialism', which antagonized both.

The weakness of such arguments is that they over-simplify the relationship between economics and international power. First, industrial production is not directly equivalent to power—otherwise Saxony and Belgium would have been great powers by 1860. High levels of capital export were just as important in giving a country diplomatic leverage: no balance of payments surplus, no empire. Secondly, to translate rising output of pig iron into effective military capability it was necessary to have a political system capable of both raising taxation in line with growth and prioritizing military expenditures. Thirdly, as was clear to many contemporaries, it was almost impossible to achieve this without increasing domestic political tension because of the distributional conflicts triggered by rising defence budgets—precisely the opposite of what 'social imperialism' was supposed to achieve.

Table 3.7 shows estimates of defence spending as a proportion of

Table 3.7 Defence spending as a percentage of GNP 1913

Country	%
Britain	3.1
France	3.9
Russia	4.6
Germany	3.5
Austria	2.8

GNP in 1913 for the five major European powers—a good measure of the extent of a country's military commitment. These figures cast doubt on the notion that Germany was somehow a more 'militaristic' state than France or Russia. Although Germany certainly had a strong militarist culture and ample economic resources, the Reich was ultimately incapable of holding its own in the naval and land arms races because of political constraints imposed by its federal system and democratic Reichstag. The fiscal constraint was even more serious in Austria–Hungary, Germany's sole reliable ally, not least because of the difficulty of getting the Hungarians to contribute to the common military budget. By comparison, Britain spent only a fractionally larger percentage of GNP on defence than Austria–Hungary and rather less than Germany, but was able to govern a vast empire, which grew from 9.5 million square miles in 1860 to 12.7 million in 1909. Some 444 million people were under some form of British rule on the eve of the First World War; yet the cost of running this huge empire was remarkably low. Russia too controlled a far larger territory than the Central Powers, and could mobilize a substantially more numerous, if less well-equipped army. This reflected the ability of the highly centralized Russian state to increase defence expenditure to take full advantage of the economy's rapid growth in the two decades before 1914. It is easy to see why the German Chancellor Theobald von Bethmann Hollweg was so worried by this. 'The future belongs to Russia,' he told his secretary in 1914. 'It grows and grows and hangs upon us ever more heavily like a nightmare ... Russia's growing claims and enormous power to advance in a few years will simply be impossible to fend off, especially if the present European constellation persists.' This was the argument most frequently used in Berlin in 1914 to justify a pre-emptive military strike against Russia and its ally France. The danger for Russia was that rising taxation was financed overwhelmingly from taxes on consumption (of which the most important was clearly the excise levied on vodka). Its regressive fiscal system proved less resilient in time of war than the more progressive systems of the other combatants.

The important point, however, is that the war was not the fulfilment of the prophecies of doom with which this chapter began. It was caused, not by a crisis of capitalism, but by a crisis of diplomacy. Indeed, capitalism surprised most contemporaries by enabling them to fight for longer and more intensively than had been thought possible. And when the economic strain eventually proved too much for some combatants, it was only in the least industrialized— Russia—that capitalism was overthrown.

In his tract *The Economic Consequences of the Peace* (1919), John Maynard Keynes looked back on the pre-war world with a mixture of nostalgia and irony, but also with his usual perceptiveness:

What an extraordinary episode in the economic progress of man that age was which came to an end in August 1914! The greater part of the population, it is true, worked hard and lived at a low standard of comfort, yet were, to all appearances, reasonably contented with this lot. But escape was possible, for any man of capacity or character at all exceeding the average, into the middle and upper classes, for whom life offered, at a low cost and with the least trouble, conveniences, comforts and amenities beyond the compass of the richest and most powerful monarchs of other ages. The inhabitant of London could order by telephone, sipping his morning tea in bed, the various products of the whole earth in such quantity as he might see fit, and reasonably expect their early delivery upon his doorstep; he could at the same moment and by the same means adventure his wealth in the natural resources and new enterprises of any quarter of the world, and share, without exertion or even trouble, in their prospective fruits and advantages . . . The projects and politics of militarism and imperialism, of racial and cultural rivalries, of monopolies, restrictions and exclusion, which were to play the serpent to this paradise, were little more than the amusements of his daily newspaper . . .

As Keynes acknowledged, nineteenth-century Europe was far from being an Eden for most of its inhabitants. But in describing its unprecedented economic fertility, the imagery of Genesis is more appropriate than that of *Götterdämmerung*.

4

Culture

James J. Sheehan

Modern culture

Modern culture, Friedrich Nietzsche wrote in 1873, 'is not real culture at all, but only a kind of knowledge about culture . . . only by filling and overfilling ourselves with alien ages, customs, arts, philosophies, religions and knowledge do we become something worthy of notice, namely walking encyclopaedias . . .'. A surprising number of Nietzsche's contemporaries shared his belief that the nineteenth century lacked the cultural integrity of former times, and therefore had to compensate for its hollowness with scholarship, collecting, and imitation. The century, Matthew Arnold lamented, did not have those passionate visions that moved men in the past: we are, he wrote in the 'Scholar Gypsy' of 1853, 'light half-believers of our casual creeds'. Gone too were the sources of artistic creativity that had inspired the ancient world and the Renaissance. 'We paint everything,' Friedrich Theodor Vischer declared. 'We paint gods and Madonnas, heroes and peasants, we paint classical, Byzantine, and Gothic pictures . . . The only style we don't have is our own'. The root of the problem, many believed, was that the century had not yet found a unifying idea, a shared identity from which people might acquire a sense of their common destiny. A great many nineteenth-century intellectuals were engaged in a search for such an idea, which might serve their culture as a wellspring of spiritual meaning and aesthetic achievement.

It is easy to sympathize with those who emphasized the derivative and divided character of nineteenth-century culture. We cannot identify a single idea or institution around which the century's cultural achievements might be organized. There is no cultural equivalent of the railroad, that quintessentially nineteenth-century invention that transformed virtually every aspect of life, from how people thought about time to the way they waged war. Nor can we find a set of cultural innovations comparable to the rediscovery of Aristotle in the twelfth century or the scientific revolutions of the seventeenth. Most of the century's leading ideas about nature, history, and society had been formulated earlier. Most of the century's distinctive cultural institutions had compelling precedents in the seventeenth and eight-eenth centuries, while the development of film, sound recording, and broadcasting, which would eventually transform the institutional basis of culture, all belong to the twentieth rather the nineteenth century.

Nevertheless, despite the dismissive remarks of contemporaries like Nietzsche, nineteenth-century culture does have a distinctive character, which comes not from any one innovation but rather from the way in which it combined and developed a variety of ideas, all with roots in the seventeenth and eighteenth centuries. In our brief summary of the century's culture, we will examine four sets of such ideas: the intellectual crisis created by an apparent decline of religious faith, the emergence of science, the particular prominence of histor-ical thinking, and the pervasive ambition to create systems of thought and knowledge. In the concluding section, we will look back on the century's central themes from the perspective of their modernist critics. But before turning to the ideas themselves, we must say a few words about their institutional setting.

Institutions

One of the most enduring legacies of the nineteenth century is the image of the alienated artist or intellectual, who lived a lonely, impoverished life on the margins of society and died before his tal-ents could be recognized. Even today we often associate creativity and alienation, assuming that those on the fringes of society can see real-ity more clearly but must pay a price for their more acute vision. In the nineteenth century, there were, to be sure, some prominent examples of this unhappy condition—artists like van Gogh, philo-sophers like Nietzsche, writers like Dostoyevsky—but the stereotype is misleading for at least two reasons. First, most of the century's leading cultural figures led fairly comfortable lives and enjoyed the admiration of their contemporaries; some grew rich from their work and basked in what passed, in those simpler times, for celebrity. Secondly, and more importantly, the image of the isolated genius distracts us from the intense and extensive institutionalization that is among nineteenth-century culture's most salient characteristics. Without taking into account the distinctive development of a range of institutions—theatres, art museums, scholarly disciplines, publishing enterprises, and many more—we cannot understand either the form or the content of the century's cultural achievements.

Consider, for example, the changing institutional basis of musical composition and performance. Until the eighteenth century, music was usually created within princely courts, churches, or local communities. Most musicians lived from the largesse of patrons, like Haydn's Prince Esterhazy, or were employees of a church, like several members of the Bach family, or went from village to village as part of some travelling troupe of entertainers. The music they made was designed for these settings: operas that could be performed at, and often by, members of the court, chamber music to embellish aristocratic gatherings, hymns and choral works to accompany religious rituals, and whatever was necessary to enliven a rural wedding or communal festival. Around the turn of the nineteenth century, the institutional setting of European music began to change. Beethoven, who was born in 1770, personified this transition: during the first half of his career he depended on patrons such as Prince Lobkowitz, who paid for the first performance of the 'Eroica' in 1803; but increasingly Beethoven became a public figure, who directed his work to a wider audience. Of course, patronage remained important, as Richard Wagner's relationship with King Ludwig II reminds us, but more and more composers and performers came to rely on the support of people who bought tickets to hear their works, joined societies that sponsored musical events, paid taxes that sustained municipal orchestras, and—last but not least—purchased printed scores for their own use. For this new public were written the works we associate with the century's greatest musicians: powerful symphonies and grand operas that could hold the attention of large audiences in spacious new concert halls, complex pieces on which celebrity performers such as Chopin or Paganini could display their virtuosity, and the songs and piano works from which generations of young amateurs might learn the musical skills so highly valued in middle-class society.

We can trace the rise of this new musical culture in the concert halls and opera houses that were built throughout Europe in the late eighteenth and nineteenth centuries. In 1742, for example, Prussia's Frederick the Great constructed an opera house in Berlin that served both court and public: admission was free, but only by invitation. When the building was remodelled in 1789, the boxes were replaced by galleries, for which tickets could be purchased by anyone who could afford them. Karl Friedrich Schinkel's Schauspielhaus, which opened with the première of Carl Maria von Weber's *Der Freischütz* in 1821, had no ties whatsoever to the court but rather celebrated the place of the dramatic arts in public culture. Similar kinds of buildings marked the role of the public in other aspects of cultural life. Art museums, for example, date from the middle of the eighteenth century, when princes opened up their collections to visitors. In the nineteenth century, governments everywhere began to construct those great treasure houses of art that still dominate our cultural landscape: Schinkel's Altes Museum in Berlin (1830), Leo von Klenze's Alte Pinakothek in Munich (1836), and Sir Robert Smirke's British Museum in London (1847). By the end of the century, virtually every major town in Europe had an opera house, a concert hall, and at least one museum.

These buildings were public in a way that neither court nor traditional community had been. They were, in theory at least, accessible to everyone, open at regular times, usually supported by public moneys. Even when museums and concert halls retained some ties to a royal patron, their audience was unrestricted, their purpose socially defined; they were *national* galleries and theatres, expressions of their nation's commitment to culture's value and pedagogical possibilities. But, while access to these institutions was public, the experiences they offered were supposed to be private: one listened silently to a concert or opera, responding only at the prescribed moment with conventional applause; similarly, one walked quietly through a museum, experiencing each work of art in isolation. This private dimension of public culture was also different from the old regime, where art and music accompanied social interaction in court and congregation and popular festivity. By affirming culture as a source of both social and individual improvement, concert halls and museums served as what the music historian Carl Dahlhaus called 'representative institutions'—that is, ways of organizing people and spaces that reflected the century's social norms and core ideals.

Nineteenth-century culture sought to be universal, available to all, relevant for everybody. Legal restrictions on who could buy a book, visit a museum, hear a concert were gradually lifted. Freedom of the press, although still severely limited in some states, was none the less an ideal advocated by enlightened people everywhere. Public education, whatever its deficiencies in practice, was the goal of governments throughout the continent. But while public culture aspired to universality, it was effectively restricted to those with the resources necessary to understand and enjoy it—the money to pay for theatre tickets, the background required to appreciate the works of art on display in a museum, the knowledge presupposed by serious novelists and intellectuals. The promise of universality, therefore, was always qualified by practical limitations that, in their own way, created cultural distinctions no less powerful than the status divisions in the old regime. Moreover, as we will see in the next section, nineteenth-century culture was also divided by conflicts over theological issues and religious practices, which had, for a majority of Europeans from every stratum, once provided a common vocabulary of symbols, rituals, and beliefs.

Secularization

For most of its history, European culture was inseparable from religious values and institutions; after the eighteenth century, this was clearly no longer the case. By the nineteenth century, intellectual life seemed to be dominated by history, economics, sociology, and natural science, not by theology or even theologically informed philosophy. The representative commissions for architects were museums, libraries, and other public buildings, not churches and religious monuments. Symphonies and sonatas, not ecclesiastical music, engaged the talents of leading composers. In short, what we think of as nineteenth-century culture was predominately secular, sustained by secular values and directed towards secular ends. For many of Europe's artists and intellectuals, the world had been—in

Max Weber's well-known description—*entzaubert*, disenchanted, drained of its sacred rituals and supernatural meanings. In 'Dover Beach', written in 1851, Matthew Arnold described the disenchantment of the world with this striking metaphor:

> The Sea of Faith
> Was once, too, at the full, and round earth's shore
> Lay like the folds of a bright girdle furl'd.
> But now I only hear
> Its melancholy, long, withdrawing roar,
> Retreating, to the breath
> Of the night-wind, down the vast edges drear
> And naked shingles of the world.

Although this ebbing of religious faith certainly gathered momentum after 1800, it would be a mistake to equate the secularization of high culture with the disappearance of religion from social, political, or cultural life. In the first place, religion's overall decline was relative, not absolute. Theology remained an active branch of learning; churches continued to be built (nearly 5,000 in England between 1800 and 1876); religious music was still written. Moreover, there is ample evidence that religious commitments continued to play an important role in most people's public and private lives. Of course the intensity of belief among Europeans varied widely: it was different for Protestants and Catholics, rich and poor, men and women, farmers and city dwellers. In some regions, like the peasant communities of Brittany (whose religiosity was the subject of some of Gauguin's finest paintings), intense piety touched every aspect of life; elsewhere, such as the Limousin, Christianity had almost disappeared.

From this variety of religious practice came some of the century's most bitter conflicts—between Protestants and Catholics, ultramontanes and anticlericals, theological liberals and conservatives—conflicts that became the basis for lasting institutional loyalties and political animosities. In England during the 1830s, for example, public life was absorbed by debates about the Anglican Church's monopoly over marriage ceremonies, the rights of dissenters, and the question of whether nonconformists could attend the ancient universities. According to the eminent historian of Victorian England, George Kitson Clark, 'probably in no other century, except the seventeenth and perhaps the twelfth, did the claims of religion occupy so large a part in the nation's life, or did men speaking in the name of religion contrive to exercise so much power'. Much the same could be said about many other European nations, which also had to confront the competing claims of religion's defenders and detractors. The apparent secularization of high culture, therefore, did not destroy religion, but it did transform it from an accepted fact of cultural life into a problem: something to be analysed, explained, defended, or attacked, and—for some intellectuals at least—something that should be replaced with a faith more in keeping with the age. Far from disappearing in the nineteenth century, religion was a matter of the greatest importance, indeed, for many intellectuals, close to an obsession.

To the radical German intellectuals who had gathered in Berlin during the 1830s, for example, theological problems were of major concern since religious reform seemed to be the first step towards a larger transformation of society. Conservatives, therefore, were not wrong when they regarded books such as David Friedrich Strauss's *Life of Jesus* (1835) or Ludwig Feuerbach's *Essence of Christianity* (1841) as both theologically heterodox and politically dangerous. The critique of religion, argued the young Karl Marx in 1843, is the basis of all criticisms. John Stuart Mill, who lived in a very different cultural and political world, came to a remarkably similar conclusion: it has been on the battlefield of religious liberty, he wrote, 'that the rights of the individual against society have been asserted on broad grounds of principle, and the claim of society to exercise authority over dissentients, openly controverted'.

But, while many intellectuals saw religion as no more than an anachronistic impediment to progress and enlightenment, others recognized that the disenchantment of the world came at a great price. Heinrich Heine, for example, who was not a poet known for his piety, regretted the cohesive force that had been lost when Catholicism's cultural power declined. In his report on the paintings in the Paris Salon of 1831, Heine contrasted the character of contemporary and Renaissance works: the former, he said, were 'like a crowd of orphans, gathered here and there, left to themselves, and none of them related one to the other'. The latter, by contrast, 'have drawn their nourishment from the breast of one great common mother . . . and, like members of one large family, live together in peace and unity, and speak the same language, though they may not utter the same words'. Twenty years later, Alfred Lord Tennyson's 'In Memoriam' asked:

> Are God and Nature then at strife,
>   That Nature lends such evil dreams?
>   So careful of the type she seems,
>   So careless of the single life.

The poet clings to the conviction that 'no life may fail beyond the grave', yet he can do no more than 'stretch lame hands of faith, and grope . . . And faintly trust the larger hope'. Even Friedrich Nietzsche, who never hesitated to express his disdain for religion, realized the cultural chasm opened by the demise of divinity. In the famous passage where Nietzsche's 'Madman' proclaims the 'death of God', he writes: 'God is dead. God remains dead. And we have killed him. How shall we, the murderers of all murderers, comfort ourselves?' How indeed?

Intellectuals feared that, with the loss of religious faith, humans were alone in the universe, subject to remorseless natural laws, deprived of immortality's sustaining hope. The end of religion also meant the end of the foundation upon which personal morality and social obligation had traditionally rested. If there were no God watching over mankind, prepared to reward the good and punish the bad, would it be possible to have either a satisfactory private life or a stable public order? This was the question posed by the novelist George Eliot in 1873, when, in a well-known exchange with F. W. H. Myers, she proclaimed that, while the existence of *God* had become 'inconceivable' and the possibility of *Immortality* 'unbelievable', the necessity of *Duty* was no less 'peremptory and absolute'. Like some grave and gloomy Sibyl, Myers recalled, 'she withdrew from my grasp, one by one, the two scrolls of promise, and left me the third scroll only, awful with inevitable fates'.

Nietzsche believed that the three concepts rose and fell together. It was, he thought, the philosopher's task to find the strength necessary to live without God, accepting the dominion of chance and the certainty of oblivion. The philosopher would have to be strong enough to reject Christian morality as well as Christian theology. Only 'moralistic little females' like George Eliot thought that it would be possible to have one without the other, thus providing another example of what Nietzsche regarded as the English tendency to compensate for every small achievement in theological emancipation with some assertion of moral fanaticism. But, in fact, few nineteenth-century intellectuals were willing to be as relentlessly consistent as Nietzsche. Most of them thought that there could be a secular substitute for religion, an alternative source of comfort and order, another way of understanding and mastering human existence. Much of the rest of this essay, therefore, will be concerned with efforts to find a substitute for the religious basis of society and culture.

Science

For many nineteenth-century intellectuals the leading candidate to take religion's place was science. Auguste Comte gave this conviction an elaborate historical and psychological foundation when, in his *Cours de philosophie positive* (1840–2), he argued that human history, like each individual human being, developed through three stages: the theological, in which the world was understood in religious terms and controlled through magic, the metaphysical, in which philo-sophical speculation was dominant, and, finally, the positivist, in which experimental science became the foundation for all knowledge and policy. Just as individuals gradually lose their childish fears and adolescent illusions, so, Comte believed, humanity was about to enter an era of cultural maturity. As he himself grew older, Comte's efforts to create a culture based on science became intense and eccentric, his worship of humanity increasingly mystical and arcane, his positivism more and more like a religion without God. But even after Thomas à Kempis's *Imitation of Christ* had become Comte's favourite book, the apostle of positivism never abandoned his faith in science as a source of secular salvation.

In practice, science and religion often coexisted; a number of the century's most significant scientists retained orthodox religious con-victions and many pious people had little trouble accepting the importance of scientific knowledge. But in the realm of public debate, science and religion frequently seemed like irreconcilable enemies, each condemned by the other as a source of philosophical error and moral collapse. Pope Pius IX, for instance, gave science's false claims to truth a prominent place among the mistaken views that were condemned in his *Syllabus of Errors* of 1864: Error Number 13 was the belief that 'the methods and principles by which the old scholastic doctors cultivated theology are no longer suitable to the demands of our times and to the progress of the sciences'.

No one espoused Error Number 13 with more fervour than T. H. Huxley, who regarded traditional faith as simply incompatible with what was now known about the natural world. 'Extinguished theologians', Huxley exclaimed, 'lie about the cradle of every infant science as the strangled snakes beside that of Hercules'. He was confident that, like Hercules, the mythological personification of heroic strength, science would grow up to perform feats against which religion's feeble power could not prevail. To an orthodox freethinker like Huxley, science would not only cleanse the world of religious illusions; it would also provide another basis of value. Neither in an unfounded belief in God nor in a vain hope of immortality, but rather in the certainties of scientific knowledge, modern men and women would find a firm foundation for those moral values that, for Huxley, as for George Eliot and virtually all of their contemporaries, remained indispensable.

It is not difficult to understand why Huxley placed so much faith in science. Its significance was acknowledged by educated people everywhere in Europe; its latest discoveries were reported in journals such as the *Westminister Review* or *Preussische Jahrbücher*; families crowded into the new museums of natural history; amateurs collected beetles and butterflies, observed the migration of birds, and sketched wildflowers. Books with scientific themes such as Robert Chambers's *Vestiges of the Natural History of Creation* (1844) or Ludwig Büchner's *Kraft und Stoff (Force and Matter)* (1855) were extraordinarily popular. In the drawing rooms of London, Paris, and Berlin, where intellectually alert men and women gathered to discuss the burning topics of the day, scientific theories seamlessly joined with political issues and literary achievements. 'Science', wrote G. H. Lewes, 'is penetrating everywhere, and slowly changing man's conception of the world and of man's destiny'.

Scientific discoveries were made everywhere in Europe during the nineteenth century. One of the century's most consequential breakthroughs occurred in the Moravian town of Brünn, where an Augustinian monk named Gregor Mendel laid the basis for modern genetics by experimenting with the peas that he cultivated in the monastery garden. But Mendel, working in isolation and not fully appreciated until after his death, was an exceptional figure in every way. Most scientists were part of an institutional network, members of the same learned societies and disciplinary organizations, subscribers to the same periodicals, participants in congresses where ideas and research findings could be exchanged. Equally important, the institutional locus for science became the research laboratory, where a team of investigators employed the latest technology to study the natural world; in the laboratory, apprentice scientists could participate in group projects, learn first-hand research techniques, and acquire the values and habits on which professional science was based. As a powerful instrument of both innovation and socialization, the laboratory combined research and teaching, the accumulation and the dissemination of knowledge.

One of the first research laboratories in Europe was established in a deserted army barracks by Justus Liebig, the author of a foundational work in organic chemistry, agricultural innovator, and longtime professor at the University of Giessen. Under Liebig's direction, students were allowed to work independently and encouraged to learn from one another; their only obligation was to report regularly on what they had accomplished. Liebig himself belonged to a transitional generation of German scientists: born in 1803, he began his career as a apothecary's apprentice but soon recognized that modern science required academic training. After mid-century, more and more scientific research was based at a university, and especially at one of the German universities whose achievements made them models for most of the world. By the 1870s, German scientists had become the recognized leaders in a number of disciplines, including chemistry, medicine, physiology, and physics, and thereby began a period of scientific accomplishment that would last well into the twentieth century. From 1900 to 1930, Germans would win twenty-six Nobel prizes, substantially more than any other country and more than a quarter of all those awarded.

In the middle decades of the nineteenth century, as in the closing decades of the twentieth, biology was the most intellectually vigorous and culturally significant scientific discipline. Consider, for example, the four extraordinary breakthroughs that occurred within a few years of one another in the 1850s. Although their significance would not be recognized until much later, Mendel's experiments had begun to yield important results by 1856. The year before, the Berlin physician and physiologist Rudolf Virchow had published his major work on cellular structures, which sought to demonstrate that cells were the basis of life and the only source of other cells—in his famous phrase, 'omnia cellula a cellula'. In 1857, Louis Pasteur, the director of the École Normale Supérieure in Paris, showed that fermentation was produced by microscopic organisms and not, as had long been believed, by some sort of spontaneous generation. And finally, in the decade's last year, Charles Darwin published *On the Origin of Species*, which offered a biological explanation for the development of all living things. Each of these ideas had what Thomas Kuhn would call 'paradigmatic' significance, in that it helped to establish the research agenda for future generations of scientists. At the same time, each would eventually have an impact well beyond its disciplinary base, in that it provided a metaphor for understanding not only biological but also social reality.

There is a certain irony in the fact that Darwin, whose discoveries were surely the most significant of the four, lived the life of a gentleman-amateur without academic credentials or connections. Born in 1809, the son of a wealthy physician, he studied at Cambridge in preparation for a career in the church—despite his lack of firm religious convictions. From boyhood, Darwin had been fascinated by the natural world and while an undergraduate he had acquired a small reputation as an amateur scientist. With his university studies complete and the prospect of Holy Orders unappealing, he was delighted to accept an invitation to sail with HMS *Beagle* on her three-year journey of exploration. Upon his return in 1836, Darwin lived briefly in London and then, from 1842 until his death forty years later, he spent most of his time in a secluded corner of Kent, where he pondered the materials gathered on his voyage and did additional research on a wide range of geological and biological subjects. Although Darwin worked alone, he was by no means isolated: through his wide network of acquaintances, membership in learned societies, and various publications, he was well known in scientific circles even before *On the Origin of Species* made him famous soon after it appeared in 1859. Despite the distractions of his new celebrity, chronic ill health, and a series of family tragedies, he continued his scientific work until the end of his life; in 1881, the year before he died, he published a monumental tome on the earthworm.

Like most truly influential ideas, Darwin's theory of evolution brought together in a particularly compelling way concepts that were already at work in contemporary culture. People read him, as Gertrude Himmelfarb observed, with a sense of recognition rather than of discovery. By the 1850s, two elements in *On the Origin of Species* had become widely accepted by scientists: first, on the basis of geological evidence, it was clear that the earth was significantly older than had traditionally been believed; secondly, many naturalists now recognized that present species of plants and animals had not always existed but rather had changed over time. To the concepts of geological time and the mutability of species, Darwin added a critical third element: a description of the mechanism through which change took place. He called this mechanism 'natural selection', by which he meant the survival and reproduction of life forms best equipped to compete for the limited resources available. It is one of the curiosities of the history of science that Darwin seems to have arrived at the basic argument in *Origin* by the early 1840s, but delayed publishing it until he received from Alfred Wallace, another amateur naturalist, a paper that described natural selection in strikingly similar terms. With Wallace's generous agreement, Darwin immediately published his own findings, first as a paper to the Linnean Society in London, then in what would become the century's most influential book.

One of the reasons why Darwin had been reluctant to publish his theories was that he anticipated the controversy they would arouse; no longer a believer himself, he none the less was reluctant to challenge the theological conventions and offend religious sensibilities. He was right to fear controversy. As his critics swiftly realized, natural selection seemed to undermine one of the most compelling arguments for the existence of God, that the complex order of nature could only have been created by the designing hand of an intelligent deity. Furthermore, by setting human beings within this evolutionary process, Darwin challenged mankind's claim to a unique place in creation, making us, as he wrote in his notebooks, 'brethren in pain, disease, death' with other animals, with whom we share a common ancestor. But perhaps more important than any particular idea in Darwin's writings was his more diffuse contribution to a cultural climate in which disbelief seemed easier, traditional faith less plausible. Darwin certainly did not disprove the existence of God, but he did offer a view of the universe in which God did not seem to fit.

Huxley was surely correct, therefore, when he wrote in an early review of *Origin* that no work had appeared in the last thirty years that would 'exert so large an influence, not only on the future of Biology, but in extending the domination of Science over regions of thought into which she has, as yet, hardly penetrated'.

Of all the great discoveries in the history of science, Darwin's theory is the most ubiquitously applied and was, at the same time, the most deeply embedded in its immediate cultural context. Among the crucially important ingredients in the theory of natural selection were not only Darwin's careful study of works by geologists like Charles Lyell and his own meticulous observations during the voyage of the *Beagle*, but also the Reverend Thomas Malthus's *Essay on the Principle of Population* (1798), whose bleak assessment of the competition among a growing population for scarce resources Darwin had read in 1838, when the basic argument in *Origin* was just beginning to crystallize. In fact, the idea of competition pervaded nineteenth-century culture. Herbert Spencer, later one of Darwin's most eloquent advocates, used the term 'survival of the fittest' for the first time in 1852, seven years before *Origins*. Samuel Smiles, whose extraordinarily popular *Self-Help* appeared in the same year, and from the same publisher, as Darwin's book, assured his readers that 'life is a struggle' in which every individual must be prepared to engage on his own. 'The nation', Smiles added, 'is only the aggregate of individual conditions, and civilization itself but a question of personal improvement'. There was an important truth in Friedrich Engels's facetious comment that 'Darwin recognizes among beasts and plants his English society'.

Darwin's concept of natural selection was only one of several biological concepts that people applied to their understanding of culture and society. For example, here is how Rudolf Virchow described the function of cells: 'They form a free state of individuals with equal rights, though not equal abilities, which persists because the individuals depend on each other and because there exists certain centres of organizations . . .'. There is, of course, nothing new about the use of technical and scientific metaphors to describe human affairs. Plato, after all, had compared the creation of the world to the work of carpenters and potters; seventeenth-century thinkers had imagined the universe to be like a clock; in the late twentieth century we sometimes compare the mind to a computer. But in the social application of biology, the distinction between metaphor and mirror was often lost: to the most fervent social Darwinians, human conflicts were not *like* the struggles of simple organisms to survive and reproduce, they were *part of* a natural process. And, precisely because these struggles—between individuals, business enterprises, nations, races—were such indisputable, inescapable facts of life, they were relatively easy to justify and absolutely essential to win.

The influence of Darwinism and similar biological metaphors came in part from a belief that natural science's methods could and should be applied to all forms of enquiry. To create a genuine science of politics, society, economics, psychology, a science that would provide the basis for prediction and manipulation, was the abiding ambition of many intellectuals in the nineteenth century and one of their most potent legacies to the twentieth. We have seen how Auguste Comte used this notion as the basis for his elaborate theories about history and human development. John Stuart Mill, while a good deal less confident and consistent than Comte, believed that 'All true political science is, in one sense of the phrase, *a priori*, being deduced from the tendencies of things, tendencies known to us either through our general experience of human nature, or as the result of our analysis of the course of history . . .'. When Engels spoke at Marx's graveside in 1883, he could find no better way to describe his friend and collaborator's achievement than to say that, 'Just as Darwin discovered the law of development of organic nature, so Marx discovered the law of development of human history'.

History

By devoting his life to the search for what Engels called 'the law of development' Marx, like Darwin, sought to fuse science and history. Darwin and Marx, like Comte, Hegel, and many of the era's other representative thinkers, believed that the meaning and value of individual phenomena could be grasped only if they were seen as part of a developmental process. For them, all knowledge was, in a sense, historical knowledge, knowledge about developments over time. The present, therefore, always had to be understood in the light of the past. Even John Stuart Mill, who is not usually regarded as an advocate of historicism, believed that 'as society proceeds in its development, its phenomena are determined . . . by the accumulated influence of past generations over the present'. We find this conviction throughout nineteenth-century culture: novelists uncovered the nature of personality by narrating the history of their characters' lives; philosophers devoted themselves to the history of great ideas; architects were trained by studying the monuments of the past, painters by copying old masters. Everywhere we look, we see expressions of an intense interest in, indeed a reverence for, the past. Museums, at first devoted to art, then to historical artefacts and natural history, spread throughout Europe. Archaeologists painstakingly uncovered the remains of ancient civilizations; folklorists rushed to record traditional customs; societies were formed to gather and preserve historical records and residues. As with so many other aspects of the century's culture, these historical concerns were not new; but after 1800 they became more widespread, articulated, and institutionalized.

Modern historicism had two sources. The first was the secularization of European culture that began in the seventeenth century. In the Christian view of the world, past, present, and future were firmly set in a temporal arc that stretched from Adam's sin in the Garden of Eden, when human history began, to the Last Judgement, when, quite literally, it would end. For every individual, as for mankind as a whole, the meaning of profane time was always subordinated to its divine origins and destination; the present, weighted with the burden of past sin, had meaning as a path to future salvation. When the ordering power of this world view waned, the meaning of human history—that is, the proper relationship of past, present, and future—became a problem, the problem that the grand historical narratives created by thinkers such as Comte, Hegel, and Marx attempted to solve. The essential difference between these grand narratives and Christianity's sacred history was neither their belief in the past's importance nor their conception of the future's promise, about which they were all in agreement, but rather their view of the historical significance of the present, which the profane historians regarded as holding the key to history's meaning and direction.

This brings us to historicism's second source, the widespread conviction among people in the nineteenth century that, because they lived in a time like no other, the relationship between their experience and that of earlier generations had become unsettled and problematic. The literature of the era is filled with depictions of how rapid and drastic changes opened a gap between past and present. Sometimes, these changes were symbolized by the arrival of that quintessential innovation, the railroad. In *Pickwick Papers*, Dickens has his hero travel by carriage, which, as his readers would have recognized immediately, located him in another era; the region in George Eliot's *Middlemarch* is being surveyed so that railroad tracks could be laid, a process that stands for the other transformations that will alter the natural and social landscape forever. Heinrich Heine regarded the opening of the rail line between Paris and Rouen in 1843 as a 'providential event', which, like the inventions of gunpowder and printing, 'swings mankind in a new direction, and changes the colour and shape of life'. No one who rode a train for the first time or was caught up in one of the great building projects that transformed one European city after another could doubt that their world was fundamentally transformed. 'Our Paris,' reads an entry in the Goncourt brothers' journal from 1860, 'the Paris where we were born, the Paris of the way of life of 1830 to 1848, is passing away . . . I am a stranger to what is coming, to what is . . .'. We have entered an era, Alexis de Tocqueville believed, in which 'the woof of time is ever being broken and track of past generations lost'. Historicism was, above all, an attempt to weave again the woof of time and recover the paths along which past generations had moved into the present. 'Only by examining the past', the Swiss historian Jacob Burckhardt told his students, 'can we gauge the speed and power of the movement in which we ourselves live'.

The nineteenth century's grand historical narratives traced the direction of this movement with their own version of the Enlightenment's conception of human progress. And in these narratives, as in the sacred histories they displaced, progress meant overcoming the sins of the past. To Comte, as we have seen, history was the story of mankind's protracted struggle against mythological and speculative illusions, a struggle that would end—indeed was now ending with the triumph of scientific reason. Like St Augustine, Marx viewed humanity as suffering from the hereditary burdens of history that, as he wrote in a famous passage, 'weighs like a nightmare on the brain of the present'. Once these burdens had been lifted by the redemptive power of revolution, it would be possible to construct a free and equal society based upon the prelapsarian goodness of human nature. While there was no room for even a secularized sort of sin and redemption in Herbert Spencer's biologically based historicism, his vision of the future was no less bright with celestial promise: 'The ultimate development of the ideal man is logically certain,' Spencer maintained, 'as certain as any conclusion in which we place the most implicit faith . . . Progress is not an accident but a necessity. Instead of civilization being artificial, it is a part of nature, all of a piece with the development of the embryo or the unfolding of a flower'.

Not everyone believed in such utopian fantasies or even in the more modest proposition that most things seemed to be getting better. Tocqueville was deeply ambivalent about the cluster of social, political, and cultural developments that he associated with democracy; cautiously optimistic about the American experiment, he remained sceptical that France could escape from the despotic dangers inherent in modernity. Joseph de Maistre was not a man to be troubled by ambivalence. He hated without qualification the modern era; everything in which the apostles of progress put such hope— individual reason, scientific enquiry, free institutions—de Maistre saw as instruments of decline and degeneration. As a believer in absolute monarchy and unwavering religious orthodoxy, he yearned for that bygone era when the executioner's axe and the inquisitor's fire had preserved people from the temptations of political disorder and theological error. Although he in no way shared de Maistre's nostalgia for the repressive powers of the old regime, Jacob Burckhardt was also pessimistic about the world in which he lived. Looking out on Europe from the sheltered perspective of his home in Basle, Burckhardt deplored the arrival of mass society with its vulgar tastes, turbulent politics, and unlimited capacity for violence. In his darker moments he saw a future dominated not by Comte's science or Marx's equality, but rather by those 'terrible simplifiers' who would manipulate the masses for their own ends.

But, however they charted its direction and assessed its possibilities, most nineteenth-century thinkers agreed that history was important. History helped people to understand their present and anticipate their future; it celebrated heroes and affirmed communities; it separated friends and enemies, winners and losers, patriots and traitors. Conservatives and radicals had different histories of the revolution, Catholics and Protestants of the Reformation,

Prussians and Austrians of German unification. History provided orators with examples with which to inspire crowds, statesmen with comparisons on which to base decisions, teachers with a treasure house from which to instruct their pupils. History mattered to everyone, but never as much as to those it had treated badly, people with national aspirations but no national state, people whose hopes for the future depended on their memories of the past. To the patriots who dreamed of a new Ireland or a restored Poland or a Greater Serbia, history was the life blood of the nation's identity, something for which it might be necessary to die—or to kill. It is well to remember that 28 June, the day in 1914 when Gavrilo Princip murdered the heir to the Austrian throne, thereby beginning the crisis that led to the First World War, was the anniversary of the medieval battle of Kosovo, the most important date in Serbian history.

Throughout the nineteenth century, the study of the past flourished as never before, resulting in some great works of history. These histories were written by men of letters like Tocqueville, whose study of the French Revolution remains among the most influential works ever written on that exhaustively studied event. Historical writing also appealed to former statesmen, such as François Guizot, who was the author, among other books, of *Memoirs to Serve as a History of my Age* (1858–67), and Thomas Babington Macaulay, whose multivolume history of England codified the conventional narrative of English history for generations. Although gifted amateurs continued to write great histories, in the course of the century the study of the past, like the study of natural science, tended to become increasingly professionalized. Serious historians were supposed to get advanced degrees, contribute to scholarly periodicals, belong to academic organizations. The research seminar played the same role in the formation of the historical profession that the laboratory did for the sciences: here apprentices learned both the techniques of research and the values and conventions necessary for professional success. In history, as in science, Germans took the lead in creating an organized discipline, which was then followed throughout Europe and America: the journal of the German historical profession, the *Historische Zeitschrift*, was founded in 1859, France's *Revue historique* in 1876, the *English Historical Review* in 1886, and the *American Historical Review* in 1895.

For both historians and scientists, the German university's distinctive blend of teaching and research encouraged scholarly productivity and at the same time ensured its transmission to future generations. German professors did foundational work on ancient Greece and Rome, the development of law and literature, and the emergence of an international system. Leopold von Ranke, who dominated the discipline from his chair at the university of Berlin, not only exploited new documentary sources and set new standards for accuracy, but also reported his findings in gracefully written books that were widely read. Born in 1795, Ranke was a conservative whose scholarly interests and political loyalties were devoted to the history of states, which he viewed as 'ideas of God', moving through historical time 'like celestial bodies, in their cycles, their mutual gravitations, their systems'. To the next generations of German historians, the state seemed less signifi-cant than the nation, which could express a people's cultural identity and their political aspirations. In the historical works of men such as Gustav Droysen, Heinrich von Sybel, and Heinrich von Treitschke, the creation of a unified German nation state was first prepared and then legitimized. From them came a narrative of the national past that still shapes the way Germans think about their history.

History had a particular significance in the aesthetic realm. Past events and personalities were important subjects for nineteenth-century artists—novelists like Alexander Dumas, poets like Tennyson, and painters like Carl Friedrich Lessing. Dumas's Richelieu, Tenny-son's King Arthur, Lessing's Jan Hus personified aspects of the national past, which usually had obvious implications for the nation's present. The past was also important as a source of artistic styles. The classical ideal guided European sculptors for several generations. Painters sought to produce masterpieces in the manner of Raphael and Rubens or to return to the innocent authenticity of the medieval craftsman. To walk through a nineteenth-century city was like a visit to a museum of past styles: classical temples such as Leo von Klenze's Glyphotek in Munich (1830), gothic structures like Friedrich von Schmidt's Rathaus in Vienna (1872–83), renaissance palazzi like Sir Charles Barry's Travellers' Club and Reform Club in London (1832 and 1840), and grand neo-baroque palaces like Joseph Poelaert's Palace of Justice in Brussels (1883). Perhaps the most prominent manifestation of the importance of history for nineteenth-century art was the museum itself, in which the treasures of the past were collected, protected, reverently displayed, and carefully restored to their 'original' form. By the middle of the century, to be part of a museum's collection was the clearest indication of artistic success and the surest guarantee of immortality.

Just as history was a popular subject for artists, art became a subject for historians. Scholars wrote biographies of great artists, analysed the meaning of their works, and developed new techniques to decide doubtful cases of attribution. In the course of the century, the grand narrative of art history, first articulated by classical scholars like J. J. Winckelmann in the eighteenth century, was refined and extended in handbooks and university lectures, and, of course, on the walls of museums.

But art history's grand narrative differed from the stories of progress that shaped so much historical theory and practice. However confident they might have been about progress in science, economics, or politics, few people could believe that their art was better than that of ancient Greece or the Renaissance. In the lectures on aesthetics that he delivered in Berlin during the 1820s, Hegel argued that art's greatest days were over; still significant as the record of past cultures, art in the modern world could no longer capture the spirit of the age. While few people were willing to go so far, most agreed that—as a German art historian wrote in 1857—contemporary art was 'far distant from the brilliance of the past art and from the universal significance it had once enjoyed'.

To practising artists, the art of the past was both model and burden, a source of inspiration and intimidation. In 1856, after admiring the Elgin marbles in the British museum, Nathaniel Hawthorne worried that the present was too much concerned with the past: 'We have not the time . . . to appreciate what is warm with life, and immediately around us; yet we heap up all these old shells, out of which human life has long emerged, casting them off forever. I do not see how future ages are to stagger under all this dead weight . . .'. As we shall see in the final section of this essay, Hawthorne's sense that life had fled from the art of the present would become a central theme in the modernist critique of historicism.

Systems

The nineteenth century was the last great age of the intellectual system, those grand syntheses that sought to contain all of reality in a single coherent explanatory order. Once again, Auguste Comte is a good example of these aspirations. According to Comte, every individual, branch of knowledge, and culture naturally sought a coherent, unified view of the world: at first theological and magical, then metaphysical and philosophical, finally, scientific and rational. The 'ultimate perfection' of this positivist system would arrive when it was able to 'represent all phenomena as particular aspects of a single general fact—such as gravitation . . . '. Now, Comte wrote,

it is time to complete the vast intellectual enterprise begun by Bacon, Descartes, and Galileo, by constructing the system of general ideas which must henceforth prevail among the human race. This is the way to put an end to the revolutionary crisis which is tormenting the civilized nations of the world.

Comte's system was both scientific and social; its purpose was not only to bring to a conclusion mankind's long search for certainty, but also to restore cohesion to a world tormented by 'revolutionary crisis'.

We can see these same ambitions in the work of G. W. F. Hegel, the last important European philosopher who tried to bring into a single system logic and history, theology and philosophy, morality and law, culture and politics, the individual and society, freedom and necessity. Born in 1770, Hegel grew up in the turbulent era of revolution and war that began in 1789. Faced with an apparently endless series of political, spiritual, and professional disruptions, Hegel devoted himself to finding a philosophy that would, in his words, 'restore the unifying power to human life'. Beginning with the publication of his *Phenomenology of the Spirit*, finished just as (and a few miles away from where) Napoleon was routing the Prussian army at Jena in 1806, Hegel created an extraordinarily rich and complex intellectual system, in which he traced three inseparable journeys: of each individual, of human thought from its origins to the present, and of the Spirit, the moving force of history that he variously identified with God and Reason. In this vast enterprise, Hegel considered epistemology, sociology, ethics, politics, aesthetics, and religion, giving each its own particular trajectory but weaving them all together into a single historical process.

The key to understanding this process was the dialectic, for which Hegel used the German word *Aufhebung*, a noun based on the verb *aufheben*, which literally means to lift up. To lift something up is both to hold it and to take it away, which is precisely what the Spirit does as it realizes itself in time. History moves dialectically, by simultaneously cancelling and absorbing what has gone before: like the oak and the acorn or the adult and the child, historical phenomena—Christianity and Judaism, Napoleon and the French Revolution—destroy their predecessors by bringing them to a new stage of existence. Unless we view them dialectically, the events of history—the violent chaos of battle, agonies of martyrdom, interminable failures of individual intellect and will—appear to be no more than a 'slaughter bench' of human hopes. But through the dialectical lens, we can see these events as part of reason's 'cunning', each contributing to the movement of history along God's path. Having such a lens is what Hegel meant when he wrote, 'To him who looks at the world rationally, the world looks rationally back'. With the dialectic, we can fulfil what Hegel called the true aim of knowledge, which is 'to divest the world that stands opposed to us of its strangeness, and, as the phrase is, to find ourselves at home in it'. Hegel himself did not find a secure home until he was almost 50. In 1818 he was called to the University of Berlin, where he occupied the chair of philosophy and quickly became the most influential German thinker of his day.

Even before Hegel died in 1831, his followers had begun to quarrel over just what this influence should be. To some of his admirers on the right, Hegel seemed to be a conservative, whose dialectic justified the status quo. After all, did he not call the state 'the divine idea as it exists on earth' and suggest that the kingdom of Prussia had a special place in God's plan? Hegel's left-wing followers drew quite different lessons from his system. To them, the dialectic, instead of justifying the established order, guaranteed that it would give way to something else, something better. They took seriously, therefore, Hegel's oft-stated commitment to reason, which they tried to turn into a critical instrument for spiritual renewal and social change.

The debate about the meaning of Hegel's system was going strong in 1836, when the 18-year-old Karl Marx arrived in Berlin to study law. Marx quickly fell in with the radical young philosophers who were exploring Hegelianism's emancipatory potential. At first repelled, then totally absorbed by what he called 'the grotesque craggy melody' of the master's ideas, Marx used them as the foundation for a vision of history that would, in the twentieth century, capture the allegiance of millions of people throughout the world. From Hegel, Marx took, first of all, the concept of the dialectic, which he used to uncover the previously hidden motor of historical development. When, in the famous opening lines of the *Communist Manifesto*, Marx wrote that 'The history of all hitherto existing society is the history of class struggles', he meant by 'history', not everything that had happened, but rather the dialectical forces that really mattered, the inner wellspring of change. Secondly, Marx adopted Hegel's ambition to create a system in which each individual piece drew its meaning from being part of a whole. Marx's system was, of course, material rather than spiritual; at its core were struggles over the means of production not Reason's efforts to realize itself. But, like Hegel, Marx believed that philosophy should seek to uncover the essential connections between apparently disparate phenomena. Seen properly, politics and economics, religion and philosophy, property rights and marriage laws, would all appear to be expressions of the elemental conflicts at the core of every social order.

Marx also shared Hegel's profound conviction that, in the modern age, mankind's long, painful odyssey had reached a dramatic new stage. History, Marx believed, was nearing its end because a new, unprecedented force had begun to emerge: this was the proletariat, a class without property or the desire to attain it, a class so alienated from existing society that it could lead mankind back to its true nature and thus to a classless community, in which people could freely share the fruits of their labour. The purpose of philosophy was to make the proletariat aware of its true nature and thus of its historical mission as the instrument of revolutionary change. Only then could humans everywhere be at home in the world—not, as Hegel had thought, through understanding and reconciliation, but rather by making the world their own.

Although their study of nature usually lacked the architectural grandeur of Hegel's philosophy or the eschatological energy of Marx's revolutionary politics, nineteenth-century scientists also tried to create systems that could connect particular phenomena. In his *Autobiography*, Darwin wrote that he understood what it meant to be a scientist, when, as a young man, he spent the summer mapping the geology of north Wales: 'Nothing before had ever made me thoroughly realize . . . that science consists in grouping facts so that general laws or conclusions may be drawn from them'. The genius of *On the Origin of Species* was, as we have seen, to group facts in a way that seemed to explain all of natural history. The German scientist Emil DuBois-Reymond expressed the conviction that biological phenomena would eventually be understood in terms of physical laws: 'If one observes the development of science', he wrote in 1848, 'one cannot fail to note . . . how new areas are increasingly brought under the dominion of physical and chemical forces . . Physiology will one day be absorbed into the great unity of the physical sciences; [it] will in fact dissolve into organic physics and chemistry'. In the following decades, scientists would suggest different bases for 'the great unity of the physical sciences', but the urge to find such a unity would persist.

We find the urge to create systems in many other aspects of nineteenth-century culture. Even the Victorian novel, as Hillis Miller once pointed out, can be regarded as a 'self-generating and self-sustaining system'. Among the persistent conventions of such novels were plots that linked each character in a hidden web of relations: Dickens's *Bleak House*, for instance, opens with a city wrapped in a fog that simultaneously contains and separates its characters; in the course of the book's complex narrative, the reader gradually sees how they share a common fate. The plot of Eliot's *Middlemarch* turns on a more subtly rendered set of connections that, as in Dickens, link people from disparate groups together. In a decisive moment in the novel, Eliot's heroine experiences 'the largeness of the world' and comes to recognize that she is 'part of that involuntary, palpitating life'. This sense of connection enables her to be at home in the world. Or, to take a different set of examples, consider these three paintings from the 1850s: Gustav Courbet's *Painter's Studio* (1854–5), Ford Madox Brown's *Work* (1852–65), and William Frith's *Derby Day* (1858). Although very different in tone and sensibility, each of them offers a systematic vision of society, Courbet with an allegory about art, Brown with a taxonomy of occupations, and Frith with a panoramic narrative of different social types. In these paintings, as in so many contemporary novels, each figure is defined in terms of how he or she fits into the larger social world.

Like the eighteenth century, the nineteenth was an age of collections, encyclopaedias, and dictionaries, which sought to bring together and classify knowledge of all sorts. By the 1830s, the natural history collections in London were so full of the results of contemporary collecting fervour that Darwin had trouble finding an institutional home for the extraordinary assembly of specimens that he had brought back from his voyage on the *Beagle*. The main purpose of the voyage was, of course, to make more accurate maps of the south American coast—another sort of systematic study of the world. People in the nineteenth century wanted to chart every inlet, assemble every ancient text, create grammars for every language, identify every species, explore every corner of the earth. Museum directors wanted to display a representative work by every great artist, zookeepers hoped to have every animal no matter how exotic, botanists every plant. In 1869 the legendary bibliophile, Sir Thomas Phillipps, declared, 'I am buying books because I wish to have one copy of every book in the world'. A similar ambition moved those who built the century's great national libraries in London, Paris, and Washington.

There were, of course, always people who viewed such ambitions with scepticism or even contempt. Gustave Flaubert, for example, satirized them in his last, appropriately unfinished novel, *Bouvard and Pécuchet*, whose protagonists set out to compile an interminable collection of commonplaces. An appropriate subtitle for his book, Flaubert thought, would be 'an encyclopaedia of stupidity'. But for most nineteenth-century intellectuals, there was nothing at all ridiculous about encyclopaedias, museums, botanical gardens, and collections of natural history. Like the great philosophical systems of Comte, Marx, and Darwin, these projects were indications that the world, however vast and complex, could be contained and comprehended. This confidence, sometimes qualified, but often without limits, gave nineteenth-century culture its distinctive energy and scale.

Modernism

The chronological boundaries of modernism are difficult to chart. In part, this is because its tempo and character differed from place to place: British, French, German, Austrian modernism shared many ideas and connections, but each had its own particular history. Moreover, the evolution of modernism varied from genre to genre. However alike they may seem in retrospect, the histories of modernism in painting and literature, architecture and social thought had different shapes and textures. Finally, a great many of the ideas, values, and sensibilities that we associate with modernism can be found throughout the nineteenth century: Schopenhauer anticipated Nietzsche, Turner the impressionists, and so on. Nevertheless, once all the precursors have been counted and the qualifications registered, it seems clear that, in the 1890s, Europe's cultural climate changed significantly. For artists and intellectuals, as well as for some of their publics, the standards and assumptions underlying nineteenth-century culture appeared less attractive and plausible. People began to design buildings, write novels, imagine the social world in what seemed like radically new ways. Around 1890, the German historian Friedrich Meinecke remembered, at the same time that the political world was becoming more troubled and crisis-ridden, culture became more vital, a vitality he described as 'a new sense for the fragmentary and problematic character of modern life'. The mission of modernism was to create a way of representing the world appropriate for this new sense of life's fragmentary and problematic character.

Friedrich Nietzsche, whose critical comments on nineteenth-century culture were cited at the beginning of our essay, is an exemplary figure in modernism's rise and spread. Born in 1844, a clergyman's son, Nietzsche received the rigorous training in the classics that characterized élite education everywhere in Europe. His extraordinary talents as a philologist earned him a professorship at the University of Basle when he was only 25. But Nietzsche's first book, *The Birth of Tragedy*, revealed how far he had strayed from conventional views of the ancient world: instead of a sober analysis of classical texts, he provided a brilliant, if often elusive, account of ancient revels and festivity, which he used to underscore the cultural deficiencies of his own age. Nietzsche soon left his position at Basle and wandered around Europe for fifteen years, writing and sometimes publishing difficult works on the nature of art, religion, language, and history. In 1889 he suffered a mental breakdown that left him incapacitated; he spent the last ten years of his life staring off into space, saying little, writing nothing. During this sad and silent decade, Nietzsche's writings attracted increasing attention. While they took very different things from the tangle of ideas and insights that made up the Nietzschean legacy, an impressive number of artists, critics, and even politicians accepted his core perception that modern culture was empty, arid, and in desperate need of revitalization.

Darwin, Nietzsche wrote, was 'true but deadly'—deadly for established religion, but no less so for the naturalistic ethical systems and progressive pieties that Darwin's admirers tried to put in its place. But about one important thing, Darwin was wrong: in a fragment written towards the end of his productive life, Nietzsche noted that his own observation of human destines had convinced him that the strongest and healthiest specimens do not survive and triumph, as Darwin had supposed, but rather were dragged down by the combined weight of mass mediocrity. 'As odd as it may sound, the strong needed to be protected from the weak, the fortunate from the unfortunate, the healthy from the degenerate and genetically unfit'. The terrible thing about the Darwinian struggle for survival, therefore, is not its cruelty but rather that the wrong side wins. The idea that the creation of a 'species represents progress is the most unreasonable assertion in the world'.

While Nietzsche's take on Darwinism was surely idiosyncratic, a great many modernists shared his belief that what science had to tell us might be true, but it was not the sort of truth from which we can derive much comfort. Sigmund Freud, for example, had no doubts about the validity of scientific methods; for a while at least, he hoped that he might uncover the physiological basis of the mind. But Freud's science offered none of the utopian hopes we saw in Spencer: 'Much is won if we succeed in transforming hysterical misery into common unhappiness'. The science of psychology had 'taught us that our intellect is a feeble and dependent thing, a plaything and tool of our impulses and emotions'. Nothing could be further from the nineteenth century's grand progressive narratives than a book like Freud's

Civilization and its Discontents, which presents a picture of a social order permanently at war against itself, an order in which individuals (at once 'bearers and victims' of civilization) must repress those urges that will return to torment them and to disrupt society.

Towards the end of the century, we can find signs of the gap between science and other modes of thought that, fifty years later, would lead C. P. Snow to speak of 'two cultures'. This gap was not, however, between natural science and literary culture, as Snow suggested, but rather between those who still believed that it was possible to explain all reality through scientific methods and those who did not. There were philosophers and economists, as well as chemists and biologists, in the first group. After 1890, these scientists continued to do important work, expanding our knowledge of the natural and social worlds. But a growing number of philosophers and social thinkers, as well as writers and cultural critics, had become hostile to science and technology. 'I hate and fear science', announced the English novelist George Gissing, because it is 'the remorseless enemy of mankind. I see it destroying all simplicity and gentleness of life, all beauty of the world; I see it restoring barbarism under the mask of civilization. I see it darkening men's minds and hardening their hearts'. But more characteristic than this rejection of science was the growing difficulty educated lay people faced in understanding exactly what scientists were doing. Consider, for example, the difference between the reception of Darwin and that of his closest modern analogue, Albert Einstein: the former's ideas were swiftly grasped and widely debated, whereas the public may have been impressed by the theory of relativity but few could say that they truly understood it.

The disciplinary study of the past, like organized scientific research, continued to thrive after 1890, but history, like science, began to occupy a different place in culture. We can find no *fin-de-siècle* equivalents of those grand progressive narratives produced by Comte, Marx, and Darwin; instead of a record of progress and emancipation, modernists often saw the past as a burden from which we are never free. In his extraordinary meditation on 'The Advantages and Disadvantages of History for Life', Nietzsche warned that the modern world was paralysed by its absorption with history. For both individuals and cultures, creativity depended on the ability to forget as well as to remember. Freud, of course, turned this notion into a complex therapeutic system that was designed to help patients master their past. But, Freud recognized, they would never entirely succeed. The past lives on and shows itself in dreams, which also point the dreamer towards the future, a future that 'has been moulded by his indestructible wish into a perfect likeness of the past'. James Joyce must have had the same thing in mind, when he has his hero exclaim, 'History is a nightmare from which I am trying to awake'.

History's changing cultural place is also revealed by comparing the characteristic structure of Victorian and modernist novels. The former usually told the story of an individual's search for identity and meaning: in the course of Dickens's *Great Expectations* and Eliot's *Middlemarch*, the protagonists find out who they are and what place in society they are meant to occupy. Often this requires triumphing over some unhappy legacy from the past; usually it ends with a marriage that will provide the foundation for a happy future. The novels of Joseph Conrad, Thomas Hardy, or Émile Zola have a very different shape. Their protagonists, like Hardy's Jude Fawley, are trapped in a world they did not make and cannot master; their pasts come back, despite their best efforts, to destroy them. And what is true for the fictional history of these characters seems equally true for the larger history of mankind. There is, Hardy wrote, 'nothing systematic in [history's] development. It flows on like a thunderstorm rill by the roadside, now a straw turns it this way, now a tiny barrier of sand that'.

We find in modernist art, philosophy, and social theory a tendency to turn away from history towards psychology as a source of knowledge and meaning. Psychology, Nietzsche believed, was an 'immense and almost new domain of dangerous knowledge' that can open up to us 'the path to fundamental problems'. Instead of seeking the fundamental truths of human existence in the random stirring of historical development, we should look for them inside ourselves, in the complex but durable structure of the mind. 'Politics is not based primarily on history', Henry Sidgwick wrote in 1891, 'but on Psychology: the fundamental assumptions in our political reasoning consist of certain propositions as to human motives and tendencies, which are derived primarily from the ordinary experience of civilized life . . .'.

Of the four themes around which we organized our summary of nineteenth-century culture—religion, science, history, and system— none was questioned more vigorously by the modernists than the

last. 'The will to a *system*', Nietzsche wrote, is 'in a philosopher mor-
ally corrupting, a subtle corruption, a disease of the character; amor-
ally speaking, his will to appear more stupid than he is . . . I am not
bigoted enough for a system—and not even for my own'. In fact,
after 1890, the era of all-embracing philosophical systems seemed to
pass. Instead, modernist culture is filled with a sense of fragmenta-
tion, just as it is filled with fragmentary projects like Nietzsche's own.
The philosopher Wilhelm Dilthey, the sociologist Max Weber, the
novelist Robert Musil all had trouble finishing their major works, all
left great unfinished projects, which future generations of scholars
have had to puzzle over.

Modernist art rarely displayed that systematic quality we can find
in the great Victorians. The sweeping narratives of Dickens and Eliot,
and the panoramic canvases like those of Brown or Frith, are replaced
by less monumental, often more intimate, increasingly more abstract
works. Simple landscapes and still lifes, the everyday existence of
ordinary people, or the private symbols of the artist's inner world—
these were the themes that attracted modernist writers and painters.
Moreover, many modernist artworks were self-consciously fragmented; Cézanne's paintings, T. S. Eliot's poetry, or Rodin's statues
all have broken surfaces that underscored their distance from the
cohesive styles of the past. The 'primary gesture' of modernism,
Stephen Spender once remarked, was its 'determination to invent a
new style in order to express the deeply felt change in the modern
world'. And no change was more deeply felt than culture's waning
capacity to capture reality as a whole, within a philosophical system,
the pages of a novel, the frame of a painting.

Let us conclude our survey of the modernist response to the nineteenth century with Georges Sorel, whose ideas provide a particularly
vivid example of the new cultural climate. Born in 1847, Sorel was
trained at the École Polytechnique, France's élite school for scientists
and technocrats. He worked for two decades as a government engineer before beginning a second career as a man of letters. In the course
of his long life (he died in 1922), Sorel wrote about a wide range of
topics and defended a bewildering variety of positions, but he is best
known for his *Reflections on Violence*, which was first published in
1908. Since Sorel had been deeply influenced by Marxist thought
since the early 1890s, it is not surprising that the class struggle plays a
central role in the *Reflections*. But Sorel did not regard class struggles

as a 'law of development', which had been discovered through the scientific analysis of history and could be used to predict and create the future: 'There is no process by which the future can be predicted scientifically, nor even one which enables us to discuss whether one hypothesis about it is better than another'. What mattered about the class struggle was neither its historical truth nor predictive power; what mattered was its psychological potential. To mobilize the inert masses, Sorel argued, one needed not history or science, but what he called a 'myth'. The myth of class conflict, he hoped, could be used to evoke an eruption of social violence that would destroy the suffocating stagnation of the contemporary world. Revolutionary violence, which for Marx was a means to move history along towards its final destination, becomes for Sorel a source of spiritual and moral renewal and thus valuable as an end in itself.

Sorel's ideas clearly foreshadowed the world of myth and violence in which men like Lenin and Mussolini—both of whom Sorel admired—would thrive. But for our purposes Sorel's *Reflections* is valuable because it underscores the distance we have travelled from the nineteenth century's assumptions about science, history, and systems. With it, we have clearly entered a cultural world that is painfully aware of what Meinecke called 'the fragmentary and problematic character of modern life'.

In the introduction to his *Philosophy of Right* (1821), Hegel remarked that it is possible to understand a historical era only when it has run its historical course, when its high point has passed and decline has begun. Understanding, therefore, always comes too late: 'When philosophy paints its grey in grey, then has a shape of life grown old. By philosophy's grey in grey it cannot be rejuvenated but only understood. The owl of Minerva spreads its wings only with the falling of the dusk'. In the fading light of the years before 1914, we can see clearly nineteenth-century culture's aspirations to replace religious faith with the certainties of science, the sacred story of redemption with a secular history of progress, the divinely established chain of being with an all-embracing philosophical system. But in the modernist response to nineteenth-century ideas about science, history, and systems, we can also begin to perceive what would follow the failure of these aspirations.

5

International politics, peace, and war, 1815–1914

Paul W. Schroeder

This chapter has a conventional approach and theme: to analyse the changing character and structure of nineteenth-century European international politics. The procedure is less conventional: to concentrate on explaining peace rather than, as commonly happens, on explaining war. Peace is more artificial and demands more explanation. Wars sometimes just happen; peace is always caused. Moreover, understanding why the nineteenth century was more peaceful than any predecessor in European history helps illuminate why it ended in a war greater than any before.

The most obvious sign of a pacific century in Europe is its relatively few and limited wars: – no general or systemic war (one involving all or most of the great powers) at all from 1815 to 1914; in two extended periods, 1815–54 and 1871–1914, no wars between European great powers. Though five wars between great powers were fought in mid-century, all important in their results, even these were comparatively limited in duration, scope, and casualties. The stability of the actors is equally striking. All the great powers of 1815 survived as such until 1914, despite some changes in rank. Except for the German and Italian states absorbed by unification in mid-century, so did most smaller states, and some new ones emerged.

I wish to thank Professor F. R. Bridge for many valuable suggestions and criticisms.

Nineteenth-century international institutions and practices likewise changed in the direction of stability. Alliances, in the eighteenth century predominantly instruments for power, security, and concrete advantages, were used primarily for much of the nineteenth century for managing and restraining both opponents and allies and preventing aggrandizement. The nineteenth-century system not only produced durable peace where conflict had been endemic (the Low Countries, Switzerland, Scandinavia, and the Baltic, and for some time the Near East) but also succeeded at times in promoting peaceful change (for example, in the creation of Belgium). It absorbed and survived forcible change by war, and proved capable of integrating new actors, even those produced or transformed by treaty violations and war, into the system. Expansion and imperialism outside Europe, in previous centuries a direct factor in Europe's conflicts and wars, remained for much of the nineteenth century largely separated from them. Most impressive of all, this international system endured and survived the strains of a century of rapid, fundamental changes in European society—industrialization, modernization, revolutions in communications, technology, and science, the rise of the strong state, mass politicization, and the growth of liberalism, nationalism, socialism, and democracy.

The Vienna system

The explanation of this remarkable record, and of its disastrous end, begins with the Vienna system, the network of treaties, institutions, and practices developed in 1813–15 during the last Napoleonic Wars and at the Congress of Vienna. There is wide agreement on some reasons for its unusual stability. It embodied a moderate, sensible territorial settlement that satisfied the main needs and requirements of the victors (Britain, Russia, Austria, Prussia, and their lesser allies) without despoiling or humiliating France. Tied into this were comprehensive negotiated settlements of many particular disputes arising out of the wars from 1787 to 1815. These settlements, combined in a network of mutually supporting treaties, gave all governments a stake in a new system of mutual interlocking rights and obligations. Backing this was a security alliance among the great powers to defend the settlement against violation or revolutionary aggression, especially by France. Finally, an old but little-used diplomatic principle was implemented, that of a European Concert, by which the five great powers became a governing council or directory for settling serious international questions, using Concert practices such as diplomatic conferences rather than bilateral or multilateral negotiations to achieve agreed solutions.

Another feature of the settlement was equally vital though less obvious: the creation of an independent, confederated, defensively oriented European centre. Throughout the eighteenth century and the revolutionary-Napoleonic era, the instability, weakness, and rivalries plaguing central Europe (the German states, Switzerland, Italy, Austria, Poland) had spawned repeated crises and wars as internecine conflicts drew in the competing flank powers. The Vienna Congress took a series of measures to turn this critical area temporarily into a zone of peace (at the cost, to be sure, of some injustice, disappointed expectations, and future trouble). It established a German Confederation uniting the German states in a permanent defensive league under joint Austro-Prussian leadership; gave Austria leadership but not direct control of the various independent states of Italy; established and guaranteed a neutral Swiss Confederation; and maintained the eighteenth-century partition of Poland by Russia, Austria, and Prussia in a modified form. Even the Kingdoms of the Netherlands and Denmark were tied indirectly into this independent, defensive centre.

If there is little disagreement among scholars about these sources of the system's stability, there is some concerning its spirit and operating principles. For many, it worked because a balance of power inhibited new bids for hegemony and monarchs cooperated against war, liberalism, nationalism, and revolution. Once these factors declined, with the balance of power shifting and new ambitions emerging, the system no longer worked. This verdict, though it contains some truth, is inadequate and misleading. The reason most governments supported the equilibrium of power, territory, rights, status, obligations, and security reached in 1815 was not that they were sated by expansion or simply exhausted by war and wanted peace. It was that they had learned that war and expansion could not provide peace and security They accepted, often grudgingly, the painful, delicate compromises of the settlement in order to achieve security in a system of rights guaranteed by law. Even in France most ministries, if not opposition groups, came to accept and support the settlement on these grounds. And when governments did need to be restrained in this era, the normal method was not balancing, confronting their power with countervailing power, but 'grouping'—using Concert means and group pressure to enforce norms and treaties. In the most important crises, balancing could not have worked, for two great powers, Britain and Russia, were more powerful and far less vulnerable than the other three, and when they worked together, as they did at major junctures in 1815–48, they settled matters. In terms of power, the system was characterized by dual hegemony, British in western Europe, Russian in the east, a hegemony that was tolerable because it was usually latent, inactive, and allowed others lesser spheres of influence.

Just as political equilibrium did not derive from balancing power by countervailing power, so conservative solidarity did not rest simply on restoring and preserving the old regime. In international politics at least, the Vienna system was not a restoration. It preserved most of the territorial, social, and constitutional–political changes brought about in the revolutionary and Napoleonic periods, and encouraged or permitted some new ones. Only later, from 1820 on, did policies of repression of dissent and simple maintenance of the status quo dominate in Russia, Austria, and Prussia and their spheres, leading to an ideological split between a liberal-constitutional West and an absolutist East. The solidarity among governments for peace created at Vienna, which transcended and outlived this split, arose from its overall success in satisfying existing demands and harmonizing conflicting claims, based on a general consensus on the practical requirements of peace and a recognition that certain limits had to govern international competition. Rivalries and conflicting aims persisted under the Vienna system as before—Anglo-French competition in Spain and the Mediterranean, Austro-French in Italy, Austro-Prussian in Germany, Austro-Russian in the Balkans, Anglo-Russian in the Middle East. But the stakes, rules, and goals were different. Now the competition was over spheres of interest and leading influence, not territorial aggrandizement, the elimination of the rival, or total control, and preserving general peace remained uppermost. The late eighteenth-century game of high-stakes poker, which the Revolution and Napoleon had turned into Russian roulette, gave way to contract bridge.

This made Concert rules and practices effective for decades after 1815 in dealing peacefully with international problems and crises, often by repressive means and never without friction and rivalry, but without great-power war or aggrandizement. The examples can only be summarized here.

Revolts in Spain, Naples, and Piedmont in 1820–1. Three great-power conferences in 1820–2 led to their suppression by Austria in Italy and by France in Spain.

The Greek revolt in 1821–5. This profound ethnic–religious revolt and war against Turkish rule repeatedly threatened to cause a Russo-Turkish war but self-restraint by Russia and Concert diplomacy led by Britain and Austria averted it.

Revolutions in Spain's and Portugal's American colonies. All the rebellious colonies gained their independence without foreign intervention, partly because Britain with its navy deterred it, but mainly because the continental monarchies, despite their sympathy for Spain and fear of republican revolution, made no serious effort to intervene.

The Eastern crisis in 1826–9. The intervention of Britain, Russia, and France to save the Greeks from being crushed by the Ottoman Sultan's vassal Egypt, though intended initially to end the fighting by diplomacy and prevent any great power from aggrandizing itself or acting unilaterally, instead escalated into an allied naval battle that destroyed the Turco-Egyptian forces. This led to a Russo-Turkish war, a Russian victory, and the danger that the Ottoman Empire would collapse with Russia picking up the pieces—a likely eighteenth-century-style outcome. Instead, Russia signed a peace treaty that increased its influence at Constantinople but preserved the Sultan's throne; the three allies negotiated the creation of an independent Greek kingdom; and this soon came under Anglo-French influence rather than Russian.

The 1830 revolutions. These revolutions, beginning in July in France and spreading to the Netherlands, Switzerland, Germany, Italy, and Poland, produced some violence, considerable political and constitutional change, and some international crises, deepening the East–West ideological divide. In international politics, however, the powers demonstrated restraint. They quickly recognized the new Orleanist monarchy to replace the ousted Bourbons in France, and managed Austro-French tension over Austrian interventions in the Papal State through conference diplomacy. They responded to a Belgian revolt overthrowing the United Netherlands, created in 1815 as a defence against France, by convening a London conference that, despite great obstacles raised mainly by the Dutch and Belgians, finally established and jointly guaranteed an independent Belgian kingdom, bringing peace until 1914 to an area for centuries the cockpit of Europe. Even Russia's crushing of a Polish revolt for independence passed without foreign intervention, serious international crisis, or territorial change.

New Eastern Crises in 1832–41. This time the threat to the Ottoman Empire came from the Sultan's ambitious vassal, the Pasha of Egypt, and his regime, twice defeated and facing overthrow, was rescued by European great powers, Russia in 1832–3 and four powers in 1839–40. The four powers' decision in 1840 finally to act without France led to a crisis and threat of war in Europe, apparently reviving the traditional power-political competition in the Near East and Europe. But the crisis really had more to do with rules and leadership in the Concert than power politics. France always favoured a Concert to defend the Sultan but wished to lead it in partnership with Britain against Russia, the permanent threat to Turkey. Instead Britain, suspicious of French aims, preferred working with Russia, and France reacted mainly out of wounded honour and lost prestige. French preparations for war, directed against Austria and Prussia, were largely a bluff, and, when the four-power concert held fast, France backed down, with the two German powers helping it do so with honour. The crisis illustrates both the Anglo-Russian dual-hegemonic structure of the system and the effectiveness of Concert grouping strategy.

Other troubles of the 1830s and 1840s. These were a mixed bag, including civil wars in Spain and Portugal between absolutists and pseudo-constitutionalists, rising discontent and tensions in Italy, especially at Rome and between Sardinia-Piedmont and Austria, another incipient Polish revolt crushed by the Eastern Powers in 1846 and followed by the annexation of the Free City of Cracow by Austria, and a small Protestant–Catholic civil war in Switzerland. All raised contentious issues between various powers; none came close to threatening international war.

Yet to claim that the system remained effective in preserving peace is not to argue that it was unaffected or unweakened by crisis and change. The 1830s and 1840s clearly show growing tensions and friction between the powers. The cause usually given for this, as for the 1848 revolutions and the ultimate downfall of the Vienna system, is the growing ideological, political, and economic gap between absolutist and moderate liberal–constitutionalist governments and groups, and the way in which absolutist regimes, increasingly weak and threatened, tried to meet demands for political, social, and economic change and the rise of nationalism by repression rather than reform.

Basically this is true, but it over-simplifies the connection between the absolutist–constitutionalist split in domestic affairs and international relations. Historians often equate the Vienna system (the treaties, rules, and practices for conducting international politics) with the Metternich system (the absolutist prescriptions for the internal governance of states). Since Austria's chancellor Prince Metternich and his allies identified the two, using the Vienna treaties to legitimate their repressive internal and international practices, and since their liberal and radical opponents likewise tarred the two systems with the same brush, this is understandable. None the less, the two were not identical or inseparable, and the actual effects of the ideological contest from 1815 to 1848 show it. Overall, the Vienna system won (peace and the treaties were preserved), while the Metternich system ultimately lost (conservative attempts to hold back constitutionalism, liberal ideas, and economic and social change lost ground throughout the 1830s and 1840s in France, the Low Countries, Germany, northern Italy, and even parts of Austria). Moreover, the ideological rifts produced heated argument but not serious international rivalries or crises between governments. All the important rivalries in Europe both antedated the ideological divide and crossed its boundaries. The ideological dispute between absolutists proclaiming a right of intervention to suppress revolutions and liberals proclaiming a doctrine of non-intervention made little difference in practice. Regardless of doctrine, states intervened in foreign revolutions within their respective spheres of influence, or did not, according to their particular interests. The ideological contest, in other words, did not directly affect the Vienna system's capacity to manage immediate international problems, nor for the most part did it lead governments into dangerous or aggressive policies. The most reactionary great-power regime in 1815–48—Charles X's in France (1824–30)—also had the most dangerously ambitious foreign policy aims.

Yet absolutist policies did undermine the Vienna system and general peace both indirectly, adding to the pressures promoting revolution and discrediting and delegitimizing it by association with Metternichian repression, and directly, by deliberately stunting the Vienna system's capacity to grow and adapt itself to new conditions. From 1819 on Metternich and his allies took the 1815 arrangements for the German Confederation, Italy, and Poland, originally capable of change and development, and reduced them to mere instruments for preserving the status quo, leaving the system still useful for crisis management but not problem-solving. On the other side, the Utopian schemes and reckless actions of nationalist and revolutionary ideologues threatened peace even more directly, while moderate reformers, especially in Britain, gave good advice without ever intending to back it with action or to take responsibility for the consequences. Britain's Lord Palmerston, for example, was often right on the kinds of measures needed to avoid revolution in Germany and Italy; Metternich right about the dangers of urging others to apply them without considering how to manage the results.

Thus its very success in preventing war and managing crises helped prepare the ground for the assault against the Vienna system.

The system undermined and overthrown, 1848–1861

Unlike some revolutions, those that swept western and central Europe from France to the Romanian Principalities in 1848 arose primarily from internal political, social, and economic discontents and movements, not international conflicts. International politics, however, played a certain role in their origins and a bigger one in their course and outcome.

One important factor was nationalism, manifesting itself in two forms, both seeking liberation but from different bonds or restraints and for different ends. The first, voiced by peoples or leaders asserting a particular identity and chafing under foreign rule, called for national 'rights' ranging from local autonomy and privileges through home rule to total independence. This kind of nationalist protest was widespread—Danes and Germans in Schleswig-Holstein, Italians in Austrian-ruled Lombardy-Venetia, Hungarians within Austria, Czechs in Bohemia-Moravia, Croats in Hungary, Poles under all three partitioning powers, Romanians under Turkish and Hungarian authority, Irish in the United Kingdom. Another kind of nationalism, voiced mainly by a rising commercial and professional middle class led or joined by free intellectuals and liberal nobles, demanded liberation from the obstacles placed in the path of the nation's political freedom, social, economic, and cultural development, and power by small, weak, or unprogressive governments. This was present in France, but strongest in Germany and Italy.

In meaning different things by national liberation and unification, the two varieties targeted and threatened different foes. The former threatened multinational empires, Austria in particular; the latter particularly targeted small princely states. The former pointed toward decentralization and federation, the latter toward amalgamation. Thus, while they might cooperate at times, the likelihood, borne out by events, was that they would ultimately clash head on. Both kinds, moreover, aroused various divergent counter-revolutionary passions and programmes—anti-Polish patriotism in Prussia and Russia, particularist loyalty in Bavaria and other German states, municipal loyalties in Italy, military, bureaucratic, and religious *Habsburgtreue* in Austria, German resistance to Czechs in Bohemia-Moravia or Danes in Schleswig, Croat and Slovak resistance to Hungarian domination, and the like. Hence the inevitable result of nationalist unity movements was increased disunity and conflict.

Nationalist movements affected international politics most directly, however, not by creating or deepening conflicts within countries or between peoples, but by providing the opportunity and means for ambitious leaders and governments to pursue expansionist aims, often old statist and dynastic ones, under new revolutionary slogans. Such 'nationalist' programmes and the responses of governments attacked or threatened by them mainly account for the international crises and conflicts of 1848–9. The Italian revolutions directly challenged both Austrian hegemony and the 1815 system, but only when Sardinia-Piedmont took the lead and attacked Austria was there an interstate war that threatened to pull in France and become general, and, when Austria crushed Sardinia-Piedmont in 1848 and 1849, the international crisis ended. The German and Danish national causes clashed in Schleswig-Holstein, but an international crisis arose only when Prussia temporarily supported the German cause with its army, and, when Britain and Russia forced Prussia to back down, the acute crisis was over. The German National Parliament at Frankfurt developed a dangerous Great German foreign policy in seeking to unite Germany, but the great international danger lay in the Austro-Prussian rivalry over who would run it. The Hungarian independence movement was a more formidable challenge to Austria than any other because early on the Hungarian movement gained legal recognition of its rights from Vienna, albeit later rescinded. It could then declare independence and fight to retain all the historic lands and peoples of the crown of St Stephen as a government in command of the Hungarian half of the regular Austrian army. Finally, it was Tsar Nicholas I's determination to keep revolution from his own lands and maintain Russian hegemony in eastern Europe that ultimately doomed the Romanian risings and the Hungarian revolution, and helped prevent war in 1849–50 between Austria and Prussia over mastery in Germany.

In other words, power politics prevailed over national movements in the international arena. More surprisingly, international peace and order temporarily won out over revolution, ambition, and war. In 1850, after numerous crises, conflicts, and threats of major war, all the pre-1848 treaties, international institutions, and borders remained intact. The events of 1848–9, unlike those of 1814–15, brought about a true restoration of the old order. What made it possible and largely accounts for both the defeat of revolutions and the preservation of peace is that all the great powers resisted the temptation to expand abroad, using their armies instead to restore their internal authority. The survival and effective use of key structural elements of the Vienna order for crisis management, notably the dual hegemonic cooperation of Britain and Russia and the application of Concert methods and principles, helps to explain this outcome.

Yet the surface restoration concealed profound changes in the international system. Crucial questions (German, Italian, and Hungarian, all part of a still larger Austrian one) had been opened up and deepened, old rivalries revived in acute form (Austro-Sardinian and Austro-French in Italy, Austro-Prussian in Germany, and Austro-Russian in the Balkans, despite their cooperation in Hungary). Liberal or democratic revolution from below was discredited, but conservative revolution from above by governments and armed force was encouraged. An insecure and adventurous republic emerged in France, with a Bonapartist conspirator, Napoleon's nephew Louis Napoleon, its President. Worst of all, the revolutions had radicalized many conservatives, formerly cautious, internationalist, and legalistic, who now saw how conservative regimes could neutralize liberalism and win over the masses by coopting nationalist goals.

This long-term perspective makes the breakdown of the Concert in the next Eastern crisis, resulting, in the first major war since 1815, appear inevitable. Yet the actual origins of the Crimean War suggest blunder and accident instead. The original confrontation between France and Russia took a long time to develop (1851–3), the issue in dispute seems superficial (nominally control of certain Holy Places in Jerusalem, really prestige and influence at Constantinople), and that issue was settled in Russia's favour before the crisis grew serious. The descent from initial crisis into actual war took almost a year (May 1853–March 1854) and went through many stages—a Turkish rejection of a Russian ultimatum, a Russian break in relations and occupation of the Romanian principalities, British and French fleet movements in support of the Turks, a Turkish declaration of war, Russian destruction of the Turkish navy, an Anglo-French offensive occupation of the Black Sea, and finally war between Russia and the western powers. At every stage European Concert solutions, usually orchestrated by Austria, were proposed and seemed capable of solving the crisis, only to be spoiled by some new development. Yet the war did not really result from bad luck or accident; beneath a contingent process lay profound causes. Three were important without being central. France, where Louis Napoleon now ruled as Emperor Napoleon III, deliberately exploited the crisis and risked war to gain prestige, destroy the Austro-Russian alliance, acquire an alliance with Britain, and thereby enjoy security and leadership in Europe. The Turks, once confident of Western support, decided on war to relieve the constant Russian pressure on them. In Britain, domestic politics within a weak divided government under pressure from a Russophobe press, Parliament, and public opinion led to confusion and unclear decisions and actions at crucial moments. But the two central factors derived from basic policy decisions in Russia and Britain, and each rested on miscalculation. The crisis arose because Russia attempted to bully the Turkish government into formally acknowledging Russian pre-eminence at Constantinople, assuming that there would be no strong European reaction. The Ottoman–Russian conflict evolved into a major war because the British government decided at various junctures after July 1853 not to allow Russia an honourable retreat under cover of the Concert, which it knew Russia was seeking, but instead to inflict a humiliating political defeat on Russia and to weaken its position in Europe and the Middle East. This policy, which risked war from the outset and finally steered towards it, rested on two assumptions: that restraining Russia by grouping it in the Concert might preserve peace now, but would not eliminate the long-range Russian threat to the Ottoman and British empires (which was true), and that British naval and financial strength added to continental land forces (Turkish, French, and perhaps also Austrian and German) could do so fairly easily and quickly, possibly even throwing Russia back in Europe and Asia.

This proved incorrect. The war, fought principally on the Crimean peninsula because Britain and France could not get at Russia effectively elsewhere, revealed the military weaknesses and inefficiency of all the contestants, especially Russia and Britain. The losses, though fairly heavy especially for Russia, stemmed from weather, disease, and logistical problems more than battle. When the allies after a year-long siege finally captured the fortress of Sevastopol, France and Austria combined to force Russia to accept peace terms and to drag Britain to the peace table. The settlement reached at the Congress of Paris in the spring of 1856 reflected the limited allied victory. Russia surrendered its special treaty rights *vis-à-vis* the Ottoman Empire (a foregone conclusion) and had to cede a small piece of southern Bessarabia to Turkey and accept the neutralization of the Black Sea, twin blows to its prestige, sovereignty, and security.

Yet, except for France, which gained military laurels and international prestige, no principal profited from the war. Russia, suffering the effects of its backwardness, partly withdrew from European affairs to concentrate on internal reform. Britain, disappointed by its war effort and distracted by troubles in Persia and India, also partially retreated from Europe. The war, far from reducing the Russian threat to the British Empire, served to convince Russians hitherto divided on the subject that Britain was a worldwide enemy and turned them towards more expansion in the Caucasus, central Asia, and the Far East. The Ottoman Empire, though it gained a brief respite from

Russian pressure and a chance for modernization, acquired no durable western support. The allies disdained it during the war and abandoned it soon after, with Russia joining France in encouraging Balkan independence movements.

The main impact of the war, however, making it a turning point in international politics, was systemic and especially affected central Europe. Austria and the European Concert lost; Prussia and Sardinia-Piedmont won. The war itself, which Austria had tried desperately to prevent, undermined the Concert and threatened Austria, an empire peculiarly dependent on international sanctions and support. The results of Austrian policy during the war proved even worse. Pressed by the western powers to join the war and by Russia, Prussia, and the German Confederation to stay out, Austria had followed a non-belligerent but pro-western course that succeeded in limiting the war and preventing Russia from winning it (two-thirds of Russia's army had to be kept on its western front) but not in ending it on Austrian terms. After a peace conference at Vienna in March–May 1855 failed, Austria helped France force Russia to accept defeat and humiliating terms. In the end it made Russia an enemy by its betrayal, angered Prussia and the German states by dragging them along in its risky pro-western policy, antagonized the western powers by refusing to fight, and convinced everyone that it was selfish, irresolute, and greedy. Yet its aim was to revive the Concert through a permanent conservative alliance with the western powers, serving to restrain Russia, defend the Ottoman Empire, and gain British and French support for the status quo (that is, Austrian leadership) against revolution and challenges from Prussia and Sardinia in Germany and Italy. Russia, Prussia, and other states were supposed to accept this for the general peace and stability it would bring.

It was a pipe dream, of course. The Habsburg Monarchy, neo-absolutist, financially shaky, full of unrest in Hungary and Lombardy-Venetia and unsolved problems elsewhere, had neither the power nor the credibility for such a position of leadership. The programme itself simply ignored liberal and national pressures and the need for change, subordinated everything to Austria's need for external tranquillity, and overlooked how unsuitable Britain and France were to be reliable partners for Austria. But the failure of this attempt to reconstruct the European Concert in mid-century on a conservative, Austrian-centred basis points to something even more significant: the absence of any liberal, western attempt to do so. The great missed opportunity for establishing a liberal international order in Europe did not come in 1848–9—the actual liberal-revolutionary foreign policy programme of those years (French, German, Prussian, Italian, Austrian, and Hungarian) were all dangerously power-political and expansionist—but in 1853–6. The western powers' defeat of autocratic Russia afforded them a chance, if they chose, to lead Europe on a liberal path in regard to trade, nationalities problems, constitutional reform, and other policies that many had advocated for decades. But neither government had clear ideas for this task or interest in it. The British concentrated on trade, empire, domestic politics, and maintaining the continental balance of power, now mainly against France. Napoleon III's ideas about reconstructing Europe were vague, impractical, and bound up with his dynastic ambitions and he proved inept in executing them. The liberal moment thus passed, leaving the field to the practitioners of *Realpolitik*.

A further blow to Austria came with the unification and *de facto* independence of the Romanian principalities that Romanian nationalists achieved in 1858–9 against Austrian and Turkish opposition through shrewd manœuvres encouraged by France and Russia and grudgingly accepted by Britain. This cost the Ottoman Sultan little, for his rights had long been nominal and an independent Romania would ultimately prove a better buffer against Russia. For Austria, however, it worsened the Hungarian problem (Transylvania had a Romanian majority) and the general threat of nationalism.

Italy, however, posed a greater strategic and power-political threat. Austria's defeat of Sardinia-Piedmont in 1849 had only hardened their rivalry. Its new king Victor Emmanuel II and leading statesman Count Cavour continued the cold war against Austria and prepared for a hot one, using the Italian national cause mainly for their particular ends—military and dynastic glory and territorial expansion, the expulsion of Austria from Italy and if possible its destruction, and victory for conservative–liberal constitutional forces led by Piedmont over democratic–republican revolutionary forces in the Italian Risorgimento. Cavour's effort in 1856 to start a war against Austria with British and French support had failed, but by 1859 he had gone far to make Sardinia a leader in fiscal, commercial, and constitutional progress in Italy, to organize and co-opt the bourgeois nationalist movement, to win sympathy abroad especially in Britain, and to blacken Austria's reputation, exploiting the revolutionary discontent in Lombardy-Venetia, Austria's repressive measures against it, and its military treaties with other Italian states to paint it as the aggressor. Having goaded Austria into breaking relations, Cavour reached a secret agreement with Napoleon III in mid-1858 to provoke a joint war with Austria to expel it from Italy, expand Sardinia, and reconstruct Italy on federal lines under French influence. This was backed by a defensive alliance in early 1859. Cavour knew that he risked replacing Austrian hegemony with French, but was confident he could manage Napoleon III.

Yet, despite growing unrest in Lombardy and mobilization of Austrian and Sardinian forces on their frontier, war proved elusive so long as Austria stood on the defence of its legal rights, and the whole conspiracy was threatened when Britain and Prussia, opposed to war and worried about France, offered jointly to mediate the Italian crisis. France countered by getting Russia to propose a general congress, intended to isolate Austria and provoke a *casus belli*. The Austrians, sensing this, initially did not flatly reject a congress but insisted that Sardinia demobilize first as a precondition. Fearing isolation, Napoleon III decided in mid-April to agree and pressed Sardinia to accept this humiliation. Cavour, near despair, contemplated resigning and exposing the plot when suddenly he was rescued by an Austrian ultimatum demanding immediate Sardinian demobilization. He evaded it, Austria declared war, France honoured its alliance commitment, Britain and Prussia condemned Austria as the aggressor and withdrew into neutrality, and Cavour had his war.

Austria's blunder is explained, though not justified, by its belief that it had to end Sardinia's provocations and the military, fiscal, and political pressures of cold war and mobilization once for all, and that this was the last best opportunity. Along with this went a fatal miscalculation born of a kind of moral hubris—the conviction that Austria's cause, the defence of its legal rights against revolutionary attacks, was so obviously right and necessary for European order that Europe would in the end support it against its enemies.

Nemesis followed hubris. After the French army had defeated the Austrian in two bloody battles in Lombardy (the Piedmontese did little fighting), Emperor Franz Joseph accepted Napoleon III's offer of a truce in mid-July. Napoleon III's decision to end the war before Austria was expelled from Italy as promised was prudent. The war had proved costly and unpopular at home, the Austrian army was still in the field, Britain was growing suspicious, Sardinia was unreliable, and, worst of all, Prussia and the German Confederation threatened to intervene. His methods, however, which included deceiving Franz Joseph, worsened his existing reputation for unreliability; diplomats' tricks are one thing, sovereigns' another. Though Cavour resigned in protest over the truce, he remained in control behind the scenes and succeeded in subverting its terms so that in the final peace Sardinia-Piedmont acquired Tuscany, Parma, Modena, and the Papal Marches along with conquered Lombardy. These gains, sanctioned by pleb-iscites, almost tripled it in size and population. The cost was the cession to France (again dignified by plebiscites) of two smaller Piedmontese territories as compensation, Savoy and Nice. The sacri-fice was painful to Italian and Savoyard patriots, but a bargain for Cavour and no boon for Napoleon. The Italian venture, as his domestic enemies pointed out, had at great cost created a new poten-tial rival for France, while the acquisition of Nice and Savoy alienated Britain and deepened European suspicions of his ambitions.

The events of 1859–60 obviously did not create a final settlement for Italy. Austria still held Venetia, the Pope and the Bourbons still ruled at Rome and Naples, and both Napoleon III and the Austrians secretly hoped to alter the outcome in different ways. Yet it could have lasted a good while. Austria was friendless, exhausted, and racked with internal problems, Napoleon III was unready for another adven-ture, and Sardinia had plenty of new territory to absorb and organize. Cavour, moreover, had little interest in the south or Italian national-ism *per se*. It required a different kind of Italian adventurer-patriot, Giuseppe Garibaldi, the greatest of all nineteenth-century freedom fighters, to launch the next act in Italian unification, one that Cavour would take over, exploit, and finish.

In May 1860 Garibaldi led an expedition of 1,000 ill-armed volun-teers from the north to Sicily to support a Sicilian insurrection against Neapolitan rule. He succeeded in driving the demoralized Neapolitan army out of Sicily and much of the Neapolitan mainland, and was checked only in late summer north of Naples. His real aim, however, was to go to Rome, overthrow the papacy, and found a democratic united Italy over which Victor Emmanuel could reign. The opportunity this presented to Cavour, who had tried secretly to stop Garibaldi while pretending to support him, was outweighed by its challenge and dangers. He, his monarch, and his allies abhorred the notion of a democratic Italy formed by popular action, but overthrowing the Pope would alienate France, outrage Catholic Europe, bring Austria back into the field with conservative support, and destroy everything that had been achieved.

Cavour's response was bold and Machiavellian. Gaining Napoleon's tacit permission, he tried first to foment an insurrection in the Papal State to justify an intervention there. When this failed, he sent the army in anyway, dispersing the papal forces and seizing most of the Pope's territory. It then invaded Naples (another neutral friendly state), and defeated the Neapolitan army, though the final mop-up took months. Garibaldi and his forces were dismissed with thanks but no reward, the Pope was confined to Rome and its environs (the Patrimony of St Peter), and Naples, Sicily, and most papal territory were absorbed through plebiscite into a new Kingdom of Italy proclaimed in January 1861.

With all its flaws, this outcome was better than any practical alternative, and achieved with surprisingly little violence and bloodshed in the interstate wars (the internal pacification of the south was another matter). Yet, from an international standpoint, these events did less to reorganize Europe on a new national basis than to advance the destruction of the old European order without establishing a new one. Three reasons prompt this conclusion. First, Italy was incomplete (Venice and Rome), would still have irredentist ambitions even after acquiring these, and, as a weak, ambitious would-be great power, would remain an incalculable, destabilizing factor in European politics. Secondly, France was now isolated and Napoleon III discredited as a leader and manager of the system, while old rivalries had been aggravated rather than healed (Austro-Italian, Austro-French, Anglo-French, Austro-Prussian). Finally, Cavour's actions in uniting Italy, however justified by danger and necessity, were so unscrupulous as to undermine any stable code of international conduct and system of mutual restraint unless convincingly renounced for the future— something neither Cavour, who died in mid-1861, nor his successors would or could do.

The creation of Prussia-Germany, 1862–1871

As everyone knows, the Second German Reich was not unified from below but created from above by Prussia through wars that ousted Austria from Germany, destroyed the German Confederation, and incorporated its non-Austrian territories into a Prussian-dominated empire. This outcome was not foreordained; other settlements of the German question were possible. Yet paradoxically, without this contingent outcome resulting in this particular Prussian-dominated Germany, it is hard to envision any stable European system emerging to replace the one finally buried in these last of the mid-century wars.

The fact that the architect of German unification, Count Bismarck, was named Prussia's Minister-President in 1862 in the course of a constitutional crisis pitting the king, the army, and the ministry against the liberal majority in Prussia's lower house demonstrates the intimate connection between foreign and domestic politics in the process. Other internal political, social, economic, and cultural factors in Prussia and Germany were involved in unification. Bismarck's motives in seeking and using power, however, were primarily international, not domestic or personal. For years he had advocated expanding Prussia's territory and power to fit its great power needs and role, absorbing or subordinating smaller states and ousting Austria from at least north Germany and possibly the south as well.

This revolutionary programme was almost certain to require war, as Bismarck recognized. Yet one cannot simply say, 'Bismarck started three wars to unify Germany'. He always tried other means first and as long as possible; technically Prussia was not the aggressor in any of them. Moreover, his main aim was always to strengthen Prussia and never to unify Germany entirely. Above all, he conducted policy, not as a puppeteer or visionary following his star, but as one player among many in Europe who pursued his overall goal step by step with limited means, seizing opportunities and avoiding traps as he went. The reason for organizing the story around him is not that he controlled events, but that he showed extraordinary skill and success in exploiting them.

His first big opportunity arose from another clash in 1863 between Denmark and the German Confederation over Schleswig-Holstein, which was set off by the Danish government's violation of the five-power London Protocol of 1852 and led to an armed confrontation. Though complicated, it was the sort of dispute that the European Concert had settled before, and another London conference was convened to do so. But Britain and Russia, Denmark's main protectors, were now rivals and distracted with other problems—Britain chiefly with North America, Russia with another Polish revolt. Napoleon III's opportunism and the Danish refusal to restore the legal *status quo ante* also obstructed a diplomatic solution. Bismarck cared nothing about the legal quarrel or the German national cause (in fact, viewed it in this context as a threat to Prussian interests), but saw a chance to gain something for Prussia, frustrate the German liberal nationalists trying to make Schleswig-Holstein a new north German middle state, compromise and snare Austria, and shore up his own threatened position in office. He persuaded Austria to join Prussia in intervening to settle the question as European great powers. The two powers demanded that Denmark restore the legal status quo and on its refusal sent a combined army to brush aside the German federal troops, first occupying both duchies and then invading Denmark. After a truce and a renewed London conference, which again broke down over Denmark's refusal to restore the *status quo ante*, Prussia and Austria pursued the war to victory, the peace treaty giving them both duchies in common. Austria had fought a war for conquests useful only to Prussia, thereby alienating its natural allies in Germany, further discrediting the Confederation, and damaging its reputation for conservative legality in Europe. Why, especially since Austria's foreign minister Rechberg knew how anti-Austrian Bismarck was? Partly because some Austrians hoped to lure Prussia into helping them overthrow the Italian settlement, but mainly because Rechberg, an old Metternichian conservative, saw German nationalism as the great revolutionary danger to both states and hoped that conservative Prussians such as the king would restrain Bismarck and revive the conservative Austro-Prussian partnership.

The question of the disposition of Schleswig-Holstein now became Bismarck's means for settling the larger German question by luring, dragging, or forcing Austria into abandoning all or most of Germany, or, if necessary, into fighting over who was its master. The events over the next two years by which the last alternative became reality are too complicated to relate here; besides Austria and Prussia, the other German states, France, Italy, Russia, and Britain were also involved and other issues (the Venetian and Roman questions, the Near East, and even the American Civil War and the Mexican revolution) played a role. A further complication was that Bismarck's aim was not, like Cavour's, relatively simple—to gain allies, start a war, make it as general as possible, and gamble on a favourable outcome—but to go to war only if necessary, keep it limited, prevent outside intervention, and control the outcome. His ultimate success, while demonstrating his skill, patience, and talent at playing the role of the injured party, depended on favourable circumstances. The German Confederation could not act effectively. The smaller states, though aware of the threat to their existence, were disunited, eager to hide or in some cases to follow Prussia for protection and guarantees. Napoleon III, still anti-Austrian and preoccupied with Italy, was confident that France would profit from an Austro-Prussian war. Russia, also still anti-Austrian and worried by Bismarck's warning that if he fell a liberal anti-Russian, pro-Polish ministry would take over, remained benevolently neutral. Italy would join any war against Austria for territorial gains, though it feared being caught fighting alone. The British preferred peace, but had other concerns overseas and mainly worried about French expansion. Austria, once it failed to secure Prussian help to recover Lombardy in exchange for Schleswig-Holstein, fell back on a stubborn, passive policy of defence, trying without success to rally German and European support against Bismarck's white revolution.

Thus the most serious obstacles Bismarck faced on the road to confrontation were domestic—overcoming the king's and others' scruples about a 'civil war' in Germany and the fiscal problems caused by the ongoing budget fight in parliament. These concerns probably account for the diplomatic truce concluded with Austria in August 1865. By February 1866, however, the king was converted to war, and in April Prussia concluded a short-term offensive treaty with Italy threatening Austria with a two-front war and assuring that at least at the outset France would not intervene. By June, these and other pressures on Austria helped Bismarck manœuvre it into taking the initiative in the final clashes over mobilization and Schleswig-Holstein that dissolved the Confederation and brought on war.

The war quickly proved disastrous for Austria and its German allies. Prussian superiority in mobilization, training, tactics and strategy, and some weapons (notably the new breech-loading rifle) far outweighed Austrian advantages in artillery and cavalry. After easily dispersing the lesser German forces and winning nearly all the early engagements, the Prussian army crushed the main Austrian one at Königgrätz (Sadowa) in early July. Bismarck, bent on harnessing the fruits of victory before outsiders, especially France, could intervene, quickly concluded a truce over the opposition of the king and some military men, making peace with Austria on terms often considered astonishingly moderate. Austria suffered no territorial losses but had to accept the dissolution of the Confederation, extensive Prussian annexations in north Germany, and a Prussian-led North German Confederation. The south German states were to be allowed their own confederation if they wished. In simultaneous separate negotiations with these south German states, Bismarck largely negated this option by tying them to Prussia in tight military alliances. In north Germany neither Prussia's allies nor its victims were given any choice. Hanover, Schleswig-Holstein, Nassau, and Frankfurt (four million inhabitants) were simply annexed to Prussia and the other small states (with another four million) incorporated into the North German Confederation. Preventing France from interfering in this revolution in the German and European balance of power was trickier, but Napoleon's indecision, French blunders, and Bismarck's wiles enabled him to evade France's search for compensations.

The settlement is often pictured as settling the struggle for supremacy in Germany; as a piece of luck for Austria, offering it a new lease on life when its last hour seemed to be striking; as a temporary stage on the road to final unification of Germany; and as the prelude to the next likely or inevitable war with France. Only the first of these verdicts is acceptable without major reservations. The war of 1866 did make Prussia master of Germany and a leading great power in Europe, a result all but a few die hards in Germany and Europe soon came to terms with and accepted. As for the second, Bismarck's treatment of Austria was realistic, but hardly generous. He took everything he wanted, aware that taking more would have imperilled his real ends. True, he wanted Austria to survive—not as a future ally, however (this is a myth), but as a defeated, vulnerable foreign state useful for holding down south-eastern Europe and for keeping nine million Catholic Austro-Germans out of a predominantly Protestant, Prussian-controlled Germany. Bismarck, moreover, always recognized the obvious fact that the dissolution of Austria would have revolutionary consequences for Germany and Europe, making Prussia's position between France and Russia even more dangerous, and that the idea of a Greater Germany was a bad, un-Prussian dream.

Austria's fate admittedly could have been much worse, and the settlement helped it survive—but at considerable cost. With its historic reason for existence, its German and Italian mission gone, and its strategic position *vis-à-vis* Prussia hopeless, its only reasons to exist were the power-political ones of security and expansion, now directed to the south-east against Russia. The internal effects of defeat were mixed. It accelerated the historic Compromise with Hungary reached in 1867, which changed Austria into a dual Austro-Hungarian monarchy, bringing some immediate relief on the Hungarian question but creating other long-range problems. The albatross of Venetia was ceded to Italy despite Austria's land and sea victories over the Italians in 1866, in fulfilment of a pre-war treaty obligation to France made to secure French neutrality. Yet, if 1866 temporarily eased Austria's worst nationality problems, it created a dangerous new one: divided loyalties among Austro-Germans looking towards Berlin.

The most doubtful views are seldom debated: that 1866 was bound to be temporary, a halfway house on the road to final unification with the south German states, and that this would probably require war with France. True, both these ideas were widely believed in 1866 and after. The North German Confederation was deliberately kept provisional so that the south German states could easily enter. In France, meanwhile, Prussia's shocking victory, France's humiliating failure in the aftermath, and the obvious new military threat to the east destroyed the pro-Prussian party at court and turned once indifferent Frenchmen into strong opponents of Prussian expansion. Yet further German unification and a Franco-Prussian confrontation over it would become inevitable only if the 1866 status quo proved untenable against the tide of German nationalism, if France decided to stop it by force, or if Prussia used violent means to promote it. None of this happened after 1866. Neither great power sought a confrontation. Prussia passed up a favourable opportunity for a national war with France in 1867 over Luxembourg. France, after meeting more rebuffs in its quest for compensation and a Prussian alliance, tried repeatedly for a defensive alliance with Austria and Italy or a united European diplomatic front against Prussia, but failed. Britain, Russia, and Austria all wished to preserve the status quo of 1866 in Germany and avoid further war. Most important, the German national movement went temporarily into reverse after 1866 in south Germany. Liberal nationalists lost ground in elections; particularist anti-Prussian parties came to power in Bavaria and Württemberg. Meanwhile particularist opposition to Prussia in north Germany declined and the North German Confederation proved such a success that many, especially liberals, called for making it permanent.

Thus, if one cannot confidently say that the 1866 settlement could have lasted and further unification been delayed for years or decades, neither can one assert the contrary. Some signs clearly pointed to this possibility, and Bismarck himself spoke of it. Moreover, the crisis that led to Franco-German war in July 1870, especially Bismarck's campaign to put a Hohenzollern prince on the vacant throne of Spain, seems highly contrived in comparison to his usual policy. He had gambled before, but only when he had to, after carefully preparing for every possible contingency and rigging the odds in his favour. His scheme here involved numerous uncontrollable risks and was virtually bound to blow up in his face, as it finally did. While his exact motives cannot be established with certainty, a sensible guess is that he, like Cavour in 1860, was gambling less to gain a prize, unification with south Germany, than to avert a loss, the possible defection of Bavaria to the Austro-French camp, which would have indefinitely postponed unification, dealt Bismarck a grave political defeat, and made the liberals in north Germany harder to handle. In any case, the collapse of his manœuvre in Spain followed by French exposure of it spawned a European crisis and threatened Bismarck with public humiliation and possible dismissal. He escaped by using France's foolishly aggressive response to enflame French national pride and German national honour against each other. When France compounded its folly by declaring war first, the reluctant south German governments were swept along into war by the nationalist tide.

This war, though bloodier, was initially as one-sided as that of 1866. Unpreparedness and strategic confusion in the French army, combined with efficient German mobilization and movements and the German ability to throw large numbers of trained reservists into combat, led by early September to the defeat, capture, or immobilization of all three main French armies. This failed to end the war, because Napoleon III, captured with one army at Sedan, was overthrown by revolution at Paris, a Provisional Republic was established, and new armies were raised and guerrilla tactics used to liberate French soil. But revolutionary *élan* proved insufficient to defeat the German army. Paris was besieged and starved into submission and the French pleas for foreign intervention fell on deaf ears. Italy instead seized Rome after the French troops protecting the Pope had been evacuated. The Pope responded by retiring to the Vatican, breaking relations, and remaining technically at war with Italy till 1929. Russia also took advantage of the war to repudiate the Black Sea clause of the Paris Peace of 1856. With Britain and Austria denouncing this, a London conference was convened with Prussia and France participating. Here the war in France was ignored despite French protests, Russia was rebuked for unilaterally violating a treaty, and the clause in question was abrogated. Meanwhile Bismarck negotiated with the south German states, especially Bavaria, on the constitution of a new federal German Reich enabling William I to be proclaimed Emperor of Germany at Versailles in mid-January 1871. A Franco-German truce in late January enabled the French provisional government to crush a rising of the Paris Commune; the final peace treaty followed in May. By nineteenth-century standards it was a harsh peace, imposing on France a heavy indemnity and the loss of Alsace and part of Lorraine, old German Reich territories acquired in the seventeenth and eighteenth centuries.

The war of 1870–1 is often considered to have substituted Germany for France as the hegemon of Europe, and to have created a lasting Franco-German enmity because of the annexation of Alsace-Lorraine. Obviously both interpretations are partly true, but they need qualification. Except possibly briefly in 1856–9, France had not been a hegemon in Europe since 1812, and Germany was at best an insecure half-hegemon after 1870. As for Alsace-Lorraine, while it remained an open wound (though by 1914 it was slowly closing) and obstructed any real Franco-German *rapprochement*, it never constituted the main problem estranging France and Germany. That problem, created in 1870 and lasting until the 1950s, was French insecurity *vis-à vis* Germany. Even the return of Alsace-Lorraine, as 1919–39 would show, would not solve this problem; only French armaments and alliances could, and these would in turn make Germany insecure.

Bismarck's main argument for annexation reflected this: since France would never accept its defeat, Germany needed a better defensive frontier. In other words, 1870–1 created a classic security dilemma; Alsace-Lorraine merely symbolized it and made it worse. Theoretically, this security dilemma could have been solved in one of three ways. First, France like Austria after 1871 could have given up trying to achieve security against Germany as an impossible task, and leaned on Germany for protection instead. For that, France was still too strong, independent, proud, and capable of alliances. Secondly, France and Germany could have become so closely integrated economically and politically that war between them would become impossible. The political and economic conditions for this would not arise till the 1950s. Thirdly, the mutual military threat could have been kept manageable by maintaining a rough parity in military capability between the powers, limiting them to a narrow common frontier, and preserving a sizeable territorial buffer between them. This was the situation created by the 1866 settlement, destroyed in 1870.

Thus the disappearance of the independent south German states becomes one of the most important changes of 1870–1 for the European system. As intermediary bodies, they had been useful not only for Franco-Prussian relations, but for Austro-Prussian, Russo-Prussian, and even Italo-Prussian ones as well. Absorbing them into Imperial Germany even worked against Bismarck's fundamental purposes for expanding Prussia. His goal was not power and territory mainly for their own sake, but in order to disentangle Prussia, freeing it from pressures and threats inseparable from its exposed geographic position by making it a true great power and master in its own house, Germany. The war of 1866 had achieved that, giving Prussia all the power and position it could safely use for this purpose. It enjoyed complete control of north Germany, close military, political, and commercial ties with the south, and a Europe in which all the great powers, including even Austria and France, were ready (if grudgingly) to live with this outcome provided Prussia went no further. The war of 1866 also gave Prussia something Imperial Germany never had: the chance for a vivifying idea, a European mission for which to use its new power. That mission, inherited from Austria, which had never effectively fulfilled it, was to organize, lead, and defend Germany as a whole, including its independent states, and keep central Europe at peace. Victory in 1871, in contrast, gave Germany more power than its neighbours were comfortable with, and no clear European mission for which to use it, leading others both to fear that power and to try to enlist it for their purposes, creating the very entanglements Bismarck had sought to avoid.

As for Bismarck, he derided the very notion of a European mission, but did come later to regret the annexation of Alsace-Lorraine and entertain doubts about the internal solidity of the Reich he had created. Convinced, not least by his difficulties in making peace in 1871, that Germany had now gone as far as it dared, he now turned Germany's interests purely into making the new system work. No one else was available for this managerial task; it is doubtful that anyone else would have tried.

The Bismarckian system in operation, 1871–1890

Bismarck's first expedient for keeping France isolated and Germany and Europe at peace was to revive the spirit of conservative monarchical solidarity, encouraging an Austro-Hungarian–Russian entente and then joining it to make the Three Emperors' League (1872–3). This proved a weak reed. A brief and artificial 'War in Sight' crisis in 1875, in which Bismarck, worried by France's rapid fiscal and military recovery, tried a small intimidation campaign against France only to have Britain and Russia warn Germany instead, revealed that reviving the Holy Alliance would not ensure Russian friendship. The more serious Eastern Crisis of 1875–8 would destroy the Three Emperors' League, forcing Bismarck into a new strategy: diverting European rivalries away from Germany to the periphery, with Germany helping to manage and settle them.

This Eastern Crisis like earlier ones grew out of the Sultan's lack of control in the Balkans, making it easy for risings against local authorities to turn into mass revolts and nationalist movements along ethnic and religious lines, drawing in great powers and new Balkan states alike. This time revolt began in Bosnia-Herzegovina in 1875, where it persisted, and spread to Bulgaria in 1876, where it was suppressed by Ottoman irregular forces by methods exaggeratedly depicted in

Europe as the 'Bulgarian Horrors', producing a strong public reaction against the Turks, especially in Britain and Russia. To this point Russia and Austria, encouraged and supported by Germany, had been working in distrustful partnership to get European and Turkish agreement on a programme of European-supervised reforms to pacify the region. Their proposals, inadequate in any case, were foiled by British coolness, Ottoman resistance, and the rebels' persistence in revolt. The Bulgarian Horrors, however, temporarily made it impossible for the British government openly to support the Turks, while Tsar Alexander II felt that he had to act to restore Russia's prestige and satisfy its public opinion. He appealed to Bismarck to repay Russia's support in 1866 and 1870 by keeping Austria neutral in a Russo-Turkish war. Bismarck refused, insisting that Germany needed both its great neighbours equally and could not allow either to be weakened. This forced Russia to agree with Austria on the conditions under which it could punish the Turks indirectly by encouraging and supporting a Serbian attack. But, despite Russian leadership and volunteers, the Turks defeated Serbia and had to be stopped by Austrian and Russian pressure—another frustration for St. Petersburg. After more failures to reach a European Concert settlement, Russia in early 1877 worked out a broader agreement in which Austria consented to a Russian war on Turkey to liberate the eastern Balkans, provided that Russia annexed no major territories itself, established no large satellite state, and gave Austria Bosnia as compensation. The conditions and concessions almost made the game not worth the candle, but cumulative frustration brought Russia to declare war in April 1877.

An initial threat of British intervention against Russia passed when it became obvious that Germany and Austria would remain neutral. Stiff Turkish resistance, however, stalled the Russian offensive for months; not until January 1878 did the Russian army finally crush the Turks and appear about to take Constantinople. Another flurry of Anglo-Russian crises passed without war in January–February 1878. A much worse one arose, however, when Russia concluded a peace treaty with the Sultan at San Stefano in March that flagrantly violated its agreements with Austria-Hungary. For the first time it joined Britain in confronting Russia; already militarily and financially exhausted, Russia faced a war it could not possibly win.

Why the Russian government allowed its negotiator, an ardent

Pan-Slav, to conclude such a treaty is unclear—perhaps as a sop to nationalist opinion, or perhaps conservatives at the Foreign Ministry decided to let their opponents try their programme and learn the consequences. In any case, Russia, needing to retreat, seized on Bismarck's offer to help revise the treaty at a European Congress. At Bismarck's insistence, Russia and Britain worked out a preliminary agreement to ensure success. On this basis the Congress of Berlin— the most splendid since Vienna—met in June–July. Hard negotiations led to agreements on the crucial issues. The huge Bulgaria of San Stefano dominating the Balkan map was greatly reduced and divided into two portions, one semi-independent of Turkey, the other merely self-governing, and Austria was invited to occupy and administer Bosnia-Herzegovina under Turkish sovereignty *sine die*. Many other territorial and other Balkan, Near Eastern, and Black Sea questions were also settled.

Two common criticisms of the Berlin Congress are that by adopting half-measures on Bulgaria, discarding the ethnic principle on which the Treaty of San Stefano was based, it prolonged unrest and condemned the Balkans, especially Macedonia, to decades of future conflict, and that Bismarck in siding secretly with Austria and Britain forced a humiliating settlement on Russia. Neither complaint is persuasive. In following ethnic lines, San Stefano ignored or violated many other strategic, political, religious, and contractual considerations, making the treaty intolerable to Britain, Austria, Serbia, Greece, and Romania, a sure prescription for new and wider war. Allowed to stand, it would have destroyed the balance of power in the whole region through Russian domination of Bulgaria, the Balkans, the Straits, and Turkey. The Berlin Treaty proved useful precisely because it was a series of half-steps and compromises that satisfied few entirely but left the door open for further change. As for Bismarck, the real Russian grievance was not that he failed to be an honest broker but that Russia wanted an ally. Helping it escape an impossible position was not enough. Nor was it Bismarck's fault that Russia's gains from fighting were apparently less valuable than Britain's and Austria's from neutrality. At the crucial juncture they held the stronger hands. Two real lessons emerge from the crisis and settlement: the European system required a manager—how war would have been avoided without one, one cannot tell; and Bismarck, by playing the honest broker and diverting rivalries to the periphery, had not succeeded in disentangling Germany or winning security and gratitude.

The collapse of the Three Emperors' League in this crisis and the strained relations with Russia that ensued pushed Bismarck a stage further in his quest for managerial expedients, from monarchical solidarity in 1871–5 and honest brokerage in 1875–8 to controlling alliances. After deliberately exacerbating the quarrel with Russia to convince Emperor William that an alliance with Austria-Hungary was necessary, in 1879 Bismarck concluded the defensive alliance the Austrian government had long sought. He promptly used it, however, to force Austria back into unwilling partnership with Russia and Germany in the Three Emperors' Alliance of 1881. This worked for a time to manage Russo-Austrian rivalry in the Balkans. Bismarck's proposal that they simply divide the Balkans along east–west lines was impractical because their various overlapping interests, strengths, and weaknesses in the region made a division into separate spheres of influence impossible and undesirable for either, but the competition could be controlled, especially if both were tied to Germany. Other Bismarckian alliances of restraint and management developed in 1881–3. Italy, at odds with France over territory, trade, and colonies, allied with Austria-Hungary and Germany in a Triple Alliance in 1882, forcing Austrians and Italians to manage their rivalry. Romania concluded a secret alliance with Austria-Hungary acceded to by Germany, and in 1881 Vienna took its small neighbour Serbia (or rather Serbia's prince) under its wing. Meanwhile Bismarck took advantage of Anglo-French rivalry in Africa to improve relations with France, and maintained reasonable relations with Britain, despite an acrid dispute arising over entering the colonial race in Africa in 1884.

This system of limited alliances of restraint seemed to give Germany great control over European politics with little danger or commitment. Yet it was a complicated, entangling, and fragile system, as the next crisis over Bulgaria in 1884–7 would prove. The Bulgarian Crisis was complicated and sometimes tragicomic in details, but fairly simple in origins and essence. Russia, ruled by the narrowly autocratic Alexander III (1881–94), managed by heavy-handed interference to alienate its loyal and grateful satellite principality, lost control of it to Bulgarian nationalists, suffered painful prestige defeats, and chose to blame its troubles on Austria and indirectly on

Germany. Out of this arose a kind of 'I dare you' Austro-Russian confrontation, which destroyed the Three Emperors' Alliance. Bismarck had to find another way to keep France and Russia apart at a time when revived French and German nationalism, Franco-Italian hostility, Anglo-French rivalry in Africa, and Anglo-Russian rivalry in the Near East and central Asia further threatened the peace. The combination he came up with in 1887 was his most elaborate and artificial. He encouraged an Anglo-Italian agreement for maintaining the status quo in the eastern Mediterranean, which Austria later joined. This served to draw in Britain, reassure Austria and Italy, and check France. A renewal of the Triple Alliance served the same ends. An agreement between the same three powers to work for the status quo in the Near East drew Britain as close to Austria as it would ever go in a commitment to resist a Russian advance in the Balkans. But earlier in February Bismarck had concluded a secret Reinsurance Treaty with Russia promising German neutrality if Austria attacked Russia and German support for Russian interests and aims in Bulgaria and the Straits.

This was obviously a system of balanced antagonisms, but that does not say much. Bismarck always considered balanced antagonisms the essence of international politics. Now, however, he was no longer balancing existing antagonisms, but promoting antagonistic policies so as to balance them and keep Germany the arbiter. Moreover, while the Reinsurance Pact did not technically violate Germany's commitments under the Dual Alliance, it did leave both sides uncertain which side Germany would support if it came to war. Granted, the juggling act preserved peace and was far better than the preventive war against France or Russia some German leaders urged and Bismarck rejected. But it did not arrest a further sickening of the peace in 1888–9. and a gradual *rapprochement* between Russia and France. Intense economic competition in the latter stages of the so-called Great Depression (1873–96) and a Russo-German customs war contributed to this. One cannot tell whether Bismarck, had he remained in office, could have devised new expedients to keep France and Russia apart and to avoid a choice between Austria-Hungary and Russia or Britain and Russia; toward the end he tried some unsuccessfully and was considering others. By Bismarck's fall in March 1890 in a power struggle with Germany's new erratic Emperor William II, however, most of his room for foreign policy manœuvre and all his domestic support was gone; most Germans greeted his fall with a sigh of relief. Probably, therefore, even Bismarck could not have managed the European system much longer. But the new Wilhelmian style would certainly be worse, and, since the only plausible alternative to German leadership was the detached, balance-of-power, muddle-through style of Britain, the question was not who would next manage the system, but whether anyone would at all.

Imperialism and world politics, 1890–1907

The initial results of Bismarck's fall and William II's 'New Course', though dramatic, did not seem dangerous. Germany's abrupt decision not to renew the Reinsurance Treaty with Russia led in 1891–4 to a Franco-Russian defensive alliance against Germany and Austria—a major turning point in the system, but also an apparent return to normalcy, restoring a balance of power in Europe. The alliance, moreover, put more pressure at first on Britain, Russia's and France's main imperial rival, than on the German powers; for the most important development of the 1890s was that centre stage in international politics shifted away from the continent to the wider world and a scramble already under way over it, the 'new imperialism'.

The hotly debated questions of what caused 'new imperialism' and what effects it had on the various European and non-European actors cannot be discussed here. In so far as they relate to our theme, the course of European international politics, the answers are fairly easy. 'New imperialism' for one thing, was not new, but an acceleration, after a slowdown from 1815 to about 1870, of a pattern of western penetration and partial domination or conquest of different sections of the non-European world beginning in the fifteenth century. 'New imperialism' speeded up the process, took in new areas (most of Africa, parts of east and south-east Asia, and the south-west Pacific), brought in new imperialist actors (Germany, Italy, the United States, Japan, King Leopold II of Belgium), and re-energized older ones (Britain, France, Russia, Spain, Portugal, and the Netherlands). As to its causes and motives, they were so many, powerful, and closely intertwined that better questions than 'Why?' are 'Why not?' and

'Why just then and not earlier?'. The answer to the latter is that at this time certain barriers (political, economic, commercial, and above all scientific, technical, medical, and military) restraining European penetration and expansion declined or disappeared. As for its causes, all the positive explanations (military and political strategy, European great-power competition, the pull of the periphery, the breakdown of traditional regimes and societies, the push of local imperialisms, men on the spot, turbulent frontiers, the white man's burden and manifest destiny, racism, the struggle for markets, the patterns of European economic development and competition, imperialism as a lightning rod for European energies, and so on) are true and apply at various points; none is the sole or main answer.

Hence the focus here must be on what imperialism did within the international system and to it. First and foremost, at least for two or three decades, it acted as a safety valve. Just as mass emigration from Europe, mainly to the New World, helped to prevent social and political revolution in the nineteenth century, so 'new imperialism' helped keep the Bismarckian and post-Bismarckian system going without general war. The second, ultimately more important, impact was to help make the system unworkable and a general war likely if not inevitable. This apparent paradox cannot be explained by narrating the events of imperialism (impossible here anyway), but only by analysing its two stages and why they affected international politics as they did, illustrating this with brief looks at particular crises and the shifts in European alignments they engendered.

Imperialism initially served as a safety valve because from the early 1870s until the mid-1890s or later it involved less a struggle between different states for critical territories and positions of power than a hunt for prizes, like an Easter egg hunt, carried on in fierce competition on the ground between individuals in and out of governments (entrepeneurs, firms, explorers and adventurers, settlers, careerists in politics and the military, and so on), but pursued more cautiously by most governments, usually aware of the dubious value and high costs of acquisitions. Even where imperialist ambitions and programmes clashed, deals and compromises were the normal outcome; there seemed enough for everyone, and losers could be compensated elsewhere.

The reasons for imperialism's ultimate destructive impact are more numerous and complex. First, interstate competition inevitably heightened as the available prizes dwindled. Pre-emptive actions to seize prizes and shut competitors out, always prominent, grew in frequency and intensity and became the dominant rule of the game. Secondly, even originally amicable deals and shared arrangements tended to break down and to produce crises and confrontations as governments sought sole possession and exclusive control rather than shared influence and exploitation (for example, Anglo-French Dual Control in Egypt; Franco-German cooperation in Morocco; the Berlin-to-Baghdad Railway; the Anglo-Russian Convention in Persia). Thirdly, as imperialist activity expanded, even ordinary commercial or political activity by one state in an unclaimed area became for another power a threat to its rights, interests, and security. Examples include British feelings, colonial and metropolitan, about Germans in South Africa; Russian and British concerns to keep Germans out of Persia, Mesopotamia, and eastern Anatolia; Britain in Egypt and the Sudan, France in Morocco; most dangerous of all, Russia and Austria mutually in the Balkans. Fourthly, and most importantly, 'new imperialism' combined with other late-nineteenth-century trends in economics, science and technology, communications, and the art of war to make world policy the dominant ideology and strategy in international politics. The survival, security, and prosperity of states in the twentieth century was believed to depend upon securing a world position, which for great powers meant the ability to compete with the established world powers, Britain, the United States, and Russia, around the globe; for lesser powers, having at least a seat at the imperialist table and share in the game.

World policy (*Weltpolitik*), often discussed as if it only or especially concerned Germany, was in fact almost universal. The enormous territorial growth of the British Empire before, during, and after the First World War represented its world policy—expansion of formal empire in order to sustain the old informal paramountcy now challenged by Russia, the United States, France, Germany, and even Japan. Russia's imperialism in central Asia and the Far East was its world policy for meeting British and German challenges and compensating for its economic and technological lag. French imperialism was a world policy for reversing its relative decline, recovering the status and prestige lost in 1870, and keeping up with Germany and Britain. The American world policy was the most overt and unselfconscious of all—a claim to exclusive hegemony over a whole hemisphere, soon

extended to the Pacific. Japan, Italy, and even Austria-Hungary succumbed to the world-policy virus; Spain, Portugal, the Netherlands,
and the king of Belgium, though without illusions that they could
compete with the great powers, were determined to stay in the game
or enter it.

Thus 'new imperialism', beginning as a relatively safe (for Europe)
scramble for prizes outside Europe, turned into a deadly struggle for
world power and position central to European politics. Germany's
world policy became the most important, not because it acted in a
particularly reckless or aggressive way (at least until 1914 it was more
cautious than most) but because its attempt to compete with Britain,
America, and Russia for world position was bound to fail. It would
have been surprising had Germany not tried for world position;
miraculous had it succeeded at a game rigged by geography and
history against it in comparison to Britain, Russia, France, the United
States, and even in some respects Japan. Germany, like France, was
handicapped in naval and colonial rivalry with Britain, by a late,
inferior starting position, the lack of a historic tradition and outlook,
and above all a geographical position both less suitable for projecting
its power outward and requiring constant division of effort between
activity abroad and defence at home. These same handicaps account
for Germany's lack of success in imperialist combinations and alliances. German tactics and methods, true, were often counterproductive (though their failings are frequently exaggerated), but no
improvement in tactics and methods could have produced success.

The shift to world policy had profound implications. The traditional nineteenth-century European power game had been played
for relative advantages, often relatively modest or symbolic ones, and
was usually deliberately stopped or held short of decision—an
irreversible victory for one power or side or the decisive defeat or
elimination of one side or any essential actor. The struggle for world
power was different, with higher stakes and goals (victory for the next
century), with a structure favouring certain powers on one side in the
European game and disadvantaging those on the other, and with a
strong tendency toward a final outcome and the elimination of
competitors.

Understanding its results requires looking briefly at three international crises of imperialism and how they affected European
alignments. The first and least important was the Fashoda Incident,

an Anglo-French confrontation in 1898 over the Sudan. The British came to Fashoda in southern Sudan following a military conquest of the Sudan from Egypt, occupied in 1882; the French occupied it first from the western Sudan and West Africa. For Britain the vital stake was not the Sudan itself, but strategic pre-emption—barring any possible threat to the Suez–Red Sea route to India and ending France's attempts to challenge its position in Egypt. France's policy, like its government, was incoherent. A small, secretive group of ardent colonialists and military men aimed to extend the French Empire from west to east across Africa, denying Britain control from the Cape to Cairo. The government, which failed to control this group's activities, wanted to pressure the British into negotiations on Egypt as a way to improve France's colonial and European positions generally. The British government, moreover, was willing and prepared to fight; the French was not, having assumed that a colonial question could not become a *casus belli*. The outcome, a humiliating French retreat, had two main effects on European politics. It did not, as often said, pave the way for an Anglo-French colonial and political *entente* (in fact, it delayed it), but it forced the French eventually to recognize that, if they wished an *entente* with Britain, it would have to be on British terms. At the same time, the direct threat of European war between great powers over a colonial issue raised the temperature and stakes of colonial and world competition.

The roots of the second crisis, the Second Anglo-Boer War of 1899–1902, go back much further, to British conquest of the Dutch Cape Colony during the Napoleonic Wars and the Anglo-Boer political and cultural clash that subsequently developed. Though as always the immediate origins of the war from 1896 to 1899 are debated, the main cause is clear enough: the determination of the virtually independent Boer Republics to maintain their independence versus Britain's determination to maintain its exclusive supremacy in South Africa, threatened by the economic growth of the Republics, by forcing them into union with the British Cape Colony after previous British attempts at federation through annexation, persuasion, and attempted *coup* had failed. (Both white communities, of course, ruled and exploited the blacks and coloureds.) Britain's political and military pressure finally prompted the Boers to open the fighting, but they only anticipated the British in doing so. The war, though costly to Britain militarily and politically (world opinion and most governments with the exception of the American and German ones favoured the Boers), ended in British victory and the preservation of its supremacy—for a time. Ironically, when a Union of South Africa was formed in 1910, it brought to pass the very Boer domination of all of South Africa that the war had been supposed to prevent, with consequences reaching down to present times.

The war's direct consequences in international politics were relatively few. That constant bogeyman of the British press, public opinion, and many politicians, the German threat, was here non-existent. Germany's policy, as opposed to its press and public opinion, was consistently pro-British, the government hoping to become Britain's colonial partner. Hence Russia and France, which considered forming a continental league against Britain, could do nothing, while the British government, having fobbed Germany off with a fool's deal over the Portuguese colonies in Africa, cashed in on German inaction while evading German advances. Thus the war again demonstrated the strength of Britain's imperial position, but also, in convincing the British that such ventures were costly and limited friendships better than isolation, helped pave the way for its later *ententes*.

The last crisis, the Russo-Japanese War of 1904–5, had major effects impossible to discuss here on Russian, Japanese, Chinese, and Korean history, the rise of anti-Western movements in Asia and elsewhere, the development of modern land and sea warfare, and much more. Here again we must concentrate on its impact on the international system, which was also profound. Under the impact of European penetration and foreign and civil war, the Chinese Empire decayed from the mid-nineteenth century while Japan rapidly adapted to Western penetration and modernized. In the Sino-Japanese War of 1894–5 the Japanese completely defeated China and imposed heavy losses on it. Russia, which had earlier reached the Pacific and established a base at Vladivostok and was rapidly building a Trans-Siberian Railway to connect it with Europe, organized an intervention with Germany and France, forcing Japan to surrender gains that would have given it dominant influence at Beijing. Russia's victory and Japan's humiliation threw China into the arms of Russia, which gained a series of political, financial, and military advantages in China in 1896–7 worrisome to other European powers, especially Britain. The contest for influence escalated in 1898 into a scramble for concrete concessions at China's expense (naval bases, commercial spheres and settlements, railway and other concessions, and so on). The competition, touched off by Germany and joined by almost everyone, was won by Russia, which gained from China the very military and commercial positions in South Manchuria it had forced Japan to disgorge in 1895. Meanwhile, from 1898 to 1900 the so-called Boxer Rebellion, a vast, diverse revolt against foreigners, missionaries, and partly the Chinese government itself, spread sporadically across China. Crushed by foreign troops especially from Japan, the movement served only to accelerate both the imperialist scramble and the Chinese government's decay, with Russia again making the greatest gains. Defeating the insurrection in Manchuria, it militarily occupied the zones of its earlier railway concessions and seemed bent on remaining indefinitely. At this same time it was also penetrating Korea.

Diplomatic efforts to check Russia, including Anglo-American efforts to promote an 'Open Door' in China and an Anglo-German agreement of 1900 in support of it, proved ineffective. The British government sought an agreement with Russia recognizing each other's informal spheres of influence in northern and central China respectively, but Russia was not interested. Only Japan, most directly threatened by Russian imperialism, organized for resistance. After provisional agreements and alliance negotiations with Russia had broken down, Japan concluded a limited defensive alliance with Britain in January 1902, ensuring that, if war came, Japan would at least face only one European foe. Before opting for war, however, the Japanese again sought a deal with Russia, essentially on terms of conceding Russia Manchuria for a Japanese free hand in Korea. Arrogance, divided counsels, confusion, and sheer incompetence kept the Russian government from taking Japan seriously until too late. In February 1904 Japan declared war and attacked the Russian naval base at Port Arthur in Manchuria.

The war surprised the world and shocked Russia by a series of Japanese victories, hard-fought and bloody on land in Manchuria but overwhelming at sea. The Russian naval base at Port Arthur was conquered and two Russian fleets destroyed or captured. By mid-1905, however, with Russia facing bankruptcy and revolution at home and Japan nearing the end of its slender resources, both sides needed peace. The peace treaty mediated by the United States satisfied neither but benefited both. Japan gained the Russian concessions in southern Manchuria and a free hand in Korea, which it proceeded to annex and colonize in 1910, while Russia escaped from the war without an indemnity just in time to deal with impending bankruptcy and the worst outbreaks of revolution in European Russia. The real losers were Korea, soon to be a Japanese colony, and China, now facing the Japanese threat alone, and the great winner in international politics, through pure luck, was Britain. A war that Britain had not wanted and that at one point had threatened to drag Britain in brought it huge gains: an end to the Russian threat in China, an extended Anglo-Japanese Alliance in 1905 protecting India, and the chance to deal with a chastened and weakened Russia over central and western Asia. The result of this was an Anglo-Russian Convention in 1907 that divided this whole area, especially Persia, into British and Russian spheres of influence, tacitly but effectively excluding Germany.

This last development marked the culmination of 'new imperialism's' impact on Europe's international politics: the transformation of alliances and alignments between 1890 and 1907 begun by the Franco-Russian alliance, advanced by Italy's partial defection from the Triple Alliance in the direction of France in 1899–1902, further developed in the Anglo-French colonial agreement over Egypt and Morocco in 1904 known as the Entente Cordiale, and finished with the Anglo-Russian Convention. Germany, in 1890 still the centre of European alliances with only an isolated France as a clear opponent, by 1907 found itself isolated with only a weakening, vulnerable Austria-Hungary as a safe ally, France and Russia as its clear opponents, and Britain leaning towards their side. Frustrated in world politics, it faced the threat of encirclement in Europe.

The standard view is that Germany brought this on itself by its dangerous growth in power, its restless, incalculable policies, and especially its attempts to make gains through pressure and threats. Two supposed major instances of the latter are its bullying of France during the First Moroccan Crisis of 1904–6 in an attempt to break up the nascent Anglo-French Entente Cordiale, and its construction from 1898 of a High Seas Fleet that challenged the British navy in Britain's home waters. Both German policies unquestionably proved counterproductive. The Moroccan Crisis drove the British and French closer together, leading to Germany's isolation and diplomatic defeat at the international Conference of Algeciras, and the naval race had much the same effect internationally and met a British naval build-up that Germany could not match.

This much in the standard view is indisputable: German policy and tactics often irritated and antagonized others, and its leaders operated from two wrong assumptions—that Anglo-French and Anglo-Russian rivalries in colonial and world affairs were irreconcilable, so that Germany could exploit them to its advantage, and that a great battle fleet would not only help Germany protect and expand its commerce and empire, but also make it more attractive as an ally, especially for Britain, and make it too risky for anyone (again especially Britain) to attack Germany. (There were also less defensible motives for fleet-building. Admiral Tirpitz, the fleet's architect, hoped to defeat Britain in war, and the Kaiser and much of the nationalist public saw a great fleet as a symbol and requirement of Germany's greatness. However, the risk and alliance theories were the ones followed by the government as a whole.) But it is one thing to show that Germany blundered and had dangerous aims; quite another to prove that these really caused the outcome, or that, had Germany not made them, the overall outcome would have been drastically changed. The difference between these two propositions is illustrated by the most important instance of Germany's aggressive provocations, the naval race. Certainly German policy was a challenge that greatly heightened Anglo-German antagonism. But, if we ask whether Germany could have been expected not to build a fleet, or if without this naval race Britain would not have made its *ententes* with Germany's rivals, the answers are anything but clear. Naval expansion from the 1880s on was a worldwide phenomenon—American, French, Russian, Japanese, even Italian, Austrian, and Turkish. Britain's own naval programme was guided more by technological and fiscal imperatives than the need to respond to Germany's. The patterns of Anglo-German world antagonism, moreover, were set before Germany began building its fleet, and did not change when in 1912–13 Germany effectively dropped out of the race. Most important, the main reason for Britain's *ententes* with Germany's rivals, as scholars have increasingly shown, was not to check Germany but to save the British Empire.

In short, the main explanation for the transformation of alliances and alignments is structural. Once the Great Game changed from European balance to imperialist world politics, Germany was bound

to lose relative to others no matter how it played the game. Besides
the handicaps mentioned earlier, Germany had few individual cards
to play compared to others. The fact that Russia and France were
serious colonial rivals of Britain worked, contrary to German belief,
to Germany's disadvantage. It compelled Britain to deal seriously
with France and Russia, especially after they allied in 1894, and to pay
something for their cooperation or a limit to their hostility, while
Germany had nothing to sell. The Germans were constantly trying to
extort payment for services that the British neither needed nor
wanted, when Britain wanted Germany to stay out of world politics,
confining itself to Europe, where it belonged. As illustration of this,
1901–2, the point in the Boer War at which, according to the leading
study of Anglo-German antagonism, the British began clearly to
identity Germany as an enemy, was also the point, according to the
best studies of German policy during the Boer War, when Germany
was trying hardest to convince Britain that Germany was the friend
Britain needed. Added to Germany's uselessness to Britain as a partner in world politics was its economic challenge, the rapid growth in
industry, commerce, and technology that made it a successful competitor in numerous British-dominated markets. In Britain and elsewhere the perception was that Germany was likely to dominate any
sphere that it could penetrate or share, giving Britain, France, and
Russia, even incipiently the United States and Japan, a common
interest in keeping Germany out.

In short, the competitive–cooperative pattern of imperialist world
politics naturally favoured a collaboration among Germany's rivals to
its disadvantage. Witness the formal and informal agreements and
cooperative actions in various regions of the world in 1890–1907 serving to exclude or restrain Germany: Anglo-Portuguese in South
Africa, Anglo-American in Latin America and the South Seas, the actual working of the Anglo-Japanese alliance in China, Anglo-French-
Russian dealings over the Ottoman Empire and the Berlin-to-Baghdad
Railway. The clearest instances are also the most important. The
Entente Cordiale of 1904, as a colonial agreement, was clearly
anti-German—designed to end Germany's ability to interfere with
British control in Egypt and to exclude Germany from an action in
Morocco (an international question in an area in which Germany had
strong interests) for which France had consulted every other party
but Germany. The Anglo-Russian Convention of 1907 was likewise

designed to exclude Germany from Persia and to ensure Anglo-Russian cooperation to check Germany in the Near and Middle East generally.

This does not suggest any anti-German conspiracy, exonerate Germany or justify its actions, imply sympathy for it, revive the old war-guilt question of the First World War, or support the German war-innocence lie in response to it. It merely applies to international politics a principle we take for granted in commerce: firms that perceive an advantage in combining to eliminate or neutralize a formidable competitor are likely to do so. Germany lost the game of world politics primarily because other major players shared an interest in making Germany lose, a result that reflects the normal nature of unregulated competition in the imperialist marketplace. Recognizing this, we can ask the next more crucial question: could this outcome have been insulated from continental European politics and kept from causing a European war? That is, could Germany have been brought to accept and live with its defeat in world politics, without resorting to violence to reverse it?

Many historians say 'No'. That is, without adopting a determinist view, they point to the actual events and developments of 1908–14 as evidence that Germany refused to accept this outcome and ultimately chose war to reverse it, and cite deep-seated flaws in German politics and society as responsible for this: the dangerous ambitions and erratic impulses of the Kaiser and his court, military independence of civilian control, deep social and political rifts and chronic political crises, the unreformed Prussian and Imperial constitutions, radical middle-class nationalism, militarist and authoritarian élites and traditions, the political immaturity of Germans generally, and so on. Undeniably these traits (far from unique to Germany) made it dangerous before the First World War, and help explain what it did during the war and after it down through the Second World War. However, they do not suffice to answer the question, a counterfactual but central and unavoidable one, of whether Imperial Germany could have been restrained in Europe despite its having lost the world game.

There are reasons for answering 'Yes, conceivably it could'. First, Germany's defeat in world policy was relative and incomplete. Excluded from certain spheres and activities and barred from some gains and colonies, it none the less continued to compete fairly successfully economically in most markets, enterprises, and consortia, and had reasonable prospects of continuing to do so. Secondly, it was still unclear before 1914 what the prizes of the imperialist contest it had lost were actually worth and how long they would last, and already apparent that some acquisitions, including Germany's own colonies, represented assets of little or no value.

A third reason, however, is decisive historically: the actual international competition before and after 1907 demonstrated that Germany could be effectively restrained. Nothing that Germany actually *did* after 1890, as opposed to its attitudes, tactics, and latent aims and ambitions, was as reckless, aggressive, and legally unjustifiable as many of the actions taken by others, especially its opponents—the British in East, Central, and South Africa or western and central Asia; the French in north, west, and central Africa; Italians in Ethiopia and Libya; Americans in the Caribbean, Latin America, and the central and south-west Pacific; the Japanese in Manchuria, Korea, and China; or Russians in the Far East and Central Asia. The only great power that was less aggressive in the imperialist scramble than Germany was Austria-Hungary, and its restraint, unlike Germany's, can be explained mainly by internal weaknesses. Clearly Germany was being successfully restrained by the international system. The contrast between Germany's uncomfortable situation, its dangerous potential, and its actual moderation in conduct shows up strikingly in Germany's military establishment. Constitutionally the military was dangerously uncontrolled; the strategy the High Command had adopted for fighting a probable two-front war (the Schlieffen Plan) was terrifyingly reckless. Yet repeatedly in times of crisis Germany's military leaders showed caution, advising the government against exploiting relatively favourable chances for war in 1904–5, 1908–9, and 1911 and actually neglecting a badly needed expansion of the army until 1912–13.

Thus the European balance system, though strained by the pressures and outcome of the world-policy game, was still working to prevent a great war in Europe. Restraining Germany was the key to this, not because Germany was the only important actor, or the only one that needed restraining, but because by 1907 only Germany was likely to decide to launch a war out of frustration or desperation, or was in a position to do so. This European balance game, however, would not long survive or succeed if the same kind of unregulated competition that had led to a decisive outcome in the world-imperialist contest came to prevail in it. Preventing this implied four basic conditions or rules. First, victory in the world game must not be used to gain a decisive advantage in the European game. Secondly, international competition, hitherto diffused outside Europe or along its periphery and conducted mainly by political and economic weapons, with military force being used mainly against non-Europeans, must not become concentrated directly on Europe and conducted by military confrontations there. Thirdly, European alliances and alignments must remain fairly flexible and permeable to be useful for managing crises, and not become rigid blocs preserved at all cost for security, rendering each alliance's policy hostage to its weaker and more threatened members. Fourthly, a rule implicitly recognized and followed throughout the nineteenth century, effective in preventing or limiting wars, must remain in force: all essential actors must be preserved regardless of shifts in relative advantage, and the European Concert must keep this goal foremost in settling disputes.

The international history of 1908–14 demonstrates how all these vital rules for preserving general European peace were broken.

The descent into the maelstrom, 1908–1914

The Bosnian Crisis of 1908–9, which started the fatal slide, arose from an action, Austria-Hungary's annexation of Bosnia-Herzegovina, that should never have caused serious international trouble at all. It aimed to remove an anomaly that had existed since 1878—Austrian occupation and *de facto* rule of these territories under nominal but empty Ottoman sovereignty—and thereby to consolidate the status quo and eliminate one flashpoint in the Balkans. It was accompanied by a retreat from a more advanced Austrian military position (the Sanjak of Novi-Pazar); had the annexation been accepted and endorsed by the other powers (as it had been in principle more than once since 1878 by Russia and Germany) it might have helped check the cold war that had been developing since 1903 between Austria and its neighbour Serbia. Most important, it was the product of a deal negotiated between the Russian and Austro-Hungarian foreign ministers Izvolski and Aehrenthal on the former's initiative, to help Russia

regain the security and prestige lost in 1904–6 by defeat and revolution. Essentially it traded Russian consent to the annexation for
Austro-Hungarian support for changes at the Turkish Straits favourable to Russia. Successfully carried through, it could have revived the
restraining partnership between Russia and Austria that had kept
them at peace and the Macedonian conflict and other Balkan issues
on ice during the period from 1895 to 1907.

Instead, this potentially valuable bargain broke down, creating a
crisis that foreshadowed that of 1914 and precipitated the arms race
and alliance competition that brought 1914 on. The deal failed partly
because of the actions of one of the principals, but also because of
actions of those not party to the bargain. When Austria announced
the annexation in October 1908, Prince Ferdinand of Bulgaria seized
the occasion to declare Bulgaria's final independence, which was
taken wrongly as proof of Austro-Bulgarian collusion. The Turks and
Serbians protested violently against the annexation, but their protests
could have been ignored or managed. Far worse was the fact that
Izvolski did not make the deal in good faith, intending once Austria
announced the annexation to call for an international conference to
consider it, thus forcing Austria to pay for the annexation with further concessions. In Izvolski's absence, however, other members of
the Russian government convinced the Tsar, who had given his consent, that the deal would outrage public opinion in Russia. Meanwhile Izvolski discovered that the British and French governments
were unwilling to support Russia on the Straits issue. Disavowed by
his regime and foiled of his hoped-for prize, Izvolski claimed that he
had been tricked by Aehrenthal and called for a conference to discuss
the annexation as a unilateral violation of the 1878 Treaty of Berlin
(already by Austrian count violated thirty-two times). The French
reluctantly endorsed the call for the sake of the alliance; the British
did so more heartily in support of the Ottoman Empire.

To see Russia at the height of this imperialist age ask Britain and
France to help it defend the sanctity of the Treaty of Berlin is rather
like watching Bluebeard summon Don Juan and Casanova to a joint
defence of the honour of Sadie Thompson. But, combined with
Turkey's protests and economic boycott and Serbia's mobilization to
back its demand for compensation, this international pressure put
Austria-Hungary under considerable strain, forcing it to call for support from Germany, whom Aehrenthal had kept largely in the dark to

show Austria-Hungary's independence. Germany responded, seeing the chance to teach Russia how useless Western support was. Thus a potentially useful bargain spawned a serious crisis and test of strength and will between opposed alliance systems.

Russia, still too weak to fight Austria much less Germany, was bound to lose. France declined to recognize the *casus foederis,* and the British, though pleased to see Russia alienated from the German powers and focused on the Balkans rather than central Asia, never intended more than limited diplomatic support. Hence once Austria had faced down the international opposition, bought off the Turks, threatened force unless Serbia demobilized, recognized the annexation, and pledged to cease its hostile and subversive activities, Russia either had to make its Serb clients comply, or stand by while Austria invaded Serbia, or fight a hopeless war. The Russian government asked Germany to intervene, hoping that it would build Russia a golden bridge for retreat. Germany did, but it was an iron one—a warning that Russia's only way out was to make Serbia back down. It did, ending the crisis but leaving Russians determined never to suffer such humiliation from the German powers again, sentiments the British and French encouraged.

The Bosnian Crisis had profound effects. It irreparably poisoned Austro-Russian relations, further exacerbated Austro-Serbian ones, tended to make Austria-Hungary even more dependent on Germany, and established a pattern by which crises became tests of the opposed alliance systems. Worst of all, it launched a race in land arms, an arena relatively quiescent in previous decades with greater attention given to naval armaments. Russia gave the initial impetus to this arms race, initially to recover from 1905, later with a great programme adopted in 1912–13 aiming at clear superiority over both German powers combined by 1917. Germany, which for a variety of reasons had not expanded its army proportionate to its population, launched a major expansion in 1913, as did the French with the introduction of three-year service. Even Britain and Belgium were caught up in a competition involving weapons, training, and offensive strategies and war plans as well as numbers. Austria-Hungary, which tried to compete but could not because of its fiscal, political, and constitutional-dualist problems, felt itself falling from the ranks of great powers. Italy, which also tried with even less success, never really attained that status. With the arms race went a militarization of diplomacy; all subsequent crises were prolonged and marked by mounting levels of tension and antagonism, difficult, unsatisfactory resolutions, and a quest for victory for one's own bloc.

The Second Moroccan Crisis (or 'Agadir Incident') of 1911 exemplified this. The initial French provocation, a direct takeover of Morocco in violation of recent treaties, was answered by German gunboat diplomacy to back its demand for compensation. An ostentatious British warning to both parties, but most directly to Germany, not to shut Britain out of any agreement raised the tension and stakes still further. In the final settlement, France gained Morocco with only minimal compensations to Germany, but the main result was to heighten both German frustration and French fears and to tighten the links between Britain and France to include naval cooperation and military consultation. The takeover of Morocco had a further snowball effect, actually foreseen and to some degree prepared for in advance. Italy now cashed in on its position between the two camps and its pledges from both sides to seize Libya, nominally Ottoman territory, not because Libya was concretely worth anything, but to raise its own prestige and ease a current domestic crisis by expansion abroad. Though the great powers reacted calmly—the Austrians took Italy seriously as a foe, and they were glad to see it distracted in North Africa—this aggression also escalated. Unable to pacify the nomadic tribes in the Libyan desert, Italy declared war on the Ottoman Sultan, formally annexed Libya, and carried its military operations into the Straits and the eastern Mediterranean, the most dangerous flashpoint in Europe.

This Italian move, perhaps the single most irresponsible action by a major power before 1914, paved the way for the worst pre-war crisis, caused by the two Balkan Wars of 1912–13. Russia contributed to it in 1912 by promoting a Russian-led Balkan League, which ultimately included Serbia, Bulgaria, and Greece, to give Russia exclusive leadership in Balkan politics. The French, tardily informed of Russia's initiative, immediately recognized it as a recipe for war against the Ottoman Empire and a direct challenge to Austria-Hungary, but went along for the sake of their alliance. Russia did not want a Balkan war (in fact, it hoped to bring the Turks in), but its Balkan clients, assured of Russian protection and seeing Turkey weakened, halted their bitter struggle among themselves over Macedonia for a joint attack on Turkey in October 1912.

This set off a year-long crisis far too complicated to relate here. From a systemic standpoint, European diplomacy, which failed at the last minute to prevent the war, barely managed in the end to prevent a general war, but the European Concert, acting through a London conference chaired by the British Foreign Secretary Sir Edward Grey, can hardly be said to have controlled the course or outcome of events. By December Turkey's forces had surprisingly collapsed, forcing Russia to intervene to stop the Bulgarians or Greeks from taking Constantinople and Austria and Italy to check the Serbian–Montenegrin–Greek advance into the proposed independent principality of Albania. Then Russian and Concert pressure failed to prevent a new war among the victors over the spoils. In mid-1913 the Serbs and Greeks, joined by the Turks and aided by Romanian mobilization and intervention, completely defeated the main victor of 1912, Bulgaria, and seized most of the spoils. The Treaty of Bucharest in August, reached largely without Concert control, ended this second war but not the crisis. A prolonged Austro-Serbian confrontation over the Serbian seizure of territories designated for Albania brought them closer than ever to actual war before an Austrian ultimatum forced a Serbian withdrawal.

Peace had been saved, but barely, and the whole European balance had been changed. In the Balkans Austria-Hungary had suffered a huge defeat. Serbia, its worst enemy, emerged from the wars almost doubled in size and confidence, while Bulgaria, Serbia's rival, was exhausted and impotent. The Ottoman Empire, the only state representing no potential threat to Austrian interests, was now virtually gone from the scene; Romania, hitherto a secret ally, was alienated, openly independent, and ardently courted by Russia and France. Italy, nominally an ally but actually a rival in the western Balkans and Adriatic, competed directly with it for control of Albania. As for Russia, though delighted by the reversal of 1909, it saw its own gains as unstable until the Balkan League was strengthened and extended and incomplete until Russia controlled the fate of the Turkish Straits. It therefore bent its efforts, now with open French support, on reconciling Serbia and Bulgaria, adding Romania and Turkey to the league, keeping Austria-Hungary isolated, and combating German influence.

In the Western, especially British, view Concert diplomacy in 1912–13 was a success, and a recipe for managing future crises. Britain had restrained Russia, Germany had held back Austria, a general war had been averted, and the overall balance of power preserved. The Balkans were not Britain's problem, and Austria's plight was its own concern and Germany's. The worst danger to Britain, the defection of Russia to Germany and a resultant continental league, seemed more remote than ever. France's President Poincaré was equally satisfied for somewhat different reasons. The two alliance blocs had survived intact, with the Russo-French one this time proving more solid, effective, and successful than the Austro-German. Maintaining these blocs rigid and unchanged was the key to peace and security. Germany, which had cooperated with Britain in the hopes of promoting British neutrality *vis-à-vis* the continent, by late 1913 had become sufficiently pessimistic on this score and about Austria-Hungary's plight to back the latter's demand for strong support to arrest its decline.

Thus by 1914 the vital prerequisites for peace were being systematically negated and those for war fulfilled. The combination that had brought the Triple Entente success in imperialism was now effective in Europe, with Russia and France expecting to attain military superiority by 1917 and Britain, though declining a direct alliance, aligned firmly with them, partly to maintain a European 'balance', but mainly to retain friendships vital to its world position. Power-political competition, once diffused on the periphery, was now deliberately concentrated on the two most dangerous fault-lines in Europe, the Rhine and the Balkans. Flexibility and permeability in alliances were replaced by a conscious separation and opposition of military blocs, intended to eliminate uncertainty and miscalculation but actually working to tie Russia's policy and fate more tightly to Serbia, France's to Russia, Germany's to Austria-Hungary, and ultimately Britain's to France. Most important, one essential actor, Austria-Hungary, had concluded from bitter experience that Concert diplomacy was no longer a means to preserve its great power status and vital interests, but a fatal snare: the other great powers, including Germany, used it to make Austria pay the collective costs of international settlements and to paralyse its capacity for action still further. Hence its government resolved to break with the Concert and to arrest its decline through strong independent action, and the German government, equally pessimistic about its one remaining ally, resolved to support it.

The scenario this suggests, in which by 1914 the question had become less whether or not general war would break out, but when and how, seems too determinist, and its implication that Austria and Germany acted out of desperation and exhaustion of alternatives sounds like an old, discredited whitewash. No such charge can apply in regard to the immediate origins of the war in the so-called July Crisis sparked by the assassination of Archduke Francis Ferdinand by Bosnian Serb terrorists. Each stage of it was contingent; each involved conscious governmental decisions that conceivably could have gone otherwise. This applies to the decision of the Austrian government to change its original plan of action from one of forcing Romania back publicly into alliance to one of eliminating Serbia as a political factor in the Balkans; to Austria's demand for German support and Germany's blank cheque; to Austria's ultimatum to Serbia and Serbia's decision partly to reject it; to Russia's advice and consent to this decision; to Austria's declaration of war on Serbia; to Russia's partial mobilization against Austria followed by full mobilization against Germany; to Germany's declaration of war on Russia; to its implementation of the Schlieffen Plan by the invasion of France and Belgium, and to Britain's declaration of war on Germany. Throughout this process the Central Powers held the initiative and other powers reacted to it; they started the war.

Yet the answer to 'Who started the war?' does not constitute an answer to 'What caused the war?' For this one needs to get beyond the usual answers, all in different ways true but also inadequate, to one that underlies them all and yields more insight. There are three such broad answers, which, oversimplified, go as follows. First, Austria and Germany caused the war by gambling on a local war to recoup their losses and gain or regain hegemony in Europe (behind which reckless gamble, it is often said, lay a desire to save their unreformed domestic structures by foreign policy victories). Secondly, Europe stumbled into war through an accumulation of unresolved conflicts, rivalries, unreconciled purposes and ambitions, hatreds, pressures, and entangling commitments that had repeatedly threatened war earlier and finally escaped control this time. The third is closer to a satisfactory answer but still inadequate: war came because the rules, norms, and practices of European politics had become so ruthlessly competitive that the very devices used to prevent war actually helped cause it. The alternative answer suggested here, which includes parts of all the above while rejecting others, is deceptively simple: the war was caused by a general long-term failure of European governments to do certain specific things necessary to keep peace viable, while at the same time repeatedly doing things that made war likely, so that the resources for peace were finally exhausted.[1]

The explanation in terms of Austro-German aggression, correct for the July Crisis, will not do as an overall answer for various reasons; only the more important will be mentioned here. First, that it begs the question of where aggression begins, and who is attacking or defending the status quo. The initial aggressive act in the crisis itself came from Serbia, part of a programme of state-sponsored terrorism in the service of a Great Serb nationalist programme and ideology directed against the very existence of Austria-Hungary. The answer also ignores the questions of whether Austria-Hungary and Germany could have afforded not to make some kind of drastic response to their situation in 1914, or been expected not to, and what alternatives not involving the risk of crisis and general war still existed. Most important, this answer with its aggressor/defender distinction assumes that the two sides at this juncture were playing two different games, one bellicose, the other peaceful, when all were really playing essentially the same game by much the same rules. No power desired general war, but all preferred it to other outcomes. Serbia preferred war to abandoning its anti-Austrian national programme, Austria-Hungary preferred it to a further decline in its status and security, Russia to another 'humiliation' like 1908–9, Germany to the collapse or defection of its last major ally and a prospective military inferiority to France and Russia, France to the loss of its Russian alliance and instant inferiority to Germany, Britain to the defeat or defection of France and German domination of the continent. All saw existing trends (and the status quo in international politics is always a trend on which calculations are based, not a static condition) in similar fashion, and concluded that the game was approaching a turning point in the near future. Three powers, seeing victory ahead, favoured

---

[1] An analogy: this is like explaining a man's fatal heart attack by going from saying (*a*) it was caused by overexertion, to (*b*) it was a coronary thrombosis caused by a blocked artery, to (*c*) it resulted from a long history of high blood pressure, to (*d*) it was caused by his consistent failure to take his medicine or his doctor's advice on smoking, diet, and exercise. One could concede that the first three explanations are all true, but still insist that only the last is satisfactory in human, historical terms.

a 'peaceful' continuation of the 'status quo.' Two others sensed impending defeat and determined to change it.

All, moreover, had the same requirement for 'peace': that their rivals accept their victory. Without question Austria-Hungary and Germany, in trying for a local war in 1914, consciously risked a general war and in a sense opted for one. But their opponents were gambling similarly in the longer term. Serbia and Russia wagered directly and France and Britain tacitly (the latter trying not to think about it) that somehow Austria-Hungary's demise, which all anticipated, would occur quietly and that Germany would accept both this demise and its resultant inferiority to its foes—a gamble less obviously aggressive but just as risky and foolish as the Austro-German one. In a sense, the European powers went to war in 1914 because they thought alike and agreed with one another.

As for saying that the war resulted from mounting pressures, strains, enmities, and crises until one finally got out of hand, the trouble is simply that there is too much evidence right to the end that governments acted on the basis of calculation. They knew what they were doing, however much they might feel that they had no other choice.

This seems to confirm the third explanation: war came because imperialism, mass politics, fervent nationalism, cut-throat economic competition, all-out arms races, and Social Darwinism had made international relations too ruthless for peaceful compromise and coexistence. Certainly this answer comes closer; this essay seems to point to it. Yet here again the evidence shows that these conditions had arisen well before 1914, and that governments even in 1914 were not the helpless pawns of them.

A deeper answer lies not in what finally triumphed in 1914, a *va banque* spirit in international competition, but in what finally disappeared, means and institutions for limiting the stakes and assuring that competition would remain within tolerable limits. In other words, the better question is not 'What caused the war in 1914?' but 'What had stopped war until 1914, and no longer could?'[2] The First World War is often explained as resulting from Germany's growth in power and bid for hegemony, so that stronger deterrence of Germany

---

[2] To resort to another medical analogy: this is like asking not what particular disease killed a patient, but why his body's defences against it succumbed.

(for example, a clear advance warning by Britain that it would stand by France) might have preserved peace. But Germany and Austria-Hungary thought they were losing, not winning, the power competition in 1914; Germany especially saw this as its last good chance to avert defeat in the near future. Moreover, the Germans anticipated and reckoned with a British entry into the war sooner or later. Most important, deterrence, which doubtless had helped stop Europe at the brink on previous occasions, was tried in 1914 and failed. The fatal problem was the absence not of deterrence but of assurance. Europe had remained generally peaceful throughout the nineteenth century not by the natural workings of the balance of power, but by restraints on it—a system of rules, norms, and practices enabling actors, especially the great powers, to act on the assumption that rivalry and competition, though inescapable, would not destroy them. The original Vienna system of guarantees had broken down and been discarded, but new versions of deterrence/assurance had emerged or survived providing enough such confidence to keep the system going. By 1914 that belief was gone, replaced by the conviction that the next, inevitable war would be one fought not within limits by governments, but to the death by whole peoples—a belief that helped postpone war till 1914 and bring it on then. The fund of assurances and mutual restraints had run out; everyone's hopes for peace rested on making others accept the unacceptable. July 1914 marks not just the onset of war, but the exhaustion of peace.

6

Overseas expansion, imperialism, and empire, 1815–1914

A. G. Hopkins

The nineteenth century was a period of unparalleled imperial expansion. Extraordinary voyages of discovery in previous centuries had enabled cartographers to inscribe other continents on what Burke called 'the Great Map of mankind'. Travellers from Marco Polo onwards had created a rich and often fanciful literature depicting the lives of noble and ignoble savages in varying states of nature. Parts of the world, notably the Americas and the Indies, had already experienced European conquest and rule. Europeans, in turn, had been influenced by what they read and by what they consumed. Colonial imports—from spices to silver, from potatoes to tobacco, from sugar to tea—had brought the exotic to town and countryside alike. It is scarcely surprising that contemporaries were impressed by their own exploratory energy and astonished by its consequences, or that they quickly developed a fascination with distant lands, as the immediate success of Defoe's *Robinson Crusoe* (1719) clearly shows.

Despite the magnitude of these developments, they were overtaken and eventually eclipsed in the nineteenth century. The application of science, especially new technology, to the means of production, communication, and coercion, gave Europe a penetrative capacity far in excess of anything available to merchant venturers and *conquistadors*. It became possible to convert mastery of the sea to ascendancy on land in new and decisive ways, and to move the frontiers of

European influence deep into the still-uncharted interior of vast continents. Since art mimics life, and life was changing with astonishing rapidity, it is no coincidence that the growth of the new science was accompanied by the rise of science fiction as a novel field of literary speculation. When Jules Verne invited his readers to embark on a *Journey to the Centre of the Earth* in 1864, the expedition, fantastic though it was, must have seemed a logical extension of the paths being cut by explorers in the real world, where, at that time, the source of the Nile was still disputed and Stanley had yet to keep his fateful *rendez-vous* with Livingstone in the middle of the Dark Continent. By the close of the century, however, exploration had been overtaken by partition, and partition, in turn, by occupation. Large segments of other continents had been annexed, and 'spheres of influence' established over much of the Middle East, the Far East, and Latin America. Even the penguins of the Antarctic, the last continent, had been obliged to acknowledge the suzerainty of the great powers. The peculiar combination of attraction and repulsion that had long characterized Europe's encounter with non-European societies found heightened expression and achieved popular appeal. But Conrad's world, as described in *Heart of Darkness* (1902), was very different from that of Defoe. By the time Kurtz met his end in the depths of Leopold's Congo, the colonial mission had been found, and innocence, like Paradise, had been lost.

Ideology and scholarship in the study of imperialism

If the broad dimensions of Europe's expansion overseas are uncontroversial, every other aspect of the subject has been exposed to intense scrutiny and debate. The intellectual giants of the period, from Adam Smith to Lenin, and including, *en route,* James Mill, Karl Marx, and J. A. Hobson among many others, formulated interpretations of the causes and consequences of imperialism that reverberated throughout the nineteenth century—and beyond to the present day. Eminent scholars, such as Seeley, Froud, and Leroy-Beaulieu, placed the study of modern empires on a professional footing for the first time, though, since they were public figures as well as academics, their knowledge served political purposes too. As the subject began, so it continued—in energetic controversy kept in vigour by the changes in the shape of the international order and of the empires contained within it.

This potent mixture of scholarship and ideology has left a permanent imprint on the historical literature: studies of the greatest subtlety jostle with work of the most blatant axe-grinding; beams of illumination meet shafts of darkness. Given the diversity and individuality of the many thousands of contributions made in the course of the present century alone, any historiographical generalization is bound to dispense injustice. Yet it is necessary to put some signposts in the ground if the main contours of the subject are to become intelligible. On this basis, and with other numerous reservations implied, it can be said that scholarly opinion was split from the outset into two camps. Although both contained multiple internal divisions, each was united in recognizing the superiority of its own objective scholarship and the ideological bias of its opponents. They agreed, exceptionally, on drawing a line of battle under the main problems requiring explanation: the causes of empire-building, the means of control, the effects of European rule, and the future of imperialism. Beyond this point, however, hostilities took the form of a war of attrition that has lasted almost to the present day.

One camp, drawing on radical intellectual sources, and typically (though not necessarily) on Marx, linked nineteenth-century imperialism to the development of industrial capitalism. According to this interpretation, the process of capital accumulation generated internal contradictions that found expression during the last quarter of the century in new and all-encompassing forms of imperialism. The struggle for control of the world was not confined to the acquisition of colonies: it culminated, in Lenin's view, in the First World War. Imperialism, like capitalism, knew no frontiers: it arose not only where there were visible constitutional ties but where economic integration created what Lenin called 'semi-colonies'. Although capitalism was everywhere aggressive and exploitative, it was also inescapably progressive in 'showing the face of the future' (as Marx put it) to the rest of the world. The spread of capitalism through the agency of imperialism was destined, in dialectical fashion, to throw up the forces that would eventually engineer the downfall of colonialism and usher in a new, socialist order. This line of argument, much elaborated and refined by its advocates, was appealing because it offered both a coherent view of the modern world and a plan of action for changing it.

The other camp, larger in number but less focused in purpose, was grouped around a liberal–conservative banner. Critics and defenders of empire here found common cause in rejecting Marxism and elaborating a range of alternative accounts of empire and imperialism. Against mono-causal economic analysis (with its alarming predictions about the demise of capitalism) was ranged a multiplicity of diplomatic, political, social, and cultural, as well as economic, explanations of empire-building; against the determinism of impersonal forces was set the role of individuals and of chance. Eurocentrism was countered by the 'ex-centric' thesis, which shifted causation to the periphery by emphasizing the role of sub-imperialists, or men-on-the-spot, such as Rhodes, Peters, and Pavie. The notion of informal empire (a liberal variant of Lenin's concept of semi-colonies) was deployed against the Marxists to demonstrate that Europe's expansion was not identified exclusively or even mainly with the 'new imperialism' that was supposed to have characterized the last quarter of the nineteenth century. Lenin's belief that capitalism was inherently aggressive was met by Schumpeter's argument that it was pacific by nature and assertive by default. The claim that imperialism was exploitative provoked alternative exercises in historical accounting to show that it brought benefits. The prediction that European influence would be overthrown by revolution was countered by the argument that evolution would produce devolution in the shape of independent states within a wider union of Commonwealth or Community.

The long-running debate between the two camps has been repeatedly surveyed and summarized, and no purpose is served by picking over it again here. This is a case where familiarity breeds respect, but also boredom. The issues in dispute remain very much alive and on the agenda, but current approaches are no longer derived, however indirectly, from the conflict between capitalism and socialism. Changes in the world at large combined with shifting intellectual interests within the scholarly community have opened the subject to new ideas and given it a new lease of life. These recent developments, some of which remain prospective, are of much greater interest today than the older, stereotyped debate, especially to readers who live in a post-imperial age.

The first important external influence was the end of the European empires in the 1960s, an event that broke up the subject as well as the constituents. As attention moved from the centre to the periphery, Eurocentric perspectives lost impetus and were overtaken by research on indigenous peoples and by the production of 'national' histories of newly independent states. Doubt was cast on the desirability as well as the possibility of continuing to write imperial history in a decolonized world. The second important external influence was the collapse (and decolonization) of the Soviet empire. The socialist experiment did not wither away: it imploded, taking with it much of the credibility of radical assessments of capitalism and imperialism. By the close of the twentieth century, decolonization had ceased to be a contemporary struggle and had become history. It is salutary to recall that India celebrated fifty years of independence in 1997: the younger generation and the middle-aged have no first-hand knowledge of colonial rule. Distance does not necessarily lend enchantment, but it ought to assist detachment.

This is not to say that we have reached 'the end of ideology' and will bask henceforth in the warm rays of capitalist triumphalism. The future is likely to play tricks on the present generation of soothsayers and historians, just as it has in the past, and ideological commitment will not be eliminated from the study of imperialism or from the study of history in general. Nevertheless, the end of the great age of empires undoubtedly has profound implications for the way in which the subject will be treated in future. Liberated from the heavy censorship of their times, which obliged them to choose between alienating either colonial peoples or the warriors shielding the Free World, scholars can begin to formulate fresh views on an old subject. To study the history of imperialism and empire is now to investigate an important slice of world history, not to be obliged to take sides in an ideological debate on topical issues.

These sweeping changes in the international order have merged with shifting scholarly priorities (with which they are entwined). In this matter, the study of the non-European world has reflected developments in European historiography. History has long since ceased to be the study of kings and princes or even mainly of constitutional and political issues. The alternative 'history from below' has itself been joined by forms of history that cut vertical rather than horizontal lines: the history of the environment, of demography, of gender, and of culture are examples of dimensions of the past that can now be put together to create a new *histoire totale*.

These intellectual trends, allied to the liberating consequences of the end of the Cold War, have begun to stimulate a fundamental reconsideration of European perspectives on the non-European world. The most prominent current influence is that of cultural history, which has led to a rash of studies of European images of other societies. This particular interest is now in danger of becoming excessively fashionable, but other contributions to cultural history, such as studies of propaganda, education, and sport, have made an impact too, and still have considerable potential. Cultural history has also joined with social history to stimulate new thinking about ethnicity and gender. Work in other branches of history is less immediately appealing at present, but arguably is at least of equal importance. The economic theme in empire-building has been rethought in ways that cut across traditional boundaries between Marxists and others, and has been extended into the non-European world through studies of the environment, the labour force, and transnational corporations, which have helped to revive interest in business history. Political and diplomatic history, the traditional staples of the subject, are being recast in a number of ways: one involves a reconsideration of the creation of 'nation' states at home and abroad; another seeks to carry the study of decision-making down to the domestic roots of politics and into the analysis of the pressure groups that formed the 'unofficial mind' of imperialism. The study of Christian missions is one example of a field of research that is experiencing a revival as a result of this development. The history of science has received new impetus from studies of the relationship between disease, medication, and the exercise of colonial authority. Finally, though the illustrations could be multiplied, fresh thought is being given to the overt coercive power of the state. Military history, for example, has expanded beyond the study of battles, and now encompasses matters such as the social basis of recruitment, the cultivation of a combative ethos in a civil society, and the 'policing' of subject peoples.

These developments present a problem and an opportunity. The problem is to some degree contained in the difficulty of generalizing about an entity called 'Europe', given the diversity of the historiography and the uneven state of the literature on the component 'nation' states. But we can now see that there is a new difficulty to add to this long-standing one: the bulk of the historiographical inheritance, valuable though it is, belongs to an era that has now passed. The opportunity arises from the fact that the post-imperial order (or disorder, as it has been called) has prompted a fresh set of questions about Europe's historic relations with the rest of the world. These questions have begun to open up new lines of enquiry and to revitalize old ones. Unfortunately, research is not yet sufficiently advanced to enable an entirely fresh synthesis to be produced. The survey that follows will try to establish bridges between the two at what seem to be the most promising crossing points. Even so, the juncture will be imperfect. The advantage, such as it is, will be to suggest how frontiers long considered closed can now be reopened.

There remains, however, one final preliminary matter: the definition of the problem under review. It is a commonplace that the terms of a debate strongly influence its course and conclusions. It is also the case that specialists on the history of imperialism and empires very rarely pause to explain the meaning they attach to key words. To do so now is to open up immense possibilities that cannot be explored in the space available. The summary statement offered here will not resolve problems that are endemic to the subject, but it should serve the more restricted purpose of guiding the reader through the present discussion.

The terms 'expansion' and 'imperialism' are often used as if they were interchangeable. To do so, however, is to lose a valuable distinction. Here, expansion will be treated as the genus and imperialism as a species. Europe's expansion overseas is an inclusive term: if imperialism is removed for separate study, expansion can be reserved for international movements (whether of people, trade, or ideas) that were not imperialistic. Imperialism can then be used to refer to a particular form of expansion, one marked by inequality and subordination, and by the integration of a client or satellite state into the more powerful host or 'mother' country. Note, however, that integration is always incomplete: an empire remains a multi-ethnic conglomerate; if it assimilates subject peoples fully, it becomes an enlarged nation state.

On this view, imperialism is a large branch of the study of power in international relations, and is not confined to constitutional or even political ties. In other words, imperialism can exist without an empire being created. As we shall see, the imperialism of intent did not always lead to an imperialism of result. When it did, the test of success was not whether the colours on the map were repainted, as they were, for example, in the case of India, but whether the sovereignty or independence of the recipient was effectively and significantly diminished, as it was, arguably, in the case of Argentina. Where the colours did change, a formal empire came into being, and with it colonies and overseas territories. But if we look only at India and Indo-China and ignore Argentina and the Ottoman Empire, we omit a sizeable chunk of the substance of imperialist relations in the nineteenth century—the 'semi-colonies' and the 'informal' or 'invisible' empire. This approach has the associated merit of separating cause and consequence. Ideologically driven accounts of imperialism inferred results, whether costs or benefits, from assumptions about motivation: if imperialism was necessarily exploitative in intent, the inevitable outcome was underdevelopment; if it was inherently benign, the consequences were beneficial. But subordination to imperialism does not, of itself, entail one result, and the result that applies at one moment may well alter with the passage of time.

These general developments and reflections must now be set in motion. There are various options, all of them imperfect, for combining narrative and analysis. The device adopted here is to take a series of photographs of Europe's relations with the non-European world from three vantage points: 1815, 1870, and 1914. The pictures taken 'before' (in 1815) and 'after' (in 1914) will show a marked contrast. The intervening position (1870) falls more or less exactly in between the two, but the year has been chosen less for reasons of chronological symmetry than because it marks, as well as any single date can, a point of departure. The global order that existed in 1815 showed distinct signs of change after 1850; by 1870 the manifestations of these changes were readily apparent; by 1914 they had transformed the world.

The European empires in 1815

The long and debilitating conflict between Britain and France was a struggle for the mastery of the world as well as of Europe. Following the Peace of Paris in 1763, France had been excluded from the two greatest prizes: North America and India. Subsequently, first under Choiseul's direction and then under the aggressive leadership of Napoleon Bonaparte, the French had attempted to reclaim and extend their lost position. It is true that Napoleon's imperial ambitions were confined mainly to Europe, but his purpose could not be accomplished without devising a global strategy to counter Britain's naval and colonial strength. The direct invasion of Britain had also been planned and nearly executed. The consequent threat to monarchy, property, and established religion had produced the unintended result of strengthening national solidarity. Reliable John Bull emerged from party politics to become a symbol of national character; lions, *rampant* and *couchant*, became popular emblems of national strength. Britain's triumph at Trafalgar in 1805 delivered supremacy over the oceans; Waterloo effectively levelled France on the continent of Europe and kept it there long enough for the Pax Britannica to become an entrenched reality for the greater part of the century.

Indeed, from the standpoint of continental Europe, the post-war years were ones of imperial retreat. The peace settlement deprived France of all its colonies, as well as its temporary wartime gains. Only a handful of unimportant territories were restored: Martinique and Guadeloupe in the Caribbean, a few islands in the Atlantic, the small colony of Guyane in South America, five tiny outposts in India, and one in Senegal. On any account, this was a poor return for a half-century of endeavour. In the longer term, it is true that France tried to re-establish its place as a colonial power: Algiers was taken in 1830; a number of islands in the Indian and Pacific oceans were annexed in the 1840s, when France made an effort to secure strategic naval bases; and Louis Napoleon (Napoleon III) launched a speculative takeover for Mexico in 1863–7. But the results did not match the intentions. Algiers was not Algeria: the conquest of the country took forty years; its settlement took even longer. The naval bases served a purpose, but for the most part were crumbs left by the British. The Mexican adventure was a fiasco. When the Foreign Legion trudged out of Mexico City in 1867, France had still to establish a significant presence in the non-European world.

Even greater disasters overtook the once mighty empires of Spain and Portugal. The Spanish empire in the New World, long a rich source of silver and legend, broke up under the disabling combination of Napoleonic conquest at home and the demands of colonists on the periphery. In the 1810s and 1820s, Spanish rule was replaced by a string of independent republics in Central and South America—from Mexico to Argentina and nearly all points in between. Spain retained Cuba, Puerto Rico, and the Philippines, but a powerful eyeglass was needed to find any other Spanish possessions in the non-European world. Portugal was also brought low. Napoleon's invasion in 1807 overturned the Portuguese government and forced the regent and his court to take refuge in Brazil. This dramatic event (facilitated by the British navy's experienced removal service) elevated the status of Brazil and opened the way to further radical political change. Brazil became an equal partner in the United Kingdom formed with Portugal in 1815, and declared its independence in 1822. With this development, Portugal lost by far its most important overseas possession. It retained footholds in Asia (principally Goa, Macau, and part of Timor), but its oriental empire had long since fallen from its position of eminence in the sixteenth century, even though nostalgia for the 'golden age' lived on—as it does today in the historiography of the subject. Portugal also had claims to central Africa, but these were larger on the map than in reality. The settlements in Mozambique were a modest legacy of its declining Indian connections; the wealth of Angola depended on the slave trade, which Portugal's 'oldest ally', Britain, had decided to outlaw.

The Dutch, having displaced the Portuguese in Asia in the seventeenth century, suffered in the eighteenth century from long-running wars with France, culminating in the ultimate humiliation of conquest (1795) and annexation (1810). As London replaced Amsterdam as the commercial and financial capital of Europe, the British had further cause to congratulate themselves on their wisdom in continuing to live on an island. The Dutch held on to their possessions in Indonesia and their few, small islands in the Caribbean, but only because they received first military and then diplomatic support from

Britain. The Anglo-Dutch Treaty of 1824 recognized Indonesia as being a Dutch sphere of influence, and provided a guarantee for a continuing imperial presence. By then, however, the Netherlands, like Spain and Portugal, was entering a period of civil turmoil that directed its attention and energy more towards domestic than overseas affairs.

This Age of Revolutions had a profound effect on the British Empire too. The loss of the American colonies in 1783 was by any standards, even those of Spain, a major imperial disaster, even if the long-term consequences for Anglo-US relations were, as we now know, more reassuring. It was long thought that the ensuing political trauma caused a reaction in Britain against further colonial annexations, and that rising anti-imperial sentiment was reinforced by the timely publication of Adam Smith's *Wealth of Nations* (1776), which condemned the mercantilist restrictions that made empire such a high-cost enterprise: 'the home consumers', Smith argued, 'have been burdened with the whole expense of maintaining and defending that empire.' The idea that there was a growing trend away from empire from the late eighteenth century provided the basis for the view that the ensuing era of free trade was essentially anti-imperialist. This assumption had a profound influence on the whole conception of the subject. In particular, it encouraged the belief that much of the nineteenth century was a period of imperial quiescence; the problem then became one of understanding the sudden renewal of imperialist rivalries during the last quarter of the century. As we have seen, this issue became crystallized in the debate over 'new' imperialism that preoccupied much of the traditional historiography.

This interpretation is no longer thought to be persuasive. Britain's record after the loss of the American colonies is scarcely that of an anti-imperial power. It held onto the rest of its empire, including British North America (subsequently Canada), the most valuable islands in the Caribbean, and India, and retained the most desirable of its wartime gains, such as Malta and Cape Town. Britain also pushed ahead with further annexations in India (including Ceylon) during the French wars, and continued to make substantial acquisitions there down to the 1840s, notably Sind (1843) and the Punjab (1849). Annexations in neighbouring Burma following the wars of 1824–6 and 1852 laid the foundation of British power there; the acquisition of the vital port of Singapore in 1819 provided a launching point for subsequent moves into the Malaysian peninsular as well as command over routes to the Far East. The occupation of other key ports, such as Aden (1839), Hong Kong (1842), Labuan in North Borneo (1846), and Lagos in West Africa (1851), was intended to achieve the wider purpose of controlling oceans and opening hinterlands. In addition, deliberate efforts were made to promote emigration and settlement, both by expanding existing colonies in British North America and Australia, and by developing new ones in South Africa (via Cape Town) and New Zealand (1840). None of these frontiers was rolled back effortlessly: force was present; hostilities often followed.

These formal extensions of empire, impressive though they are, do not convey the full extent of Britain's growing presence in the non-European world. Overseas expansion also increased Britain's informal influence in ways that conform to the definition of imperialism offered earlier. In 1838, for example, a free-trade treaty agreed with the Ottoman Empire safeguarded the position of European minorities, subjected tariffs to external control, and eliminated state monopolies. The treaty was followed by a package of modernizing reforms offered on terms that the Ottomans could scarcely refuse. After a show of force, a similar free-trade treaty was signed with Persia in 1841. At about the same time, Britain fought two wars with China in 1839–42 and 1856–60, and gained Hong Kong and a string of Treaty Ports (headed by Shanghai) that were intended to promote British trade with the largely untapped interior. But the greatest scope for creating an informal 'empire' lay in Latin America. As Canning, the Foreign Secretary, put it in 1824 in a now celebrated phrase: 'Spanish America is free, and if we do not mismanage our affairs badly, she is English.' The idea was to shape the newly independent republics through trade, investment, and the export of British liberalism, so that they would become valued (and dependent) commercial partners and also congenial allies. The degree of success resulting from this endeavour has been the subject of a considerable debate among modern scholars, and has now become the classic historical test of theories of informal or invisible empire.

If it is agreed that the first half of the nineteenth century saw substantial formal additions to the British Empire, and if it is further agreed that Britain's informal presence and influence also expanded (even if the degree of expansion is contested), then it is clearly impossible to accept the proposition that there was a long period of anti-imperialism between two phases of empire, one old and one new. We are faced, instead, with the problem of explaining a whole range of notable extensions to Britain's effective presence in the non-European world during the first half of the nineteenth century.

As might be expected, there are many explanations on offer. The most influential, by far, focuses on the Industrial Revolution, which began in the late eighteenth century. Industrialization distinguished Britain's economic development from that of other European states at this time; it seems reasonable to suppose that it can also account for Britain's much greater success overseas as well. Unfortunately—for simplicity has powerful attractions—the case, as stated, needs revision as well as merely elaboration. Overseas trade was less important in the early stages of the Industrial Revolution than was once thought; where it was important, the outstanding connections tended to be ones that already existed—for example, with the West Indies and North America. Moreover, free trade was not promoted by a rising bourgeoisie carrying *The Wealth of Nations* in one hand and a cheque book in the other. New industries grew up within the protection of mercantilist restrictions, which most manufacturers were anxious to cling to for as long as possible, and free trade was not established fully until 1850, following the abolition of the Corn Laws in 1846 and the Navigation Acts in 1849.

This does not mean that we are obliged to turn away from economic interpretations of imperialism or to fall back on explanations based on chance and circumstance. The Industrial Revolution is still important in accounting for Britain's increasingly expansive presence in the non-European world, but its role has now to be recast. Clear signs of a systematic connection between the process of industrialization and imperialism date from the 1830s and 1840s, when Palmerston's gunboats and treaty-gathering agencies were fully employed, and when emigration schemes were being busily canvassed. However, this activity was a manifestation not of the triumph of industry but of its emerging difficulties. The staple exports (especially cotton goods) were suffering from overproduction and falling profits and needed new markets, which could not be obtained readily in protectionist Europe. At the same time, population growth was outstripping domestic food supplies, and rising unemployment was generating a challenge to civil order, as the

Chartist movement vividly illustrates. The decision to abandon mercantilism was not the culmination of the effortless advance of industry, but a hazardous experiment designed to provide new markets for manufactures and new sources of food for the urban population. Speaking in 1849, Peel was certain that the abolition of the Corn Laws had enabled Britain 'to pass triumphantly through that storm which convulsed other nations' in the previous year.

The explanation of British 'exceptionalism' does not stop with a revised view of the development of modern manufacturing. It has been argued recently that the established historiography has exaggerated the place of the Industrial Revolution in modern British history, and that attention needs to be shifted to the development of finance and commercial services, symbolized by the rise of London as the pre-eminent centre of world trade and by the emergence of the pound sterling as the leading international currency. London and the Home Counties were major centres of service-sector employment; the City generated vital overseas earnings; and the leading figures in the Square Mile wielded considerable influence in political circles. On this view, imperial expansion was designed not only to solve industry's problems but to maximize the City's earnings, and to make Britain the warehouse of the world rather than its workshop.

What is particularly interesting about both the revised view of the role of industry and the new emphasis on the City is the way in which both arguments are tied to broader developments in society instead of being cut off and placed in a separate box to be consulted only by specialists on international history. This observation applies equally to considerations of defence, which also have to be given prominence in accounting for Britain's overseas expansion. The small, offshore island had long been obliged to give the highest priority to the need to protect itself against larger and more powerful neighbours, first Spain and then France. The main strategy was to develop the navy, the 'senior service', and with it a 'blue-water' policy that spanned the world. Naval strength was supported by mercantilist policies; wealth created by seaborne commerce generated valuable foreign earnings and a degree of independence from land-based predators. The long-suffering infantry also played its part: Wellington's victories elevated the status of the army and confirmed that it served the interests of the nation rather than, as was feared in the eighteenth century, the ambitions of potential tyrants. Trafalgar and Waterloo provided a permanent advertisement for the vital importance of the armed services in upholding the peculiar combination of conservatism and reform that was to characterize the British way of life after 1815, and help to explain the survival of a martial ethos throughout Gladstone's era of liberal internationalism—and beyond it.

Viewing the world from the standpoint of 1815, it is apparent that the first half of the nineteenth century was a period of markedly uneven development in Europe's relations with non-European societies. Once great empires were in retreat or had collapsed; Britain alone was creating new frontiers of expansion, formal and informal, overseas. Taken as a whole, this endeavour can be seen as a long-term strategy for winning the peace. By maximizing its comparative advantage in finance, shipping, and commerce, and by creating reliable political allies abroad, Britain hoped to bring into being an international regime that would support its own emerging liberal economic and political order. Even so, the frontiers established overseas had yet to be pushed very far inland, except in India, and the attempt to create an informal empire in Latin America (as elsewhere) had achieved only limited success. The imperialism of intent was evident, but it had yet to be matched by an imperialism of result.

1870: The struggle for the mastery of the world

From the vantage point of 1870 it is possible to follow with some clarity the appearance of major economic, political, and cultural trends that began to emerge from about the middle of the century, and to look ahead to see how they found expression in the period of intense imperialist competition that characterized the years leading down to the First World War. The question of how these elements can be related and weighed to explain late nineteenth-century imperialism will be reserved for the next section of the chapter, when the observation point provided by the terminal date of 1914 enables the advantage of hindsight to be brought to bear on this daunting and still baffling problem.

By 1870 a number of interlocking economic and technological

changes had begun to transform the landscape of continental Europe. Industrialization had spread in a slow and patchy way from the early years of the century. By the last quarter of the century, particular regions of Germany, France, and Belgium had sizeable industrial sectors, and Germany, the most advanced of the continental powers, was starting to pioneer the products of the second industrial revolution, such as chemicals and electrical goods. The application of steam power, which was fundamental to improvements in manufacturing productivity, enabled striking gains to be made in transport efficiency too: railways were built from the 1830s; transoceanic steamship services began in the 1850s. These developments cut the cost and sped the movement of goods and people dramatically. The application of another miraculous innovation, electricity, had a similar effect on information flows following the invention of the land telegraph in the 1840s and the submarine cable in the 1850s. Improvements in technology also transformed the means of destruction, making possible larger and more powerful navies and, through the invention of automatic loading and mobile field guns, brought the prospect of total war a good deal nearer.

These innovations impinged on the overseas world very soon after they were adopted in Europe. During the 1850s regular steamship services began to ports in sub-Saharan Africa, railway construction started in India, Australia, and Latin America, and the first transatlantic telegraph cable was laid. By the 1870s these initial connections had been multiplied, even though getting to continents still proved easier than getting across them: railway-building in most of Asia and Africa awaited the coming of European rule at the close of the century. New engineering skills enabled the great canals of Suez (1869) and Panama (1914) to part four continents. Modern weapons arrived even sooner: Enfield rifles were available to deal with the Indian Mutiny in 1856; Gatling's primitive machine gun was in use from 1862 (though it let Gordon down in Khartoum in 1885); Maxim's much improved version came on the market in 1889 (in time to slaughter 11,000 Sudanese at Omdurman in 1898). Considered as economic assets, these engines of destruction were essentially labour-saving devices that greatly cut the cost of coercion. They had the considerable merit (for those who possessed them) of enabling the few to dominate the many.

These developments greatly strengthened the connections between

Europe and the rest of the world. The volume and value of trade expanded to reach unprecedented levels. Even more significant were changes in the structure of the international economy as increasing specialization produced the classic pattern of exchange whereby Europe exported manufactures and the rest of the world concentrated on producing raw materials and foodstuffs. The shoots of a 'green revolution' could be seen in the growth of export enclaves across the world, as cereals, vegetable oils, cotton, jute, coffee, cocoa, rubber, silk, and timber were carried by steamships to the ports of Europe in exchange for the staples of the great manufacturing centres, notably textiles and metal goods. The mining revolution was even more visible, as rich deposits of gold and other minerals, such as diamonds, copper, and tin, were found, often dramatically, on distant frontiers. It was at this point, in the second half of the century, that the Industrial Revolution began to have an important effect on economic relations with the world beyond Europe.

The expansion of world trade was closely associated with the export of capital and the movement of people. After about 1850, financial flows from Europe were of growing importance in funding development in the rest of the world. At first, capital was directed mainly to governments, whether to assist antique structures, like the Ottoman Empire, to modernize or to help entirely new states, like the Latin American republics, to come into being. From the 1870s, a growing proportion of finance was raised for private ventures, above all for railways. With increasing scale and specialization, a new set of large banks and complementary commercial and shipping firms emerged to manage the international economy. The integration of commodity markets was matched by the integration of capital markets; the activation of a new (and now familiar) set of connections was signalled in 1873, when a financial crisis in the United States was transmitted to the other industrializing countries and, via them, to the exporters of 'primary' products.

The opening of new frontiers generated a fresh exodus from Europe. Emigration was fuelled by population growth, unemployment, and (in some parts of Europe) political instability; it was also extended further as knowledge of new opportunities grew and as the cost of taking them fell. France was the exception that illustrates the rule: a falling birth rate, continued employment opportunities on the land, and the generally unattractive prospects offered by its own colonies combined to keep the rate of emigration down—to the chagrin of colonial enthusiasts. Nevertheless, by about the middle of the century the large-scale, enforced movement of Africans across the Atlantic was finally halted and was replaced by a flow of free, if often desperately poor, migrants: English, Scots, Welsh, and Irish settled in North America; Spanish and Italian emigrants went to Latin America. The other 'colonies of settlement', such as the Cape, Australia, and New Zealand, which had been reserved but scarcely settled, also began to fill out. These flows expanded greatly during the last quarter of the century, by which time new sources of supply and new destinations had emerged to blur the initial lines of connection between home and host.

The movement of peoples between and within the other continents affected by the influences transmitted from Europe is almost buried under this familiar story. As Europeans made the still hazardous voyage across the Atlantic, increasing numbers of Chinese found their way to Singapore and other parts of south-east Asia, Indian settlers and transient workers expanded their age-old ties with East Africa and extended them south to Natal and the Cape, and Africans, Vietnamese, Malays, and many others travelled long distances to work in mines and on plantations—often in circumstances that raised doubts about the effectiveness of the abolition of slavery. Taken as a whole, what was happening globally by 1870 was the movement of one factor of production, labour, funded by another, capital, to take up opportunities on a third, immobile factor, land.

Economic development and population movement brought a return trade in information and images on a wholly unprecedented scale. This was the last great era of exploration, when there were still some continents to be discovered and just enough support to make discovery possible—but not enough to make it too easy. (Stanley, however, always contrived to travel with a portable bed and ample supplies of champagne.) Deserts were crossed, mountains were scaled, forests were traversed, icebergs were negotiated. The most famous explorers, like de Brazza, Livingstone, and Stanley, became both legends and icons, feted by governments and commemorated by having rivers, lakes, and towns named after them; Carl Peters was later added to Hitler's pantheon. The heroic age of discovery came to an end when Amundsen reached the South Pole in 1911; by then, the ethos of trial by endurance and self-sacrifice had become a very masculine model of man. Scott's death in the Antarctic in 1912 set an example that many unsung heroes were to follow on the battlefields of Europe between 1914 and 1918.

The muscular Christian also explored, endured, and sacrificed. The effort to convert souls travelled in harness with the effort to transform economies and societies. In both cases results fell far short of intentions in the first half of the century. By 1870, however, there had been a revival of missionary energy and activity that continued down to 1914, especially in Africa and Asia. Cardinal Lavigerie, one of the most militant of European crusaders against Islam, founded the Society of Missionaries in 1868, when he was Archbishop of Algiers. Livingstone, who died in Africa in 1873, was revered in Europe as a missionary as well as an explorer. General Gordon, Christian soldier and guardian of the frontier against Islam, became a martyr: his death in Khartoum in 1885 inspired others to join Europe's campaign to redeem the heathen.

The information gathered from these diverse sources and places was processed in new or expanded ways. Studies of Britain and France have shown how increasing literacy, combined with the growth of the popular press, brought news of the wider world to a non-specialist audience, and how fact and fantasy were mixed to produce malleable representations and misrepresentations of other societies. Novelists, good, bad, and indifferent, achieved popularity, sometimes even fame, by capitalizing on this new-found interest. The 1880s saw the publication of a clutch of celebrated adventure stories, headed by Pierre Loti's *Le roman d'un spahi* (1881), Stevenson's *Treasure Island* (1883), and Rider Haggard's *King Solomon's Mines* (1885). By the turn of the century, the colonial novel had become a well-recognized literary genre, and a new generation of armchair imperialists had been brought up on tales of triumph over odds and adversity in 'uncivilized' parts of the world. Images of distant lands, typically mixed with imperial and patriotic themes, found many other popular outlets: in the poetry of Newbolt and Kipling, in theatre and the music hall, in advertisements in newspapers and on billboards, and in photographs and postcards—where the *Mauresque* (the portrayal of North African women) became particularly popular in France.

Scholarship also played its part in conveying ideas about the non-European world. Geography, geology, oceanography, anthropology, botany, zoology, tropical medicine, and history were among the academic disciplines that were greatly stimulated by overseas expansion and became caught up, more often than not, with imperialism and empire. The new 'sciences' of eugenics and phrenology made their presence felt though their influential claims about the classification and ability of various 'races'. Empire, its heroes, and the values they exemplified also entered into the training of the young, especially in Britain, through the education system, sport, and youth organizations such as Boy Scouts (1908) and Girl Guides (1910).

The study of European representations of non-European societies, often referred to as Orientalism, is currently the most popular branch of new research on imperialism. The reasons for this renaissance cannot be explored here, except to say that they include a concern to identify alternative, cultural sources of colonial oppression following the collapse of the economic basis of standard Marxist accounts, and the need to find a voice for ethnic minorities in the contemporary world. The general conclusion of studies written from this perspective is that European observers produced derogatory and often racist stereotypes of other societies, even when they thought they were being objective and scientific.

The problem with this interpretation is that it imposes a stereotype of its own on what was a very diverse and continually evolving set of images. In reality, very different presentations of other societies, noble and barbaric, were already available in the eighteenth century. The nineteenth century saw the further development of racist literature, but also the growth of anti-imperialist thinking. These dissenting thoughts were not confined to leading intellectuals and politicians, such as Anatole France and Jean Jaurès, but included eminent explorers and missionaries who identified with the societies they came to know. These sentiments extended to the many European writers, painters, composers, and designers who were inspired by what they saw or understood of these very different societies. Gaugin went to live in Tahiti; Stevenson settled in Samoa. Thus, while there is a strong case for emphasizing the expanding volume and variety of European images of other societies in the late nineteenth century, and for confirming the belief that much of it served the interests of European expansion, there are good grounds, too, for resisting the temptation to reduce such multiple impressions to a crude stereotype, even if it is intended to serve a well-meaning cause.

The significance of the political changes that could be seen in 1870 are fully acknowledged in the chapters that complement the present one. Here, it is necessary only to refer to the central processes of state- and nation-building that preoccupied most of Europe in the nineteenth century. State-building was the more dramatic development because it entailed visible and often instant changes to boundaries and constitutions, as happened, for example, when the Netherlands and Belgium separated and became independent states in 1830. The movements that led to the unification of Italy in 1870 and to the creation of Germany in the following year were greater in scale and scope because they altered the balance of power as well as the configuration of Europe. Even where boundaries remained more or less fixed, existing states experienced major internal change as the process of nation-building was moved on, whether by central governments or by revolution. Strategies of incorporation were not always successful: assimilation by means of internal colonialism could easily provoke provincial reaction; centres lost as well as gained power. Austria was obliged to concede equality to Hungary in 1867, albeit still within the dual monarchy of Austria-Hungary. Spain and Portugal experienced revolution or insurrection after 1848 as well as before, and continued to oscillate between monarchical and republican forms of government. France and Britain already had a strong sense of nationality, but both were obliged to deal with internal dissent and separatist claims, even though the Breton challenge did not match that of Ireland. The British formula for giving substance to the notion of a United Kingdom was based on slow and cautious reform. The French, true to the revolutionary spirit of *terreur et rupture*, trod a rougher road; in addition, they were more readily exposed to external aggression. Political instability after 1815 continued with the revolutions of 1830 and 1848 and merged with the catastrophic defeat at the hands of Prussia in 1870 to produce the Third Republic, which presided over the great era of French colonial expansion.

These developments did not flow to the world beyond Europe as readily as trade, capital, and ideas, but they are highly relevant, nevertheless, to an understanding of overseas expansion and imperialism. At one level, it has been argued that late-nineteenth-century imperialism was an expression of the changing balance of power in Europe; at another that it was the product of nationalism. These possibilities will be touched on in the next section of the chapter. For the present, it is sufficient to note that state-building and to a greater degree nation-building were processes that enlarged the political arena, whether formally through extensions of the franchise or effectively through appeals to a wider and increasingly literate public. This opened up the twin prospects of manipulating and responding to public opinion. The *parti colonial* took advantage of the more open political system operating under the Third Republic to promote its cause; the jingoistic fervour that accompanied the Anglo-Boer War (1899–1902) is probably the best-known example of popular support for imperialism. The result, in both cases, was that imperialism became an increasingly prominent item on the political agenda after 1870.

As noted at the outset, there can be no doubt that this was a time of intense imperialist rivalries, even if it is conceded that the period before 1870 was one of informal expansion rather than of quiescence. Virtually the whole of Africa was partitioned and subsequently occupied, principally by Britain and France, between 1879, when the French advanced into Senegal, and 1912, when they established a protectorate over Morocco. Further east, the British expanded into the Malay peninsular between 1874 and 1909 (forming the Federation of Malay States in 1896), annexed Upper Burma in 1886 (following the third Anglo-Burmese War in 1885), and established protectorates over Sarawak, Brunei, and North Borneo in 1888. The French advanced into Cochin-China, Annam, Cambodia, and Tonkin from bases established in the 1860s, created the Union Indo-Chinoise in 1887, and declared a protectorate over Laos in 1893.

These dramatic moves underline the central role of Britain and France in late-nineteenth-century imperialism, but it is important to note that other European powers, old and new, shared in the spoils. The Dutch consolidated and developed their holdings in Indonesia. The Portuguese, having lost Brazil earlier in the century, managed to hold on to Angola and Mozambique, though their position depended on the continuing goodwill of the major powers, especially Britain. Spain was less fortunate. After crossing swords unsuccessfully with the United States in the Spanish-American War of 1898, it was forced to cede Cuba, Puerto Rico, and the Philippines, a transfer that signalled the emergence of Britain's ex-colony as an imperial power in its own right. Russia pressed ahead with plans for extending its land-based empire in central and east Asia, taking territory from China and expanding into Manchuria until halted by Japan's victory in the

Russo-Japanese War of 1904–5. The presence of the aspiring colonial powers was felt mainly in Africa. Germany acquired sections of West, East and South-West Africa in 1884–5 (and a handful of islands in the Pacific as well). Italy, having failed to conquer Abyssinia in 1895–6, acquired Libya in 1911. The vast private estate established in the Congo by King Leopold II of Belgium during the 1880s came under direct Belgian rule in 1908.

Substantial though it is, this roll-call of annexations fails to capture the full extent of Europe's expansion during this period because it does not take account of the spread of informal influence and, on some accounts, the creation of informal empires. Although Latin America, the Middle East, and China did not become European colonies, their independence was significantly compromised. A number of Latin American republics, headed by Argentina, were dominated by British finance and trade, and their political élites were beguiled by British liberalism. The Ottoman Empire fell increasingly under the control of Britain, France, and Germany after defaulting on its external debt in 1876; Britain and Russia divided Persia into spheres of informal influence in 1907. China resisted foreign incursions until prised open by the rising power of Japan after the Sino-Japanese War of 1894–5. There followed a scramble for concessions and influence that resulted in large segments of China being partitioned informally between Britain, France, Russia, and Germany. China retained its formal independence, but Yuan Shi-k'ai, who was appointed President of the Republic in 1912, after the revolution of 1911, was first interviewed for the job in London.

Europe and the world overseas in 1914

The terminal date of 1914 offers a retrospective view of developments during the previous half-century. It is evident that major economic, political, and cultural changes were taking place in Europe, and also that the overseas world was being brought under European control by both formal and informal means. The problem is to decide how these two sets of events were related. As suggested at the outset, the established answers to this question have lost credibility. Marxist-inspired approaches are flawed by their insistence on a mechanical and now

dated view of economic development; the most influential alternatives are compromised by their excessive preoccupation with the need
to refute Marxism. Moreover, the opposition of economic and political forces (and other dualities) sanctioned by this debate now seems
too crude to be acceptable. The problem is not how to choose
between two possibilities, but how to relate and weigh a complex of
motives. Elements of the existing historiography of course remain
very valuable, but the kaleidoscope now needs to be shaken to see if a
different pattern can be produced.

A useful starting point is the basic distinction drawn earlier
between expansion and imperialism. It is apparent that Europe was
expanding overseas, in fits and starts, from the sixteenth century
onwards and that the process accelerated in the nineteenth century
because the great powers acquired the means of penetrating other
continents and also the motives—economic, political, and cultural—
for doing so. Given this context, the more precise question to be
addressed is why expansion was converted into imperialism (and
then into empire) at certain times and in certain places. This outcome
was not inevitable. Britain exported manufactured goods, capital, and
people to the United States on a large scale in the nineteenth century,
yet it did not attempt to re-annex its former colonies or to turn them
into an informal empire. Similarly, French capital and expertise
played a significant part in modernizing Russia's economy and army
at the close of the century without making the Tsar a pawn of Paris.
The explanation is contained in the examples: the relationship
between the parties was one of approximate equality; it was not
possible, even if it were desirable, for one to dominate the other.

For expansion to become imperialism and for imperialism to be
translated into empire, two conditions had to be met: the motive had
to be strong enough for the attempt to be made, and the inequality
between the expanding and the receiving states had to be sufficiently
large to make the prospect of domination practicable. This starting
point opens the way to a more refined approach, one that considers
expansion and imperialism as being uneven processes with respect to
both place and time. The formula takes account of the importance of
spatial variations among different European states and the need to see
how changes in the mix of motives and the international standing of
individual states altered with the passage of time. As these variables
have not yet been applied systematically, the examples that follow

must be thought of as illustrating an approach rather than proving a thesis.

The most distinctive spatial variation was the difference between Britain and the states on the European mainland. As an offshore island, Britain had long capitalized on the opportunity to develop its naval power and seaborne commerce. The results of this orientation were striking: in the nineteenth century about two-thirds of Britain's exports went to regions outside Europe, headed by North America, Latin America, and Asia; its capital exports showed a similar preference for areas of white settlement (including Australasia) and Asia (especially India). Not surprisingly, Britain was dependent to a much greater extent than other European countries on earnings from overseas investment, shipping, and commercial services to balance its international payments. Its continuing ability to settle its accounts depended on a growing network of increasingly specialized and far-flung connections, all of which had to be, in Palmerston's phrase, 'well kept and always accessible'.

It is not hard to see why Britain should have been the leading expansionist power, and also the one most likely to translate expansion into imperialism if trade flows or investments were endangered, or be tempted to do so if new commercial prospects appeared on the horizon. This is not to suggest that British imperialism was simply a function of economic imperatives. To understand why Britain became a great imperial power it is necessary to look beneath external manifestations of its international presence and to incorporate other crucial components of the state, notably the foundations of continuing political stability, the capacity to combine economic change with social conservatism, and the legitimating ideology that underpinned authority but outlawed authoritarianism, as well as to rethink the nature of modernization to give weight to activities other than industrialization.

No other European power came near this degree of commitment to overseas expansion and empire in the nineteenth century. Two-thirds of French exports remained in Europe; the figure was even higher for the remaining colonial powers. Foreign investment fell into the same pattern: the greater part of French foreign investment in the late nineteenth century went to Russia, Spain, and Italy, and not to its overseas colonies. Similarly, the small proportion of German investment that found its way outside Europe gravitated to the Americas, the Ottoman Empire, and China, and avoided Bismarck's newly acquired and uniformly impoverished colonies.

The striking difference between Britain and its rivals raises the interesting problem of whether the relationship between the continental powers and the non-European world requires an entirely separate set of explanations. If Britain is taken to be the 'early start' country and the 'late starters' are regarded as being engaged in a process of catching up, a case can be made for treating the British path as the norm and for supposing that other countries followed scaled-down or lagged versions of it. This route has been followed by all theories of imperialism that seek to emphasize the role of industrialization in empire-building. It can be seen particularly clearly in the long-standing debate between Marxists and others on the relative importance of prestige and profit in French imperialism. A detailed examination of the composition of the *parti colonial* concluded that French imperialism was essentially a quest for *la gloire* pursued more by military officers and sundry journalists, explorers, missionaries, and eccentrics. On this view, French imperialism was the highest stage, not of capitalism, but of nationalism. However, detailed work on Lyons, the centre of the silk industry, has drawn attention to the prominent part played by provincial businessmen in promoting the French advance into Indo-China, and a more wide-ranging study has shown that there was a close fit between French industry and the colonies, even though the greater part of French trade and investment went elsewhere. These interpretations have yet to be reconciled.

The process of industrialization has also featured prominently in the debate on German imperialism, where the concept of social imperialism has been deployed to link the growth of the colonial movement with rising urban unemployment in the 1880s. It has been applied, too, in revisionist approaches to Portuguese and Italian imperialism, which have attacked the traditional emphasis on non-economic motives and have emphasized instead the important part played by the emerging industrial sector in seeking raw materials and markets. According to this interpretation, the smaller colonial powers differed in scale but not in kind from the role model, Britain.

This line of enquiry has the merit of identifying a common theme, industrialization, and of connecting it to the European presence overseas. But it has limitations and can be misleading. As noted earlier, economic and cultural forces are no longer seen to be contending for paramountcy, as they were in the older historiography. Moreover, the economic dimension of imperialism is not contained within the process of industrialization, important though that was. Revisionist research on Britain, summarized above, has emphasized the significance of non-industrial forms of capitalism. If this view is accepted, the 'British model' is not what it has long seemed to be. After 1870, the late-start countries were catching up with what Britain used to be, not what it had become: the greatest financier and the most efficient conveyer belt in the world. The best comparison may be one that is rarely made: between Britain and the Netherlands, where finance and commercial services were also important engines of overseas expansion and imperialism.

Even where comparisons can be made, however, vast differences in scale distinguished Britain from its rivals. Overseas expansion and empire-building were central features of British history in the nineteenth century; elsewhere in Europe they were rarely more than adjuncts. Books written about 'Imperial Germany' usually spend very little time on its overseas colonies; discussion of informal expansion often comes to a halt with the Baghdad railway. This emphasis represents accuracy, not dereliction. The German empire was formed by the land-based expansion of Prussia; colonies were primarily settlements within Europe. It is scarcely surprising that Bismarck's interest in Germany's overseas colonies stemmed more from diplomacy than from economics: their usefulness in creating difficulties between Britain and France far outweighed their value as resources and markets, which was indeed minimal. Given these huge contrasts in structure, scale, and attitude, it would seem wise to vary the proportions when mixing the ingredients to produce an explanation, or rather explanations, of European imperialism.

It is possible, of course, that these patterns rearranged themselves as the nineteenth century unfolded. One influential argument to this effect holds that Britain's supremacy reached its high point in the mid-Victorian era, when she managed an extensive informal empire, and declined thereafter, when foreign rivals began to exert their newfound industrial strength. As far as Britain was concerned, there was no 'new imperialism' in the last quarter of the century, as Marxists claimed, because expansion was already taking place through the imperialism of free trade. The scramble for territory after 1870 was started by young or rejuvenated states on the continent of Europe.

Britain was a reluctant participant; she had become a defensive power, and could no longer manage the world from afar, in splendid isolation.

This is an ingenious and illuminating argument, but it is open to serious objection. It is perfectly true that Britain's dominance in world affairs was not threatened for a generation or more after Waterloo, but it is also true that its influence overseas was limited during that period by technological and other constraints. There was an imperialism of intent, but it resulted in a degree of informal influence rather than in an informal empire. In the second half of the century, and particularly after 1870, there was an evident challenge to Britain's position, but the most striking outcome of the contest was not its demotion but its confirmation as the superpower of the day. Britain's share of world trade in manufactures was indeed being reduced by new competitors, but its dominance of overseas investment, shipping, and allied commercial services was growing absolutely and at a pace that kept it far ahead of other European powers. Moreover, Britain was in the forefront of those who were using the new technology of communications to push coastal frontiers inland. If it is agreed, following this argument, that Britain was an expanding power, not a declining one, it is much easier to understand how it finished up holding or controlling far more of the non-European world than any of its rivals, and why even the French were left with what Lord Salisbury famously referred to as the 'light soils' of the Sahara.

The most striking continuity throughout the period, therefore, was the special position of Britain as the power most committed to overseas expansion and having the greatest empire. This generalization holds for 1815, 1870, and 1914 and all points in between. What changed were the circumstances in which this dominance was exercised. The era of competitive imperialism obliged Britain to exert itself to a greater extent than before: crises in distant and sometimes unknown parts of the world – none more obscure than Fashoda—came close to causing conflict between the great powers. The effort was expended not simply to defend an existing position, but to take advantage of new opportunities that were opening up for reasons that were independent of the appearance of foreign rivals. These changing circumstances can be designated 'new imperialism', providing the term is freed from its restrictive Marxist meaning of a crisis of advanced industrial capitalism. This is not to deny the importance of fluctuations in the performance of manufacturing across Europe and the attendant problems of unemployment and civil order. But the new imperialism was a much broader phenomenon, as we have seen, and was bound up with decisive changes in technology, with the enlargement of the political arena, with the spread of literacy, with the burgeoning ideology of dominance, and, in the case of Britain, with the development of an unprecedented financial capacity and the associated growth of the tertiary sector of the economy. These features help to account for British 'exceptionalism' and for the extraordinary extent to which its domestic history was bound up with its empire. They also allow scope for varying the emphasis in other parts of Europe to reflect differences in economic structures and political alignments, and the often marginal nature of involvement with the overseas world.

Whether the effort, large or small, was worthwhile is a question that repeatedly imposes itself, not least because it is unanswerable. No one has yet devised an accounting technique that can attach numbers to human lives and national prestige. Even if this could be done, it would be impossible to decide where to draw the line: the balance would look very different in 1815, 1870, and 1914—and in 2000. Are the costs borne by one generation balanced by the gains accruing to the next, and then counterbalanced by subsequent losses? Even the most creative of accountants would have difficulty reconciling these uncertain credits and debits.

What can be said, within the strict limits imposed by measurability, is that recent research has tried to disaggregate judgements about national gains and losses by looking more closely at different regions and sectors. Work on Britain, for example, has emphasized not only the well-known connection between manufacturing in the Midlands and the north-east of the country and the Empire, but also the overseas orientation of the City and the Home Counties generally. What emerges from this analysis is the extent to which specific interest groups gained disproportionately from overseas expansion and empire.

Elsewhere, the gains were spread thinly, and the costs of running the Empire were borne by the generality of tax-payers. Research on the French empire points in the same direction. Textiles and metal goods found profitable niches in the colonies; large proportions of specific imports (such as rice, sugar, olive oil, phosphate, and groundnuts) were drawn, in return, from the Empire. The costs of managing the Empire were carried, in the shape of high prices and other subsidies, by French tax-payers. Beyond this point, the analysis tends to fray at the edges in both cases. Were the costs to the tax-payer offset by the psychic income derived from being a citizen of a great power, or does this proposition mistake acquiescence for enthusiasm? Did the true benefit of empire manifest itself at times of acute crisis, such as the two world wars in the twentieth century, or was the possession of empire a cause of war in the first place? These questions are large enough to merit further consideration, but too large to be explored here. When placed with the complementary issue of whether the colonies gained or lost from empire, it is apparent that the subject as a whole requires a separate and sizeable study.

Conclusion

The main conclusions of this survey have been attached to the preceding sections of the chapter. Rather than summarize the summaries and risk confirming the mistaken belief that history is no more than the record of what is already known, it might be better, or at least more interesting, to end by referring briefly to what is unknown and might still be discovered, and by glancing ahead to what was to come after 1914.

The study of Europe's relations with the non-European world is an old subject that is now being reinvented. History is not value-free, but the particular ideologies that inspired and shackled the study of empires during their existence have withered away, and there is an opportunity to look afresh at themes and events that appear to have been exhausted or overlooked by fashion or rendered inaccessible for lack of source materials. There was a time, for example, when the history of colonial rule dealt exclusively with the rulers and ignored the ruled. That imbalance has been corrected, and rightly so, but with the result that many current judgements on colonial policy and on the European presence in general rest on studies that were completed a generation or more ago and now need to be re-examined. The present fashion for studying images and representations has done little to fill this gap: amidst some research of high quality, there is now a library of predictable and repetitive work, much of which steers clear of empirical reality. Atoning for the errors of Marxism seems, in some circles, to require the excision of material existence. Consequently, large opportunities await a new generation of historians: standard themes in the economic and political history of colonial rule need to be rethought; the opening of official archives has made sources available for studying the process of decolonization; fresh documentation can be discovered simply by asking neglected questions, as has begun to happen with the history of expatriate firms. These illustrations are no more than indications of a range of possibilities spanning several centuries. The point to stress here is that the subject remains vital and enticing. The world being its stage, scale alone guarantees its importance; the questions it raises go to the heart of issues of power and morality in global relations; the legacy of empires remains visible in the international order and disorder around us today, and for that reason alone commands attention and requires explanation.

By 1914, the rapidity and extent of Europe's expansion overseas had changed the boundaries of the world and altered the lives of millions. When the real 'war of the worlds' between empires old and new began in Sarajevo, space and time had contracted to the point where it was even possible to discern, in the distance, the outline of the 'global village' that was to characterize the post-imperial international order later in the twentieth century. Faced with the challenge of motor cars, flying machines, telephones, and wireless transmissions, writers of science fiction had to invent a new and even stranger universe if they were to keep ahead of reality. Europe's empire-builders continued to challenge the imagination by moving reality on: the war of 1914–18 saw parts of the world re-partitioned, the inter-war years saw the application of new technology to the management of overseas possessions, the Second World War was fought partly to restore and confirm the European empires, and the post-war settlement included grand schemes for a renewed colonial occupation. The impetus behind the assertive imperialism of the late nineteenth century had by no means run its course in 1914; Conrad's 'great knights-errant' still had much work before them.

Conclusion: into the twentieth century

T. C. W. Blanning

The introduction to this volume ended with an invocation from Matthew Arnold, expressing the nineteenth century's longing for release from world-weariness:

> Thou waitest for the spark from heaven! and we,
> Light half-believers of our casual creeds . . .
>
> .   .   .   .   .
>
> Ah! do not we, Wanderer, await it too?

That was not a *fin de siècle* sigh, but was written in 1852, at the high noon of Victorian self-confidence, the year after the Great Exhibition. Plenty of other examples could be found from even earlier in the century, from Lord Byron, for example:

> Society is now one polished horde,
> Formed of two mighty tribes, the *Bores* and *Bored*.

It was a condition with political implications, as the French politician Alphonse de Lamartine revealed when he observed before the Revolution of 1848 that *'La France s'ennuie'* (France is bored). In 1847 the sensation of the Paris Salon was a huge painting by Thomas Couture, *The Romans of the Decadence*, a brilliant combination of visual titillation and moral message. Draped languorously on couches, a party of semi-clad and naked Romans drink, eat, and caress each other, while others dance and frolic in wild abandon. As statues of great figures of the past gaze over the orgy in mute censure, at one side two virile German 'barbarians' observe the scene thoughtfully. Couture's painting had been inspired by two lines from Juvenal's Sixth Satire:

> We suffer today from the fatal results of a long peace, more
> damaging than war,
> Luxury has rushed upon us and avenges the enslaved universe.

This indictment of the modern world would have been even more timely if it had been exhibited at the Salon of 1869—or indeed at the Salon of 1913—for by then the forces Juvenal and Couture held responsible for decadence had intensified: the peace had been longer and the luxury was greater. Both were about to be blown away, for the 'spark from heaven', to which Arnold had looked forward, did arrive eventually, raining in from the guns of August 1914. It was not to be extinguished for four years, by which time the blaze the spark had ignited had incinerated much of Europe.

Such was the destructive force of the First World War and so hor-rific were its long-term consequences that mighty efforts have been made to trace its origins back into the nineteenth century. As we have seen, there is plenty to find there, for the century had begun as it ended, in war and revolution. Particularly disturbing, as the century neared its end, was the political polarization that affected almost every country in Europe. As the centre shrank, the extremes on both left and right gathered strength. The phenomenon indicated by the title of George Dangerfield's influential study *The Strange Death of Liberal England* could be found all over Europe. In the 1860s and 1870s liberals had seemed to be carrying all before them, taking power in one country after another and introducing their characteristic pol-icies of constitutionalism, a property-based franchise, civil liberties, and free trade. The beginning of the end was the Great Depression, which began in 1873. It may not have been very great in objective terms, especially not by the standards of the twentieth century, but at the level of perception it marked a watershed. The palmy days of self-sustained, endless growth seemed to have gone for ever.

Now the liberals found themselves in the position of the sorcerer's apprentice, unable to control the forces they had unleashed to make their lives easier. The nationalism they had deployed against the cosmopolitanism of the aristocrats was now turned against them by radical right-wing groups. The *laissez-faire* economy which had generated so much economic growth also created an increasingly militant proletariat, organized in social-democratic parties. The civil liberties the liberals had fought for were now used against them by opponents more adept at exploiting the popular press, voluntary associations, or public meetings. They had opened the door to political participation for property-owners like themselves but now found it difficult to shut it against the growing clamour for universal manhood suffrage, not to mention votes for women (only Finland and Norway had given women the right to vote by 1914). Many episodes from the late nineteenth century exemplify the crisis of liberalism. Perhaps the most ominous was the election of Karl Lueger as mayor of Vienna in 1895, following the success of his Christian Socialist party in winning two-thirds of the seats on the city council. He was all the things the liberals disliked: radical, democratic, populist, clerical, loyal to the dynasty, socialist, and anti-Semitic. Despite the services he rendered to his city, it is difficult not to experience a feeling of unease when finding that one of the main boulevards in Vienna is still named the 'Karl Lueger Ring'.

The oxymoronic nature of the title of Lueger's party demonstrates the appeal of anti-modernity in the late nineteenth century. The force that had eroded old certainties, whether they derived from belief-systems or work patterns, was increasingly arraigned as a negative destroyer. It was to take shelter from the bracing but cold wind blown in by liberal competition that shopkeepers, artisans, and peasants huddled around traditional-sounding programmes. A mushrooming metropolis such as Vienna, whose population increased from just a quarter of a million in 1800 to over two million by 1914, was a natural breeding ground for *anomie*, that 'condition of instability resulting from a breakdown of standards and values or from a lack of purpose or ideals' identified by Émile Durkheim (1858–1917) as the central modern malaise. The contributors to this volume have provided us with many graphic examples.

These and other critiques of modernity deserve to be taken seriously, not least because they were often expressed by contemporaries of exceptional intelligence and sensitivity. When Richard Wagner writes 'My whole politics consists in nothing more than the most visceral hatred of our entire civilization' or Émile Zola uses the dying Nana as a metaphor for modern Paris ('a pile of blood and pus dumped on a pillow, a shovelful of rotten flesh'), we must sit up and take notice, however overstated these verdicts seem to be. Hegel was right: there is such a thing as the *Zeitgeist* ('spirit of the times' in its less succinct English translation) and it is creative artists who are best attuned to it. Nor are their opinions without political consequences. It was a visit to a performance of Wagner's *Tannhäuser* in Paris in 1895 that galvanised the Zionist leader Theodor Herzl. Among other things, it led him to articulate a new view of politics, one based less on means–ends rationality than on an appeal to the subconscious: 'Dream is not so different from deed as many believe. All activity of men begins as dream and later becomes dream once more.' So Herzl was able to appreciate the importance of myth and symbol in the political process and also to offer an important insight into the process of German unification:

Believe me, the politics of a whole people—particularly if it is scattered over all the world—can only be made with imponderables that hover high in the air. Do you know out of what the German Empire arose? Out of dreams, songs, fantasies and black–red–gold ribbons . . . Bismarck merely shook the tree that fantasies had planted.

Herzl's experience of anti-Semitism in France in the 1890s, especially during the Dreyfus Affair, and the shock of Lueger's victory in Vienna, convinced him that Jews could expect nothing from liberal assimilationism. So he turned his back on Europe, proclaiming at the first World Congress of Zionists, held at Basle in 1897, the need 'to create a publicly guaranteed homeland for the Jewish people in the land of Israel'. Herzl died in 1904, forty-four years before the state of Israel was created.

Disillusionment with liberalism could take many other forms, both passive—such as cultural pessimism, or active—such as terrorism. The murdered victims of the latter included the Tsar of Russia (1881), the President of France (1894), the prime minister of Spain (1897), the Empress of Austria (1898), the King of Italy (1900), the President of the United States of America (1901), the King and Queen of Serbia (1903), the King and Crown Prince of Portugal (1908), the Russian prime minister (1911), another Spanish prime minister (1912), and the heir to the throne of Austria-Hungary and his wife (1914). It was the last-named atrocity, of course, that precipitated the July Crisis and the First World War. By that time, most of the more important states in Europe were showing signs of chronic instability: Austria-Hungary was wracked by ethnic conflict and awaiting the death of the emperor

Francis Joseph (on the throne since 1848) with a mixture of hope and trepidation; the Russian Empire's half-hearted experiment with constitutionalism in the wake of the revolution of 1905 was running into the sands; the United Kingdom was breaking up over Irish Home Rule; a revolution in Portugal in 1910 abolished the monarchy in favour of a republic; Spain, pulled apart by Basque and Catalan nationalism, lurched from one crisis to another, including an aptly named 'Tragic Week' in Barcelona in 1909; Italian politics were a byword for corruption and violence, exemplified by the 'Red Week' of 1913, when much of central Italy was out of control of the government; even the most prosperous and stable of the major states, Germany, was experiencing difficulty in advancing to a full parliamentary regime.

The First World War was to make this chronic instability terminal. The Austro-Hungarian, German, and Russian empires disappeared altogether. In Italy, Benito Mussolini became prime minister in 1922 and set about replacing the constitutional monarchy with a fascist dictatorship, the same year in which the Irish Free State seceded from the United Kingdom. In Spain General Miguel Primo de Rivera carried out a military *coup d'état (pronunciamento)* the following year. Portugal followed suit in 1926.

To recite this sequence of events suggests that the malaise did reach far back beyond 1914. Yet the temptation to which the introduction succumbed should now be offered greater resistance. In particular, we must try to forget that we know what happened after 1914—that the war lasted four years, brought the Bolshevik, fascist, and Nazi revolutions, led to a second and even more destructive conflict, and with it the Holocaust, and so on and so forth. In the previous volume in this series it was argued that the French Revolution created both the *Ancien Régime* and the Enlightenment because it provided the teleological lens through which they were viewed by later observers. In the same way, it could be said that the First World War created the nineteenth century—not the other way round. In the interests of intellectual integrity, we should at least attempt the impossible and try to view the period before 1914 on its own terms.

The cultural pessimists who had sounded the death knell of modern civilization before 1914 might well have taken a less jaundiced view of the established order (and might well have been less impatient for 'the spark from heaven') if they had known of the horrors that were to come. But they did not. The prescience of Sir

Edward Grey, the British Foreign Minister, who observed on 3 August 1914 that 'the lamps are going out all over Europe, we shall not see them lit again in our lifetime', was exceptional. Many more believed that the war would be quick, easy, and victorious. Just as British officers were scrambling to get over to France to see action—and win medals—before the show was over, the German Kaiser told his troops departing from Berlin that they would be 'home when the leaves fall' (*Daheim wenn das Laub fällt*).

The constitutional monarchism that most European states came to prefer in the course of the nineteenth century—the only republics in 1914 were France, Switzerland, Portugal, and San Marino – may have been unexciting but had provided a framework for conflict resolution within which a great deal of economic, social, and cultural progress had been achieved. As the chapters in this volume have demonstrated, such important indicators as per capita income, life expectancy, communications, housing conditions, literacy, and recreational variety all showed spectacular improvement in the course of the century. To be sure, there was what Niall Ferguson has termed a 'development gradient' as one moved east across the Elbe and south across the Alps, but, for most people in most places, conditions were improving. Even Christians could look past growing secularization at home to a rapidly expanding empire for their God abroad: as John Roberts has written, 'the nineteenth century had turned out to be the greatest missionary age since that of St Paul'.

It had also been the greatest age of European expansion. In 1914 some 80 per cent of the world's land surface, not counting uninhabited Antarctica, was ruled by European powers or colonists of European origin. Russia and the United Kingdom alone ruled a third of it. The entire coastline of Africa, with the exception of Liberia, was controlled by European powers. Moreover, even those areas not under direct rule were subject to constant interference. As Tony Hopkins tells us, when Yuan Shi-k'ai was appointed President of China in 1912, he was interviewed for the job in London. Yet there were signs that the world was changing. No one would have thought of interviewing the prime minister of Japan in London, especially not after Japan's crushing defeat of Russia in the war of 1905, the first achieved by an Asiatic power against a European enemy. There were also signs that the subject populations of the European empires were beginning to stir: July 1914 saw not only the war crisis in Europe, but also Mahatma Gandhi's return to India from South Africa. More threatening still, so far as Europe's relative position in the world was concerned, was the irresistible rise of the United States of America, whose population had increased twelvefold in the course of the century and whose industrial output was now equal to that of the United Kingdom, Germany, and France combined.

The First World War both hastened Europe's decline and made it incomparably more painful than it might otherwise have been, but it did not cause it. Nevertheless, 1917 has a good claim to be a truly pivotal moment in European history, for it was then that Europeans lost control of their own affairs. The arrival of American troops both sealed the defeat of Germany and ensured that the peace settlement would be framed according to American interests. As the final two volumes in this series will show, the *Pax Americana* had come to stay. This conclusion is being written in the last year of the twentieth century, at a time when American bombs and missiles are being deployed in an attempt to resolve a dispute inside a European country. If the nineteenth century was the century of Europe, the twentieth century has belonged to America.

Further Reading

Politics

M. S. Anderson, *The Ascendancy of Europe 1815–1914* (London, 1985), is an admirable introduction. Important thematic works include Michael Mann, *The Sources of Social Power*, ii. *The Rise of Classes and Nation-States, 1760–1914* (Cambridge, 1993), Jerome Blum, *The End of the Old Order in Rural Europe* (Princeton, 1978), Benedict Anderson, *Imagined Communities: Reflections on the Origin and Spread of Nationalism* (2nd edn., London 1991), Ernest Gellner, *Nations and Nationalism* (Oxford, 1983), Adrian Hastings, *The Construction of Nationhood: Ethnicity, Religion and Nationalism* (Cambridge, 1997), R. J. Evans, *The Feminists: Women's Emancipation Movements in Europe, America, and Australasia 1840–1920* (London, 1979), and Spencer M. Di Scala and Salvo Mastellone, *European Political Thought 1815–1989* (Boulder, Colo., 1998). For details of political systems and their workings, see Eugene N. Anderson and Pauline R. Anderson, *Political Institutions and Social Change in Continental Europe in the Nineteenth Century* (Berkeley and Los Angeles, 1967), and Robert Justin Goldstein, *Political Repression in Nineteenth-Century Europe* (London, 1983). Jonathan Sperber, *The European Revolutions 1848–1851* (Cambridge, 1994), analyses a crucial event. Among the vast number of studies of countries, the following is a small selection: on Britain, Michael Bentley, *Politics without Democracy 1815–1914* (London 1984), and Roy Foster, *Modern Ireland, 1600–1972* (London, 1988), on the larger continental states, Mary Fulbrook (ed.), *German History since 1800* (London, 1997), Robert Tombs, *France 1814–1914* (London 1996), Richard Pipes, *Russia under the Old Regime* (London, 1977), and Alan Sked, *The Decline and Fall of the Habsburg Empire, 1815–1918* (London, 1989). Space does not permit coverage of every country, but the following round out the picture: E. H. Kossmann, *The Low Countries 1780–1940* (Oxford, 1978), Denis Mack Smith, *Italy, A Modern History* (Ann Arbor, 1959), David Kirby, *The Baltic World 1772–1993* (London, 1995), Raymond Carr, *Spain 1808–1975* (2nd edn., Oxford, 1982), Jonathan Steinberg, *Why Switzerland?* (2nd edn., Cambridge, 1996), Norman Davies, *God's Playground: A History of Poland* (Oxford, 1981), and Barbara Jelavich, *History of the Balkans* (Cambridge, 1983).

Society

The introduction of Nicholas B. Dirks, Geoff Eley, and Sherry B. Ortner (eds.), *Culture/Power/History: A Reader in Contemporary Social Theory* (Princeton, 1994), surveys recent developments in social and cultural theory.

M. L. Bush, *Social Orders and Social Classes in Europe since 1500: Studies in Social Stratification* (London, 1992), is a collection of essays combining some theoretical perspectives with national case studies. Particularly strong on central and eastern Europe is Dominic Lieven, *The Aristocracy in Europe, 1815–1914* (London, 1992). Pamela Pilbeam, *The Middle Classes in Europe, 1789–1914: France, Germany, Italy and Russia* (Basingstoke, 1990), adopts a thematic approach that covers the various types of middle class. Jürgen Kocka and Allen Mitchell (eds.), *Bourgeois Society in Nineteenth Century Europe* (Oxford, 1993), focuses on a series of comparisons centred on the German experience. Geoffrey Crossick and Heinz-Gerhard Haupt, *The Petite Bourgeoisie in Europe, 1789–1914: Enterprise, Family and Independence* (London, 1966), explores an often-neglected social milieu. Dick Geary (ed.), *Labour and Socialist Movements in Europe before 1914* (Oxford, 1989), is a collection of essays on national labour movements by specialists. Bonnie Anderson and Judith Zinsser, *A History of their Own: Women in Europe from Prehistory to the Present*, ii (London, 1990), is a very readable synthesis. Laura Frader and Sonya Rose (eds.), *Gender and Class in Modern Europe* (Ithaca, NY, 1996), provides a series of essays concentrating on work and politics. An innovative approach to social history is adopted by Dror Wahrman, *Imagining the Middle Class: The Political Representation of Class in Britain c. 1780–1840* (Cambridge, 1995). James Sheehan, *German Liberalism in the Nineteenth Century* (Chicago, 1978), has much to say on the social context in which liberalism flourished. William Sewell, *Work and Revolution in France: The Language of Labour from the Old Regime to 1848* (Cambridge, 1980), represents an early but approachable example of labour history taking the 'linguistic turn'. Ira Katznelson and Aristide Zolberg (eds.), *Working-Class Formation: Nineteenth-Century Patterns in Western Europe and the United States* (Princeton, 1986), is starting to look outdated in its approach, but contains some excellent case studies. Jacques Rancière, *The Nights of Labor: The Workers' Dream in Nineteenth Century France* (Philadelphia, 1989), is difficult, but ultimately seductive. A controversial attempt at 'postmodern' history is Patrick Joyce, *Democratic Subjects: The Self and the Social in Nineteenth-Century England* (Cambridge, 1994).

The European economy, 1815–1914

The trilogy of E. J. Hobsbawm, *The Age of Revolution, 1789–1848* (London, 1962), *The Age of Capital, 1848–1875* (London, 1975), and *The Age of Empire, 1875–1914* (London, 1987), although informed by the author's Marxist beliefs, remains the best general introduction to the nineteenth century, admirably balancing and relating the economic, social, cultural, and political dimensions. Although now rather dated, the two collections of essays edited by Carlo M. Cipolla—*The Fontana Economic History of Europe*, iii. *The*

Industrial Revolution (Glasgow, 1973), and iv. *The Emergence of Industrial Societies* (Glasgow, 1973)—remain useful in providing concise introductions to specific aspects. Peter Mathias and M. M. Postan (eds.), *The Cambridge Economic History of Europe*, vii. *The Industrial Economies: Capital, Labour, and Enterprise. Part 1: Britain, France, Germany and Scandinavia* (Cambridge, 1978), and Sidney Pollard (ed.), *The Cambridge Economic History of Europe*, viii. *The Industrial Economies: The Development of Economic and Social Policies* (Cambridge, 1989), are somewhat cumbersome, but these two volumes contain some superb chapters, notably Tilly's on Germany in volume vii and Schremmer's on public finance in volume viii. Alexander Gerschenkron, *Economic Backwardness in Historical Perspective* (Cambridge, Mass., 1962), provides the classic developmental model applied to European industrialization. Sidney Pollard, *Peaceful Conquest: The Industrialisation of Europe 1760–1970* (Oxford, 1981), is the best account of the diffusion of industrial technology and manufacture; he is especially good on the regional distribution of economic change. D. S. Landes, *The Unbound Prometheus: Technological Change and Industrial Development in Western Europe from 1750 to the Present* (Cambridge, 1969), remains the most readable history of technological change in the period. Charles P. Kindleberger, *A Financial History of Western Europe* (London, 1984), is an indispensable book that brilliantly combines banking and fiscal history. Hartmut Kaelble, *Industrialisation and Social Inequality in 19th Century Europe* (Leamington Spa, 1986), provides an exceptionally good introduction to the social consequences of industrialization, full of useful data on income and wealth distribution drawn from a wide range of monographs. Clive Trebilcock, *The Industrialisation of the Continental Powers, 1780–1914* (London, 1981), is an excellent survey that is especially good at relating economic developments to great power rivalry. Paul Bairoch, 'Europe's Gross National Product: 1800–1975', *Journal of European Economic History* (1976), 273–340, is an ambitious but useful attempt to give orders of magnitude to the growth of European countries' GNP. No student can get far without B. R. Mitchell, *European Historical Statistics, 1750–1975* (London, 1975), an indispensable compendium of statistics.

Culture

Robert Rosenblum and H. W. Janson, *19th Century Art* (New York, 1984), is a handsomely illustrated survey of both painting and sculpture. Nikolaus Pevsner, *A History of Building Types* (Princeton, 1976), is both a useful introduction to architecture and a guide to cultural institutions. Also good on the visual arts are Hugh Honour, *Romanticism* (London, 1968), and Linda Nochlin, *Realism* (London, 1971). Carl Dahlhaus, *Nineteenth-Century Music* (Berkeley and Los Angeles, 1989), offers a challenging analysis of music and its institutional setting. More conventional but very useful are the two relevant volumes in the Man and Music series, namely Alexander Ringer (ed.), *The Early Romantic Era: Between Revolutions: 1789 and 1848* (London, 1990), and Jim Samson (ed.), *The Late Romantic Era: From the Mid-Nineteenth Century to the First World War* (London, 1991). Owen Chadwick, *The Secularisation of the European Mind in the Nineteenth Century* (Cambridge, 1975), discusses the problem of religion as seen by the century's most important thinkers. Hugh McLeod, *Religion and the People of Western Europe, 1789–1970* (Oxford, 1981), is still the best one-volume introduction to the social history of nineteenth-century religion. R. C. Colby *et al.* (eds.), *Companion to the History of Modern Science* (London and New York, 1996), is a collection of articles surveying various disciplines and themes. Adrian Desmond and James Moore, *Darwin: The Life of a Tormented Evolutionist* (New York and London, 1991), is a detailed biography that emphasizes the historical rootedness of Darwin's ideas. David Lowenthal, *The Past is a Foreign Country* (Cambridge, 1985), is an extended essay on the role of the past in modern culture. Maurice Mandelbaum, *History, Man and Reason: A Study in Nineteenth-Century Thought* (Baltimore, 1974), provides a history of ideas about the past. The best single book on Hegel and his legacy is John Toews, *Hegelianism: The Path toward Dialectical Humanism, 1805–1841* (Cambridge, 1980). H. Stuart Hughes, *Consciousness and Society: The Reorientation of European Social Thought, 1890–1930* (New York, 1958), may now look out of date but in fact is still a valuable introduction to modernist ideas about society. Carl B. Schorske, *Fin-de-siècle Vienna: Politics and Culture* (New York, 1980), has proved an influential analysis of modernism in Vienna; it is especially good on art and literature. Eugen Weber, *France, fin de siècle* (Cambridge, Mass., 1986), is both informative and highly entertaining.

International politics, peace, and war, 1815–1914

For a fuller guide to the massive monographic literature, see the American Historical Association's *Guide to Historical Literature*, 2 vols. (3rd edn., Oxford, 1995), ii, section 47. A detailed account of the international relations of the first half of the century is to be found in Paul W. Schroeder, *The Transformation of European Politics 1763–48* (Oxford, 1994). For the period 1848–1914, A. J. P. Taylor, *The Struggle for Mastery in Europe 1848–1914* (Oxford, 1954), is still a classic. Norman Rich, *Great Power Diplomacy 1814–1914* (New York, 1992), gives an excellent overview of the entire century. Pierre Renouvin and Jean-Baptiste Duroselle, *Introduction to the History of International Relations*, analyses the *forces profondes* behind international politics, drawing mainly on the nineteenth and twentieth centuries. For the most persistent and dangerous problem of European diplomacy, the Eastern Question, M. S. Anderson, *The Eastern Question 1774–1923: A Study in International Relations* (London, 1966), is still the best introduction. Barbara

Jelavich, *Russia's Balkan Entanglements 1806–1914* (Cambridge, 1991), traces Russia's leading role and mainly frustrating experiences in it. Raymond F. Betts, *The False Dawn: European Imperialism in the Nineteenth Century* (Minneapolis, 1976), is a helpful general introduction to European imperialism. Wolfgang J. Mommsen, *Theories of Imperialism* (Chicago, 1982), contains stimulating discussions of some of the major controversies. See also the titles listed in the following section. For the theoretical debate, Kenneth Bourne, *The Foreign Policy of Victorian England 1830–1902* (Oxford, 1970), surveys British policy for most of the period, with accompanying documents. F. R. Bridge, *The Habsburg Monarchy among the Great Powers 1815–1918* (New York, 1990), is authoritative for Austrian policy. Dietrich Geyer, *Russian Imperialism: The Interaction of Domestic and Foreign Policy 1860–1914* (New Haven, 1987), is penetrating on Russian policy. The best study in English of German unification and German policy under Bismarck is Otto Pflanze, *Bismarck and the Development of Germany*, 3 vols. (Princeton, 1990), while Paul M. Kennedy, *The Rise of Anglo-German Antagonism 1860–1914* (London, 1980), is indispensable for an understanding of Anglo-German relations. James Joll, *The Origins of the First World War* (2nd edn., London, 1992), is a splendidly thoughtful discussion of this controversial theme and an outstanding volume in the Longman series on the origins of modern wars, all of which can be recommended.

Overseas expansion, imperialism, and empire, 1815–1914

Two general accounts offer different entry points: D. K. Fieldhouse, *Economics and Empire 1830–1914* (London, 1973), provides detail on the frontier, where European and indigenous societies met. Andrew Porter, *European Imperialism 1860–1914* (Basingstoke, 1994), contains a full list of recent references. The following studies of individual countries underline the variety of Europe's relations with the non-European world while also providing numerous additional references: P. J. Cain and A. G. Hopkins, *British Imperialism: Innovation and Expansion 1688–1914* (London, 1993), Ronald Hyam, *Britain's Imperial Century 1815–1914* (2nd edn. Basingstoke, 1994), Lance E. Davis and Robert A. Huttenback, *Mammon and the Pursuit of Empire: The Political Economy of British Imperialism 1860–1912* (Cambridge, 1987), C. M. Andrew and A. S. Kanya-Forstner, *France Overseas: The Great War and the Climax of French Imperial Expansion* (London, 1981), Robert Aldrich, *Greater France: A History of French Overseas Expansion* (Basingstoke, 1996), Jacques Marseille, *Empire colonial et capitalisme français: Histoire d'un divorce* (Paris, 1984), Gervase Clarence-Smith, *The Third Portuguese Empire 1825–1975* (Manchester, 1985), Maarten Kuitenbrouwer, *The Netherlands and the Rise of Modern Imperialism: Colonies and Foreign Policy, 1870–1902* (Oxford, 1991), Hans-Ulrich Wehler, *The German Empire 1871–1918* (Leamington Spa, 1985), and Wolfgang J. Mommsen, *Imperial Germany 1867–1918: Politics, Culture and Society in an Authoritarian State* (London, 1995). There are innumerable case studies. The most celebrated also deals, fortunately, with the most celebrated case: Ronald Robinson and John Gallagher with Alice Denny, *Africa and the Victorians: The Official Mind of Imperialism* (2nd edn., London, 1981). H. L Wesseling, *Divide and Rule: The Partition of Africa, 1880–1914* (Westport, Ct., 1996), is valuable for a fully European perspective on the process. Three sets of essays provide guides to influential interpretations: Roger Owen and Bob Sutcliffe (eds.), *Studies in the Theory of Imperialism* (London, 1972), William Roger Louis (ed.), *Imperialism: The Robinson and Gallagher Controversy* (New York, 1976), and Raymond E. Dumett (ed.), *Gentlemanly Capitalism and British Imperialism: The New Debate on Empire* (London, 1998). The *Journal of Imperial and Commonwealth History* is the leading journal in the field.

Chronology: the 'Long Nineteenth Century', 1789–1914

1789   MAY   Meeting of the Estates General.
      JULY   Fall of the Bastille.
      AUG.   Promulgation of the Declaration of the Rights of Man.
      OCT.   The royal family and the National Assembly brought to Paris.
      NOV.   Expropriation of the Church begins.
           Leblanc invents process for deriving soda from sea salt.

1790   Death of Joseph II, succeeded by his brother Leopold II.
      JULY   Civil Constitution of the Clergy.
           Burke, *Reflections on the Revolution in France.*
           Mozart, *Cosí fan tutte.*

1791   MAY   New Polish constitution.
      JUNE   Louis XVI's flight to Varennes.
           Beginning of Saint-Domingue slave revolt.
           Mozart, *The Magic Flute.*
           Tom Paine, *Rights of Man.*
           Revolution government abolishes all guilds in France.
           Brandenburg Gate completed.

1792   Death of Leopold II, accession of Francis II.
      APR.   Wars of the French Revolution begin.
      AUG.   France becomes a republic.
      SEPT.   Massacres in Paris.
      SEPT.   Battle of Valmy.

1793   JAN.   Execution of Louis XVI.
      MAR.   Counter-revolutionary revolt in the Vendée begins.
      APR.   Committee of Public Safety established.
      AUG.   *Levée en masse.*
      SEPT   Terror begins.

Second partition of Poland.

Last witch executed in Poland.

Central Museum of the Arts opened in the Louvre.

Revolutionary government in France abolishes all seigneurial claims, restrictions, and obligations.

1794 JULY Battle of Fleurus.

JULY Fall of Robespierre.

Prussian *Allgemeines Landrecht* (General Legal Code) promulgated.

1795 British occupation of Dutch colonies.

Third partition leads to the extinction of the Polish state.

Treaties of Basle end wars between France and Prussia and France and Spain.

Belgium annexed to France.

Crompton's spinning mule is adapted for power.

1796 Bonaparte conquers northern Italy.

Catherine the Great of Russia dies; with the accession of her son, Paul I, Russia suspends its role in the First Coalition.

Trevithick begins to apply steam power to traction.

Edward Jenner introduces vaccination against smallpox.

1797 Treaty of Campo Formio ends war between France and Austria.

1798 General Bonaparte leads an expedition to conquer Egypt.

Battle of the Nile, a British fleet commanded by Nelson destroys Napoleon's fleet.

Irish rebellion.

War of the Second Coalition.

Wordsworth, *Lyrical Ballads.*

Coleridge, *Lyrical Ballads.*

Malthus, *Essay on the Principle of Population.*

Haydn, *Creation.*

Aloys Senefelder invents lithography.

1798–9   Tennant and Macintosh invent bleaching powder for cloth.

1799 MAR.   War between France and Austria resumes; Russia enters the war on the side of Austria; the French are expelled from Italy.

OCT.   Bonaparte returns from Egypt.

NOV.   Bonaparte seizes power in France.
Collapse of Dutch East India Company.
First water-driven spinning mule is set up in Saxony.

1800   Battle of Marengo, Bonaparte defeats the Austrians.

Battle of Hohenlinden, Moreau defeats the Austrians.
Friedrich von Hardenberg *alias* Novalis, *Hymns to the Night.*
Alessandro Volta demonstrates first electric battery.

1801   Treaty of Lunéville ends war between France and Austria.

Assassination of Paul I, accession of Alexander I.
Bonaparte's Concordat with the Pope.
Act of Union unites Great Britain and Ireland.

1802   Treaty of Amiens.

Chateaubriand, *The Genius of Christianity.*

1803   War resumes between France and Britain.

France sells Louisiana to the USA.

Imperial Recess decrees sweeping territorial changes in Germany, which ensure French domination.
Widespread secularization of monasteries in Germany.
Beethoven's Third Symphony, 'Eroica', composed (first performed 1805).

1804   Francis II, Holy Roman Emperor, proclaims himself also Emperor of Austria as Francis I,

Bonaparte proclaims himself Emperor Napoleon I, is crowned by the Pope Pius VII.
Code Napoléon enacted.

1805   Bonaparte reorganizes Italy under direct French control.

AUG.   The third coalition consisting of Britain, Austria, Russia, and Sweden is formed against France; war resumes on the continent.

OCT.   Austrian army capitulates at Ulm.

OCT.   Battle of Trafalgar.

DEC.   Baffle of Austerlitz; Napoleon inflicts a crushing defeat on an Austro-Russian army.

DEC.   Treaty of Pressburg; Russia withdraws from the war.

1806 MAR.   Napoleon makes his brother Joseph King of Naples.

JUNE   Napoleon makes his brother Louis King of the Netherlands.

JULY   Napoleon reorganizes Germany as the 'Confederation of the Rhine'.

AUG.   Formal end of the Holy Roman Empire when the Emperor Francis II abdicates and becomes Francis I of Austria.

OCT.   Prussia declares war on France.

OCT.   Battles of Jena and Auerstedt, Prussia defeated.

1807   Russia rejoins war as Prussia's ally; indecisive campaign in Poland.

JUNE   Decisive French victory at Battle of Friedland.

JULY   Treaty of Tilsit ends war; France and Russia enter alliance. Portuguese royal family flees to Brazil.

Fichte, *Addresses to the German Nation.*

Caspar David Friedrich, *The Cross in the Mountains.*

Britain abolishes the slave trade.

Humphry Davy isolates sodium and potassium from their compounds.

1808   Napoleon imposes his brother Joseph as King of Spain; Spanish people rise in revolt, assisted by the British army.

Rome occupied by French troops.

Goethe, *Faust*, Part I.

1809 APR.   War resumes between France and Austria.

MAY   Austrians defeat Napoleon at the Battle of Aspern-Essling.

JULY   Napoleon defeats the Austrians at the Battle of Wagram.

OCT.   Treaty of Schönbrunn ends war between Austria and France. Papal States annexed to France.

1810   Napoleon marries the Archduchess Marie Louise, daughter of the Emperor Francis I.

Napoleon annexes the Netherlands to France.

Napoleon annexes the north-western coast of Germany.

Revolts against Spanish rule in Venezuela and Rio de la Plata (future Argentina).

1811   'Luddite' machine-breaking riots in Britain.

1812   Battle of Salamanca, defeat of French in Spain by army commanded by the Duke of Wellington.

Goya, *The Disasters of War.*

JUNE   Napoleon with his German and Italian satellites invades Russia.

SEPT.   Napoleon fights the indecisive Battle of Borodino and enters Moscow a week later.

OCT.   Napoleon's retreat from Moscow begins.

DEC.   Remnants of Napoleon's army leaves Russia.

Henry Bell's *The Comet,* the world's first commercial steamship, begins operations on the Clyde.

1813 FEB.   Treaty of Kalisch between Prussia and Russia.

JUNE   Wellington defeats the French at Vittoria, prompting King Joseph to flee to France.

AUG.   Austria declares war on France.

OCT.   Napoleon is defeated at the Battle of Leipzig and loses control of Germany.

DEC.   Prussian army under Blücher begins the invasion of France.

Colombia declares independence from Spain.

Rossini, *Tancredi.*

1814 MAR.   Allies abandon attempt to negotiate with Napoleon and conclude Treaty of Chaumont for wartime and post-war alliance.

MAR. Wellington captures Bordeaux.

APR. Napoleon abdicates, is exiled to the island of Elba; Louis XVIII returned to French throne.

SEPT. General negotiations for a comprehensive peace settlement begin at Vienna.

Uruguay declares independence from Spain.

1815 MAR. Napoleon returns from Elba

JUNE (18th) Battle of Waterloo; Napoleon abdicates and is exiled to St Helena.

Congress of Vienna completes restructuring of Europe.

SEPT. Russia, Austria, and Prussia form the 'Holy Alliance'.

NOV. Britain, Russia, Austria and Prussia form a Quadruple Alliance to maintain the Vienna settlement.

NOV. Second treaty of Paris reduces France to frontiers of 1790.

Humphry Davy invents miner's safety lamp.

1816 Chile declares independence from Spain.

1817 Wartburg Festival, liberal-nationalist demonstration by German students.

1818 Hegel becomes Professor of Philosophy at the University of Berlin.

Prado Museum founded at Madrid.

1819 Carlsbad decrees suppressing political activity in Germany.

First steam-powered ship (the Savannah) crosses the Atlantic.

Peterloo Massacre at Manchester.

Schopenhauer, *The World as Will and Idea*.

Géricault, *The Raft of the Medusa*.

Singapore founded by British East India Company.

1820 Revolutions in Spain and Portugal.

Spain cedes Florida to the United States.

1820–21 Revolts in Naples and Piedmont and their repression.

Conferences at Troppau and Laibach; European Concert splits over right of intervention.

1821   Peru and Panama declare independence from Spain.

Michael Faraday discovers electro-magnetic rotation.
Death of Napoleon on St Helena.
Carl Maria von Weber, *Der Freischütz*
Klenze, *Valhalla* (completed 1842).
Constable, *Haywain*.
Hegel, *Philosophy of Right*.

1822   Greek declaration of independence.

Brazil declares independence from Portugal.
Congress of Verona.
Pushkin, *Eugene Onegin*.

1823   French invasion of Spain to restore Bourbon authority.

New South Wales becomes a Crown colony.
Daniel O'Connell forms Catholic Association of Ireland.
Beethoven, *Missa Solemnis*.
Schinkel, *Old Museum*, Berlin (completed 1830).
Robert Smirke, *The British Museum* (completed 1847).

1824   Death of Byron at Missolonghi.

Delacroix, *Massacre of Chios*.
Beethoven, Symphony No. 9 ('Choral').

1825   Decembrist revolt in Russia following death of Alexander I.
Financial crash.
Coronation of Charles X of France at Rheims.
Opening of Stockton–Darlington railway, the first line to carry passengers.
Financial crisis in London.
Portugal recognizes the independence of Brazil.
Bolivia declares independence from Spain.
Manzoni, *I Promessi Sposi*.

1827   Anglo–Russian–French alliance and intervention in Greek

War leads to destruction of the Turkish–Egyptian fleet at the Battle of Navarino.

Joseph Niepce produces photographs on asphalt-coated plate.

Death of Beethoven.

Schubert, *Die Winterreise.*

1828   Russo-Turkish War, Russian victory, French occupation of southern Greece.

1829   Treaty of Adrianople ends Russo-Turkish War, leads to independent kingdom of Greece (1832).

Catholic emancipation in Ireland and Britain.

George and Robert Stephenson's Rocket wins Liverpool–Manchester railway competition.

1830 JUNE   French invade Algiers.

      JULY   Revolution in Paris; Charles X flees; Louis Philippe becomes king.

      AUG.   Revolution in Belgium.

      SEPT.   Revolts in Hesse, Brunswick, and Saxony

      NOV.–   1831 revolt in Poland.
      SEPT.

Delacroix, *Liberty Leading the People.*
Victor Hugo, *Hernani.*
Stendhal, *Scarlet and Black.*

1831   Belgium achieves recognition of independence from the Netherlands.

Insurrection in Lyons.
Darwin sails to South America on *HMS Beagle.*
Chloroform invented.

1831–2   Risings in Italy, especially in the Papal States, suppressed.

1832   Great Reform Act in Britain.

Britain declares sovereignty over the Falkland Islands.
Mazzini founds 'Young Italy'.
Hambach festival, radical German demonstration.

Karl Friedrich Gauss and Wilhelm Weber build first electric telegraph at Göttingen.

Death of Goethe; posthumous publication of his *Faust*, part II.

Berlioz, *Symphonie fantastique.*

1832–3   First Turco-Egyptian War; Russia intervenes to save the Ottoman Sultan.

1833   Treaty of Unkiar-Skelessi: Russia allies with Ottoman Empire.

Holy Alliance renewed over Poland and the Ottoman Empire.

1834   Workers' revolt in Lyons.

New Poor Law in England.

Prussian customs union (*Zollverein*) founded.

Carlist Wars begin in Spain; Britain and France ally to exclude the Holy Alliance.

Slavery is abolished in all British possessions.

1835   Donizetti, *Lucia di Lammermoor.*

1836   Chartist agitation begins in Britain.

Glinka, *A Life for the Tsar.*

Charles Barry wins the competition to design the new Houses of Parliament (built 1840–70).

Meyerbeer, *Les Huguenots.*

1837   Accession of Queen Victoria.

August Borsig's iron foundry opened in Berlin.

Electric telegraph patented.

1838   H. G. Dyer and J. Hemming invent ammonia process for making soda.

Louis Daguerre invents process for producing a silver image on a copper plate.

Charles Dickens, *Oliver Twist.*

1838–48	Chartist Movement in England.

1839   Second Turco-Egyptian War; joint European intervention again saves Ottoman Sultan from defeat.

Treaty of London, fixing Belgian–Dutch borders, guaranteeing Belgian neutrality and establishing independent Luxembourg.

Britain annexes Aden.

Chartist convention and petition in England.

'First Opium War' between Britain and China.

James Nasmyth designs steam hammer.

Charles Goodyear vulcanizes rubber.

1840   Dispute between France and the other powers over the Turkish–Egyptian settlement produces major European crisis.

Napoleon's ashes returned from St Helena and interred at the Invalides.

Treaty of Waitangi confirms British sovereignty over New Zealand.

Justus Liebig discovers elements of artificial fertilizer.

Proudhon, *What is Property?*

1841   Straits Convention restores Concert, settles Eastern Question.

Friedrich List, *National System of Political Economy.*

Ludwig Feuerbach, *The Essence of Christianity.*

1842   Hong Kong ceded to Britain.

British conquest of Assam and Burma begins.

British driven out of Afghanistan.

Tahiti made a French protectorate.

Gogol, *Dead Souls.*

1843   Legalization of export of machinery from Britain.

France annexes Ivory Coast and Dahomey.

Carlyle, *Past and Present.*

1844   Revolt of Silesian weavers.

Engels, *Condition of the Working Classes in England.*

1845   Great Famine begins in Ireland.

1846   Polish revolt in Galicia; Cracow annexed by Austria.
             Repeal of British Corn Laws.

1847   Civil war in Switzerland.
             Discovery of gold in California.
             Economic crisis in Europe.
             Charlotte Brontë, *Jane Eyre*.
             Emily Brontë, *Wuthering Heights*.

1847–8   Banquet campaign in France.

1848 JAN.   Revolts in Sicily and Naples.

  FEB.   (22–24th) Revolution in Paris; proclamation of French Second Republic and universal male suffrage.

  MAR.   Uprisings in Munich, Vienna, Budapest, Venice, Cracow, Milan, Berlin.

  MAR.–   Hungarian independence declared.
  APR.
          Abolition of serfdom in central Europe.

  APR.   Chartist demonstration in London.

  MAY   Frankfurt parliament meets.

  JUNE   (17th) Rising in Prague crushed.

  JUNE   (22–24th) Insurrection in Paris crushed.

  JULY–   Northern Italy reconquered by Austrians.
  AUG.

  OCT.   (31st) Vienna bombarded into surrender.

  DEC.   Emperor Ferdinand of Austria abdicates, is succeeded by Francis Joseph.

  DEC.   Louis-Napoleon Bonaparte elected President of French Republic.
          Marx and Engels, *The Communist Manifesto*.
          J. S. Mill, *The Principles of Political Economy*.

1849 FEB.   Roman Republic proclaimed.

  JULY   French troops suppress Roman Republic.

  AUG.   Hungarian nationalists defeated.

AUG. Austrians recapture Venice.

Britain annexes Punjab.

Courbet, *A Burial at Ornans*.

1850 Cross-Channel telegraph cable.

Millet, *The Sower*.

Faraday makes public his theory of magnetism.

1851 DEC Louis Napoleon Bonaparte's coup d'état.

Isaac Singer invents sewing machine.

Discovery of gold in Australia.

The Great Exhibition, London.

1852 DEC. Louis Napoleon Bonaparte proclaimed Emperor as Napoleon III.

Burma becomes a province of India.

Pereire brothers found Crédit Mobilier.

Charles Dickens, *Bleak House*.

Holman Hunt, *The Light of the World*.

1853–6 Crimean War.

1854 Abraham Gesner manufactures kerosene.

Heinrich Goebel invents first electric light bulb.

1856 Peace of Paris ends Crimean War, opens Italian Question.

Henry Bessemer develops steel converter.

William Henry Perkin makes synthetic mauve dye from naphtha.

Indian Mutiny.

Sinn Fein founded in Ireland.

1857 Millet, *The Gleaners*.

1858 JULY (20th) Cavour and Napoleon III sign the agreement of Plombières, an alliance against Austria.

Bernadette Soubirous experiences a vision of the Virgin Mary at Lourdes.

1859 APR. (2nd) Austrian army invades Piedmont.

  MAY (3rd) France declares war on Austria.

  JUNE Austrians defeated at Magenta and Solferino.

  JULY (11th) Truce of Villafranca.

    French occupy Saigon.

    Charles Darwin, *On the Origin of Species.*

    First practical storage battery invented.

1860   Sardinia-Piedmont annexes Lombardy and much of central Italy; France annexes Nice and Savoy.

  MAY Garibaldi and his 'Thousand' sail for Sicily.

  AUG. (22nd) Garibaldi invades the Italian mainland.

1861   Victor Emmanuel II assumes title of King of Italy.

    Emancipation of the serfs in Russia.

    Friedrich Siemens and Pierre and Emile Martin develop open-hearth process for making steel.

1862   Bismarck appointed Minister-President of Prussia.

    Albert Memorial.

    Garnier, Opera house, Paris (completed 1875).

1863   Revolt in Poland against Russian rule is suppressed.

    Salon des Refusés, Paris.

    Manet, *Le Déjuner sur l'herbe.*

1863–65 Legal and local government reforms in Russia.

1864 JAN. Austria and Prussia go to war against Denmark over Schleswig-Holstein.

  OCT. (30th) Peace of Vienna; Denmark cedes Schleswig-Holstein to Austria and Prussia.

    Tolstoy, *War and Peace.*

    Newman, *Apologia pro vita sua.*

    Pius IX, *Syllabus errorum.*

    The First International, London.

    Pasteurization invented.

| 1865 | | Transatlantic telegraph cable completed. |

Pierre Lallement builds first pedalled bicycle.

| 1866 | APR. | War between Austria and Prussia. |
| | JULY | (3rd) Prussia defeats Austria at the battle of Königgrätz (Sadowa). |

Peace of Prague (German Confederation abolished, Prussia greatly expanded, North German Confederation formed).

Venice ceded to Italy by Austria.

Invention of dynamite by Alfred Nobel.

Dostoevsky, *Crime and Punishment*.

Financial crisis in Britain.

| 1867 | | Austro-Hungarian Compromise creates federal dual monarchy. |

British Second Reform Act widens suffrage to male householders.

Collapse of the Crédit Mobilier.

Zola, *Thérèse Raquin*.

Manet, *The Execution of the Emperor Maximilian*.

Ibsen, *Peer Gynt*.

Karl Marx, *Das Kapital*, vol i.

| 1868 | FEB. | (28th) Disraeli becomes Prime Minister for the first time. |
| | DEC. | (9th) Gladstone becomes Prime Minister for the first time. |

Discovery of Kimberley diamond deposits.

Dostoevsky, *The Idiot*.

| 1869 | | Opening of Suez Canal. |

Matthew Arnold, *Culture and Anarchy*.

| 1869–70 | | 'Liberal empire' in France. |

| 1870 | JULY | (19th) France declares war on Prussia. |
| | AUG. | (19th) French army besieged at Metz. |

SEPT. (2nd) French defeated at Sedan; Napoleon III is taken prisoner.

SEPT. (4th) Republic proclaimed in France.

SEPT. (20th) Italian forces enter Rome.

Zénobe Gramme makes the first dynamo with ring armature.

Adolf von Bayer synthesizes the dye indigo.

1871–8 German *Kulturkampf.*

1871 JAN. (18th) William I of Prussia proclaimed German Emperor.

JAN. (28th) Paris capitulates.

MAR. (18th) Rising of the Paris Commune.

MAY (10th) Peace of Frankfurt; France cedes Alsace and Lorraine to Germany.

MAY (28th) End of the Paris Commune.

George Eliot, *Middlemarch.*

1873 Financial crisis in Europe, beginning in Vienna; Great Depression begins (lasting until 1896).

League of the Three Emperors (Germany, Austria, Russia).

First Impressionist Exhibition.

Constitution of French Third Republic.

1875 Revolt in Bosnia-Herzegovina touches off Eastern Crisis.

German Social Democratic Party founded.

Britain acquires majority shareholding in Suez Canal Company.

1876 Queen Victoria proclaimed Empress of India.

Alexander Graham Bell patents the telephone.

First performance of Richard Wagner's *Der Ring des Nibelungen* at Bayreuth.

Thomas Edison invents the phonograph.

Renoir, *Le Moulin de la Galette.*

Brahms, *Symphony No. 1.*

Thomas Edison makes first electric filament lamp.

Sidney Thomas and Percy Gilchrist perfect 'basic' process for steel production.

Protective tariffs introduced in Germany.

1877–8   War between Russia and Turkey.

1878   Congress of Berlin sorts out the Eastern Question (for the time being).

Anti-socialist law in Germany.

Theodor Fontane, *Before the Storm.*

Degas, *Dancer on the stage.*

1879   Germany and Austria-Hungary sign the Dual Alliance.

First electric tram exhibited, at Berlin.

1880–1   First Boer War brings recognition of Boer semi-independence.

1881 MAR.   Assassination of Alexander II of Russia.

  AUG.   Irish Land Act.

Tunis becomes a French protectorate.

1881–6   Welfare reforms in Germany.

1882   Germany, Austria-Hungary, and Italy form the Triple Alliance.

French occupy Hanoi.

British occupy Egypt and the Sudan.

Gottlieb Daimler builds petrol engine.

Wagner, *Parsifal.*

1883   French invade Madagascar.

Nietzsche, *Thus Spake Zarathustra.*

Death of Wagner.

1884   Russia begins to lose control of Bulgaria, causing serious Eastern crisis.

Charles Parsons constructs first practical steam turbine.

Hiram Maxim devises recoil-operated machine gun.

Seurat, *A Bathing-Place.*

Sacconi, *The Victor Emmanuel Monument,* Rome (completed 1923).

Germany begins to found a colonial empire in Africa.

1885   Congo Free State established under Leopold II of Belgium.

Gottlieb Daimler invents internal combustion engine.

Carl Benz builds single-cylinder engine for car.

Discovery of gold in Transvaal.

Cézanne, *Montagne Ste-Victoire.*

Van Gogh, *The Potato-Eaters.*

1886   British annex Upper Burma.

1887   Germany and Russia conclude Reinsurance Treaty.

British annex Zululand.

'Bloody Sunday' in London.

Boulangist crisis in France.

Cyanide process for extracting gold and silver.

1888   North Borneo, Brunei, and Sarawak made British protectorates.

J. B. Dunlop invents pneumatic tyre

Strindberg, *Miss Julie.*

William II becomes German Emperor.

1889   Eiffel Tower opened.

1890   Bismarck dismissed; Germany drops Reinsurance Treaty.

Germans occupy Ruanda-Urundi.

Britain cedes Heligoland to Germany in return for Zanzibar and Pemba.

Baring's financial crisis in London.

J. G. Frazer, *The Golden Bough.*

Ibsen, *Hedda Gabler.*

1890–8   Manhood suffrage introduced in Spain, Belgium, the Netherlands, and Norway.

1891   Pope Leo XIII issues the bull *Rerum novarum* on social issues.

1892   Rudolf Diesel patents his eponymous engine.

1893 JAN.   (13th) Independent Labour Party founded in Britain.
Alliance between France and Russia.
Tchaikovsky, *Symphony No. 6 (Pathétique)*.

1894   President Carnot of France assassinated.
Britain occupies Matabeleland.
Uganda made a British protectorate.
Italy invades Ethiopia.
Togoland made a German protectorate.
Alfred Dreyfus condemned for treason.

1894–5   Sino-Japanese War; Russia leads tripartite European intervention to frustrate Japanese victory.

1895   Louis and Auguste Lumière invent the cinematograph.
Guglielmo Marconi invents the wireless radio.
Röntgen discovers X-rays.
Lumière brothers invent motion-picture camera and projector.
Oscar Wilde, *The Importance of being Earnest.*
Oscar Wilde sentenced to two years' hard labour for sodomy.

1895–8   Russia gains dominant political, military, and economic hold on Manchuria and North China.

1896   Italian army defeated by Ethiopia at the battle of Adowa.

1897   Anti-Semite Karl Lueger becomes mayor of Vienna.
Spanish prime minister assassinated.

Discovery of gold in the Yukon, Canada.

Germany begins to build a major battle fleet.

Germany touches off scramble for naval bases and other concessions in China.

1898 JULY 'Fashoda incident'—confrontation between Britain and France in the Sudan.

Empress Elizabeth of Austria assassinated.

War between the United States of America and Spain.

Marie and Pierre Curie discover polonium and radium.

1899 SEPT. (19th) Dreyfus pardoned.

OCT. Second Boer War begins.

Peace conference at The Hague establishes an international court of arbitration.

Houston Stewart Chamberlain, *The Foundations of the Nineteenth Century.*

Freud, *The Interpretation of Dreams.*

1900 British Labour Party founded.

King Umberto I of Italy assassinated.

Boxer Rebellion in China.

Russia occupies Manchuria.

First flight of a Zeppelin airship.

1901 Max Weber, *The Protestant Ethic and the Spirit of Capitalism.*

President McKinley of the USA assassinated by anarchist.

Thomas Mann, *Buddenbrooks.*

Completion of Trans-Siberian Railway.

1902 Limited Anglo-Japanese Alliance signed.

Lenin, *What is to be Done?*

1903 King and Queen of Serbia assassinated.

1904 **8 Apr.** Entente Cordiale between Britain and France.

Russo-Japanese War begins.

Chekhov, *The Cherry Orchard.*

Otto Wagner, *Post Office Savings Bank*, Vienna (completed 1912).

Gaudi, *Casa Batlló*, Barcelona.

1905 JAN. (22nd) 'Bloody Sunday' in St Petersburg begins revolution in Russia.

FEB. First Moroccan Crisis.

OCT. (17th) Nicholas II promises a constitution and an elected parliament.

OCT. Norway regains independence from Sweden.

Schlieffen Plan.

Group of German Expressionist artists known as 'The Bridge' founded.

Einstein's theory of relativity.

1906 Constitution granted in Russia.

1906 Launch of HMS *Dreadnought.*

1907 Manhood suffrage in Austria.

AUG. Britain and Russia sign a convention.

Picasso, *Les Demoiselles d'Avignon.*

1908 Austria-Hungary annexes Bosnia-Herzegovina; Bosnian Crisis erupts.

King and Crown Prince of Portugal assassinated.

Fritz Haber introduces industrial process for synthesizing ammonia.

Georges Sorel, *Reflections on Violence.*

Braque, *Houses at L'Estaque.*

Peter Behrens designs the AEG Turbine Factory, Berlin.

1909 Louis Blériot flies across Channel in monoplane.

Diaghilev opens his season of *Ballets russes* in Paris.

1910   E. M. Forster, *Howard's End*.

1911   Assassination of the Russian prime minister Stolypin in Kiev.

Italy goes to war with the Ottoman Empire, seizing Libya and the Dodecanese Islands.

Second Moroccan Crisis.

Group of German arists known as 'The Blue Rider' founded at Munich.

Rutherford's theory of atomic structure.

1912   Russia promotes the Balkan League under its protection manhood suffrage in Italy.

Social Democratic Party becomes the largest party in the German parliament.

Spanish prime minister assassinated.

Jung, *The Theory of Psychoanalysis*.

1912–3   First and Second Balkan wars.

1913   Freud, *Totem and Taboo*.

Stravinsky, *The Rite of Spring*.

Proust, *Swann's Way*.

1914 JUNE   (28th) Assassination of the Archduke Franz Ferdinand at Sarajevo.

JULY   (24th) Russia threatens war if Austria-Hungary attacks Serbia.

JULY   (25th) Austria-Hungary mobilizes against Serbia.

JULY   (30th) Russia begins general mobilization.

AUG.   (1st) Germany declares war on Russia.

AUG.   (3rd) Germany declares war on France and invades Belgium.

AUG.   (4th) Britain declares war on Germany.

AUG.   (5th) Austria-Hungary declares war on Russia.

AUG.   (25–30th) German army commanded by Hindenburg routs invading Russian army at Tannenberg.

SEPT. (5–14th) German invasion of France is halted at the battle of the Marne.

SEPT. (27th) Russians invade Hungary.

James Joyce, *Dubliners.*

Walter Gropius, *Model Factory* at the Werkbund Exhibition, Cologne.

Maps

Map 1 Europe in 1789.

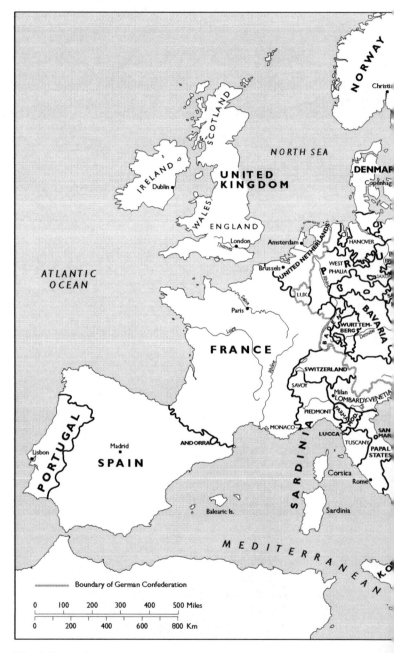

Map 2 Europe in 1815.

Map 3 Europe in 1914.

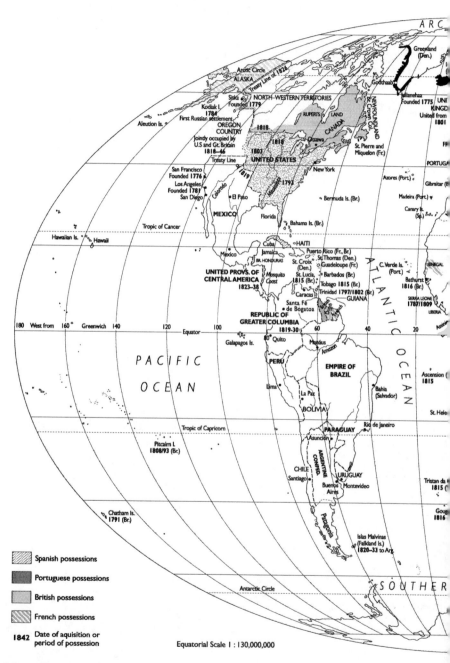

Map 4 European possessions 1830.

Map 5 European possessions 1878.

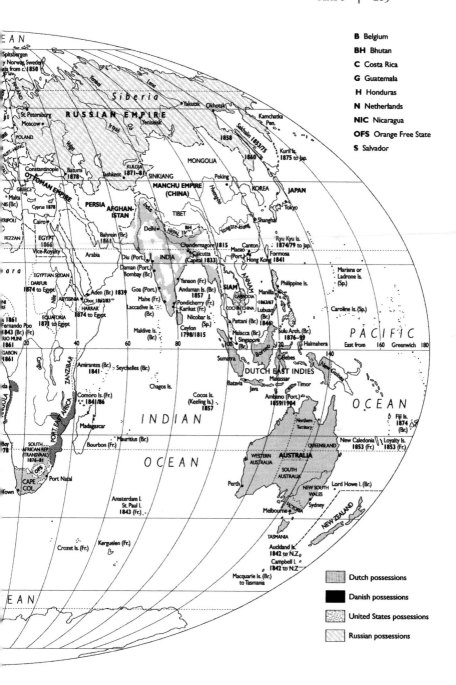

B Belgium
BH Bhutan
C Costa Rica
G Guatemala
H Honduras
N Netherlands
NIC Nicaragua
OFS Orange Free State
S Salvador

Dutch possessions
Danish possessions
United States possessions
Russian possessions

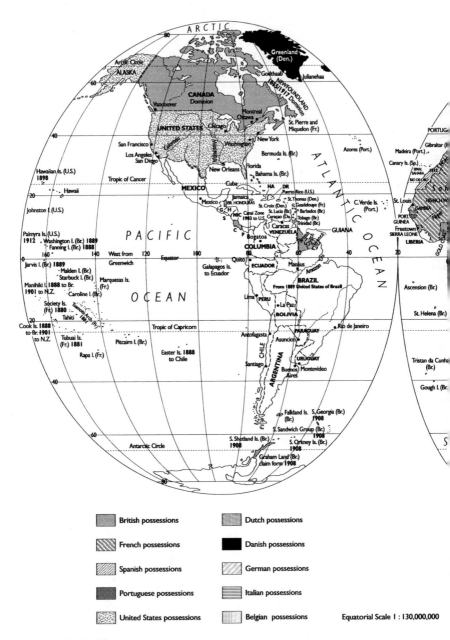

Map 6 The World 1914.

A Albania

B Belgium

BH Bhutan

C Costa Rica

DR Dominican Republic
(from 1905 U.S. special rights)

G Guatemala

H Honduras

HA Haiti (from 1915 U.S. special rights)

N Netherlands

NIC Nicaragua (1909/12 U.S.
special rights. 1912 mult.
occup.)

P Panama (1903 indep. Rep.
under U.S. Protection)

S Salvador

1842 Date of aquisition or period of possession

Index